FROM SYMBOLISM
TO STRUCTURALISM

EXPLORATIONS IN
INTERPRETATIVE SOCIOLOGY

GENERAL EDITORS
PHILIP RIEFF
Benjamin Franklin Professor of Sociology
University of Pennsylvania

BRYAN R. WILSON
Reader in Sociology, University of Oxford
Fellow of All Souls College

Also in this series
MAX WEBER AND SOCIOLOGY TODAY
Edited by Otto Stammer
Translated by Kathleen Morris

THE SOCIAL FRAMEWORKS OF KNOWLEDGE
Georges Gurvitch
Translated by Margaret A. Thompson and
Kenneth A. Thompson

Forthcoming
LUCIEN LÉVY-BRUHL
Jean Cazeneuve
Translated by Peter Rivière

THE CARNETS OF LÉVY-BRUHL
Translated by Peter Rivière

FALSE CONSCIOUSNESS
Joseph Gabel
Translated by Margaret A. Thompson and
Kenneth A. Thompson

FROM SYMBOLISM
TO STRUCTURALISM

Lévi-Strauss in a Literary Tradition

JAMES A. BOON

> Tout est réciprocité, allusion et allégorie, dans la vie et dans l'art. Celui qui posséderait la faculté de saisir immédiatement toutes les analogies, celui-là serait l'artiste immortel, et du même coup le psychologue par excellence (Mauclair cited in Lehmann: 210).

> Lévi-Strauss often manages to give me ideas even when I don't really know what he is saying (Leach 1967a: xvii).

HARPER & ROW, PUBLISHERS
NEW YORK, EVANSTON, SAN FRANCISCO, LONDON

JAMES A. BOON: FROM SYMBOLISM TO STRUCTURALISM
LÉVI-STRAUSS IN A LITERARY TRADITION

Copyright © 1972 by James A. Boon

For information address Harper & Row, Publishers Inc.,
49 East 33rd Street, New York, N.Y. 10016

International Standard Book Number (cloth): 06–136086–4
Library of Congress Catalog Card Number: 72–75621

Author's Preface

This book is all suggestion, containing nothing final. Since its strategy requires us to maintain a considerable analytic distance from the very human phenomena at issue, it seemed that a few initial, more personal comments as to its nature and scope might be helpful. The book compares the work of one contemporary French social anthropologist, Claude Lévi-Strauss, and several past French creative writers, known as Symbolists. Such a comparison is to begin with unusual. First, it is obviously not academic. Second, the comparison is not a means, but (for the purpose of this work) an end. It leads to no pat conclusion. I only try to convince you more and more as we proceed that the comparison is valid, that the analogy between Lévi-Strauss and Symbolists is extensive and deep, and that pursuing it tells us more about both. With the exception of a long and indispensable digression into linguistics, I try to restrict the inquiry to this analogy and to pursue it to its limits.

Thanks to such a restriction on scope, we can circumscribe a more intensive examination of the critical and analytic principles that are more exactly our subject of study. The book contents itself with describing a *way* of approaching various colorful human productions. The way matters most. Once it is comprehended much more could be discussed: for example, who besides Lévi-Strauss and some Symbolists have worked out a similar doctrinal methodology; or what is it that makes it all seem so 'French'. However, I only allude to these topics in passing. This is because, again, I felt the *way* mattered most, deserved our first attention, and related more generally to more worthy concerns. And when I had finished with the way, it seemed I had a book, or at least an essay.

There are from the start four types of readers who might encounter this book: (1) those who know from a little to a lot about both Lévi-Strauss and the Symbolists; (2) about Lévi-Strauss but not the Symbolists; (3) vice versa; (4) those who know nothing about either. Each of these types simply represents a different slant on things (ignorance = innocence is too a valid slant); no one slant has a decided advantage. The book will be easier to read for someone with a little background in Lévi-Strauss; it might be easier to understand for someone with a fair background in French Symbolist literature. It is probably easiest to enjoy by not reading against it and by not being put off if occasionally it goes too far. Type (4) might have the roughest going, but I like to hope his chances for reward (and enjoyment?) are the highest; at least type (4) is the least likely to have his vested interests offended.

Thus, the book is not meant to be 'exclusivistic.' It may sometimes seem so, because we must eventually assemble a set of concepts that really can make sense only in the framework it has sought carefully to establish. If the reader feels for a moment that he has been excluded—that he has been talked above or around—I hope he will read on patiently, for the same point is bound to come up again, perhaps next time in a more accessible fashion.

Consider this book an unfamiliar city. Consider its author your guide. Your reading the book is analogous to the guided tour. Many persons are uneasy if they begin a tour without first seeing a map of the area to be traversed, although the map might in fact bear little relation to the procedure of their tour or the plan behind it. Analogously, many persons would expect the present tour to begin with a general, standard description of on the one hand Lévi-Strauss and on the other hand the Symbolists: who, what, where, when, why. . . . But this book is in part an argument against the worth of such a start, claiming that it would distract us from understanding the body of ideas that are at issue. We start rather with certain critical attitudes and move on to illustrate various propositions and analytic approaches without ever talking much about Lévi-Strauss or the Symbolists *per se*. Or rather we insist that the *per se* is really the composite of critical attitudes and analytic that these writers reveal. Rather than giving you the low-down on Mallarmé or Proust—e.g. who they were, what they wrote, why and for whom—I try to guide you to features of their *work* which will point us toward the ramifications of our critical propositions. While the features I mention might occasionally be based on opinion, I generally back up these views with brief examples of text from the author in question or at least with others' opinions. Moreover, I try to demonstrate any point being argued on the spot. This procedure lends to the book a curious rhythm, and the reader finds himself shifting from grand generalization to more exacting textual critique. By and large, whenever we suddenly find ourselves before a terse quotation, having just been through a maze of literary or ethnological theory, the former is being offered to clarify or exemplify the latter. We are aiming for interior 'clicks.'

This brings us to a word about style. An author should never talk about his own style. My style provokes descriptive terms like 'precious' or 'baroque.' But consider our plight! For as the reader will quickly come to sense, we are involved here in what Kenneth Burke has called 'critics-who-write-critiques of-critical-criticism' (Burke 1964: 174). When one is working at the level of fourth degree analytic remove, there are bound to be many loose ends along the way. Often, especially at terminal paragraphs, I tend to pick up the loose ends and carry them out to the point of embellishment. This is a risky tactic and sometimes seems not worth the effort. But I think it is usually worth the *chance*, since the embellishment aims always to be additive (i.e. it should not wipe out any ground that has been gained) and it just might push through to a new level of understanding achieved through the rapid retrospection it requires. There is, after all, embellishment, and there's embellishment. And if some of this book's trills leave the reader wondering whether he is up against an instance of insight or of buffoonery, I hope he will consider that uncertainty an opportunity for reflection and not a ruse by an inconsiderate author.

To the best of my discernment every hint within these pages either echoes a prior or foreshadows a subsequent assertion made

explicit. Hints and suggestion in this sort of work are not aimed
at obscurantism. They provide the cash crop (in the form of
the reader's ever mounting re-cognitions) harvested from working through the derivation of a closed set of sensory-based terms.
Moreover, it is not as though every hint in whatever sort of work
could be just as easily an explicit statement. In the present book,
for example, such explicitness would have tripled the length
(and concision, too, is a virtue). As for hints, then, I hope they
will be welcomed, and if not that, ignored—but never rejected
in disdain.

Notwithstanding all that precedes, many professionals in anthropology will care little to know that certain poets had come
to conclusions similar to those of one-of-their-own. Many professionals in French literature would be disturbed to see their
authors put into service to elucidate the work of a social theorist.
In fact the only point where these two narrower professional
interests might coincide would be in reacting to the present book
in a chorus of: What does it matter? The book, then, is not
directed toward professional interests. It is directed toward
readers who are interested in working together to understand
delineable processes involved in the creation of various human
significant forms such as myth, poetry, social structure, some
music, ethnology, and literary criticism. I have known and read
a lot of anthropologists interested in this variety of understanding, as well as a lot of poets, critics, philosophers, students, and
especially interdisciplinary-oriented teachers. I think that Lévi-
Strauss and Symbolist authors, although they are radically
different students of man, have arrived at very similar insights.
And I want to show you how it is that I think so.

Those interdisciplinary-oriented teachers without whom this
book might never have appeared are J. Theodore Johnson,
David M. Schneider, Martin Silverman, Milton Singer, and
Karl D. Uitti. With deep appreciation I acknowledge their
help and encouragement. Out of the host of persons encountered
along the course of constructing this work, grateful memories
set into relief Blanchard Bates, Margaret Blaker, Jennifer Bur-
dick, David Crabb, Ray DeMallie, J. K. D. Feather, Paul
Friedrich, Lucas Kamp, Bess Keller, Edmund Leach, Claude

Lévi-Strauss (by correspondence), G. Daniel Massad, John
Moore, James Peacock, Jim Rauh, Sam Stanley, William Sturtevant (special thanks for his careful reading), Sol Tax, Hervé
Varenne, and Irving Zaretsky. The alphabetical order belies the
heterogeneity of the assortment. Many were a great help in
practical matters (sometimes unbeknownst to themselves); a few
served as positive inspiration (sometimes unbeknownst to themselves); others still provided an equally essential negative foil
(sometimes unbeknownst to themselves) for the material I was
writing. Such is the dialectic involved in assembling a book
while profiting from the experience of *others*.

Transcending all efforts toward classification, and well-
beknownst to her, has been the assistance, interest, and patience
of my wife Olivian; we have labored together throughout.

J. A. B.

Contents

		Page
Author's Preface		v
INTRODUCTION	A 'Way In.'	1
I SURFACE AFFINITIES	Contents and Interests Shared by Lévi-Strauss and Symbolists.	17
II STRUCTURAL ANALYSIS	A View from Baudelaire's 'Les Chats.'	38
III POETIC EVERYMAN	By Way of the Modern Poem (and Language) to Regain a Sense of Myth.	62
IV POETIC STRAW MAN	Self-aware Syntheses of *Pensée Sauvage.*	108
V CRITICAL RAMIFICATIONS	The Symbolist Narrative of *Tristes Tropiques* And Rousseau Mallarméan *Mythologiques* And Music Marcel Proust, mythically.	139

Contents

VI INTERPRETATIONS Through Literary Corres-   209
AND CONCLUSION   pondences toward a Cross-
cultural *Esprit*.

References   232

Index   246

DUE TO MY FAMILY

Social life imposes on the consanguineous stocks of mankind an incessant traveling back and forth, and family life is little else than the expression of the need to slacken the pace at the crossroads and to take a chance to rest. But the orders are to keep on marching (L-S 1956: 285).

Introduction

A 'WAY IN'

C'est avec précaution qu'il faut prononcer le mot 'structuralisme' (*Esprit* 1963: 546).

Symbolisme? comprends pas. Ça doit être un mot allemand, hein? Moi, d'ailleurs, je m'en fiche (Verlaine cited in Gibson: 16).

The search for correspondences of this sort is not a poet's game or a department of mystification, as people have dared to say of Rimbaud's *sonnet des voyelles*: that sonnet is now indispensable to the student of language who knows the basis, not of the color of phenomena, for this varies with each individual, but of the relation which unites one phenomenon to another and comprises a limited gamut of possibilities. These correspondences offer the scholar an entirely new terrain, and one which may still have rich yields to offer (L-S 1961b: 126-7).

Thus we shall hope to attain a plan in which logical properties will be manifested as attributes of things just as directly as flavors or odors whose particularity—excluding any mistake—nevertheless refers back to a combination of elements which, diversely chosen or arranged, would have suscitated the consciousness of another odor (L-S 1964a: 22; my trans.).

Such are the aspirations of French anthropologist Claude Lévi-Strauss, specialist in preliterate peoples' mythologies as seen through concepts derived from linguistics. In terms of sensory correspondences he describes the aim of the method he calls 'structural' as being to 'set up an inventory of mental enclosures' as it seeks to prove 'the existence of a logic of sensory qualities' (L-S 1964a: 18, 9).

. . . the primitive nobility of the human soul. The races— that our civilization, confused and perverted, voluntarily treats as savage, with a totally ludicrous pride and fatuity— understand as well as the child the high spirituality of dress- ing up (Baudelaire 1951, tome III: 'Eloge du maquillage,' my trans.).

A language must be found. Moreover, every word being an idea, the time of a universal language will come! This language will be of the soul for the soul, containing everything, smells, sounds, colors, thought holding on to thought and pulling. The poet would define the amount of the unknown awakening in his time in the universal soul: he would give more—than the formulation of his thought, than the annotation *of his march toward Progress*! Enormity be- coming normal, absorbed by all, he would really be *a multi- plier of progress*! (Rimbaud: 309).

Conversely, two nineteenth century French poets, Baudelaire and Rimbaud (the latter's words here reflect the former's in- fluence)—both specialists in corresponding sensory percep- tions—describe some ideas about primitive humanity and lan- guage which underlie their philosophies of poetry.

Indeed, Lévi-Strauss trespasses on territory covered by certain literary figures, and they encroached on the field that he has since made his specialty. A quick glance at the above quota- tions might even incline us to check for a possible reversal of sources. The anthropologist has taken into account material traditionally treated by the poet, who in turn professed concerns embraced by the anthropologist (-linguist), and both have sensed a universal logic, a mental harmony common to all. The mutual terminology noticeable in the quotations extends to the authors' most basic doctrines. Lévi-Strauss explores the

nature of 'symbols' and would at some level agree with Baudelaire that 'the universe is a vast storehouse of images and signs
which must be digested and transformed' (Hyslop: 27). Similarly, writers influenced by Baudelaire assert that 'there is a
structure underlying all experience . . .' (Lehmann: 113). 'Symbols,' 'signs,' 'systems,' 'analogies,' and 'transformations' pervade
both ways of thinking, and all these concepts seem to bear on Lévi-
Strauss' notion of 'code' as a 'means of fixing significations by
transposing them into terms of other significations' (1966a:
172).

Out of this sensed analogy between several literary figures on
the one hand and Lévi-Strauss on the other stems the present
book. My aim is to explicate Lévi-Strauss' (and only Lévi-
Strauss') method and doctrine of structuralism by viewing it
through the optic of literary—for want of a better term—
'Symbolism.' But let us avoid for a moment these monumental
-isms, in order to appreciate at a more down-to-earth level the
nature of our inquiry. Primarily, I want to discuss how Lévi-
Strauss is 'striving towards a genuine topology of imaginative
functions . . .' (*TLS* 1967: 522) through his programmatic
analyses of particular sorts of native texts and of particular unconscious patterned customs. Eventually we consider Lévi-
Strauss' ideas on the limits of human understanding and on the
source of experiential significance. These ideas might be called
the doctrine discernible behind his method, the latter alone being
the primary foundation of 'structuralism.' Yet such an analytic
distinction is ultimately untenable, at least, as we shall see, within the context of Lévi-Strauss' motivation.

The procedure of the inquiry is a simple one. I compare Lévi-
Strauss to some other writers who have likewise been concerned
with *texts* (with the works of others as well as their own) and
with the bases (their own and others') for *constructing* significance out of the interrelated sensory units comprising those
texts, which are themselves constructed out of the interrelated
sensory units comprising experience as it is conceived. For the
moment let us think of a 'text' simply as some assortment of
elements revealing complex connections among themselves. Use
of this term will at first be confusing, since an author's work is

B

also called a text. However, I want to imply that this latter sort of text is merely posited and can never be known in its own right. The author's work can only be critically 'known' across more abstracted 'texts'—i.e. any body of interrelated elements posited by the reader—through which it is assimilated. In other words I am purposefully establishing a notion of how literature is experienced by anyone other than its author which parallels Lévi-Strauss' notion of how cultures are experienced by an outside observer. This matter should become clearer as we proceed.

These writers—of necessity known to me only through their works and not at all in and of themselves—are a very heterogeneous assortment. They include a lot of Baudelaire and Mallarmé, a little of Rimbaud and Verlaine, scatterings of minor poets and critics in the circles of some of the former (especially Mallarmé), a bit of the more poetic side of Jean-Jacques Rousseau, and what I take to be the essence of Proust. At times I will talk about each of these persons—i.e. about their texts—individually, always remaining aware that

> In point of fact there is no such thing as Shakespeare's Hamlet (Wilde: 374).

At other times I will gloss over their individuality and designate them 'Symbolists.' Abrupt as this latter move might seem, there are clear precedents. For example, my French literature anthology note the 'general usage . . . to designate as Symbolists not only the followers of Mallarmé but also certain of their forerunners . . . [and] many of their present-day successors . . .' (Guthrie and Diller: 451).[1] However, such precedents are actually of little worth, since it might well be that I am not thinking of 'Symbolism' in the same way as the proponents of those precedents; and there is nothing in an -ism. To render more apparent what I mean by calling these authors 'Symbolists,' I might instead call them 'Sensory-intellectualists' or 'Interregnum-constructionists,' or, following a suggestion by Fiser (1943), 'musicalists.' For the aspects of their works that concern us, and that appear to me to explain many more or less

[1] See '. . . Symbolism in Literary History' in (Wellek 1970).

intuitive notions regarding the nature of French literary 'Symbolism,' involve techniques and theories in two areas: (1) corresponding sense perceptions from different orders of experience; (2) self-conscious, intellectual constructionism as a creative mode. Yet, when not treating these writers individually, I will call them 'Symbolists.' And any quotations from other sources which contain the term 'Symbolism' or 'Symbolist' are included only if the work of the author in question is being cited as demonstrating the Symbolist criteria mentioned above.

Without a doubt there are many more poets, novelists, and critics who could be called Symbolists—as loosely defined by these correspondence-constructionist criteria—and there are many aspects of the writers I call Symbolists which fall outside of those criteria. Indeed, it would be surprising if there had not at all times and in all places been Symbolist 'authors'; in fact, we shall eventually surmise that there have been, especially in the absence of alphabets! I am merely drawing on the works of some Symbolist writers who were perhaps more explicitly so or more aware of themselves as such—especially inasmuch as they carried on a particular method of poetry and criticism pioneered by Baudelaire. It should further be remembered that I am *using* these Symbolist works, or aspects of them or commentary on them, in order to illuminate features of Lévi-Strauss' studies. Therefore, no adequate representation of any individual Symbolist work can be expected. The task at hand is rather to review a little of what Fiser has called 'the *esprit* in which the great symbolists conceived their works' (1943: 10; my trans.), all the while bringing Lévi-Strauss to bear on the matter.

Thus, the present study is an exposition of how I think Lévi-Strauss thinks (organizes his thoughts)—as manifested in his texts—and of how he thinks natives in preliterate cultures organize their thoughts—which latter are likewise manifested, however inadequately translated, in different cultures' 'texts,' i.e. in the myths recited, in the customs enacted, in the rites performed, as observed by Lévi-Strauss directly or across ethnographic reports. Moreover, the present work is a demonstration that other French men of letters have organized thoughts and thought of their experience in similar ways. Thanks to this analogy we can hope to establish a quiet dialectic. The other men of letters should give us more insight into Lévi-Strauss and the ways of thinking he describes; simultaneously the findings of structuralism should shed at least a little light on Symbolism. Such reciprocal enlightenment is the ideal fruit of anthropology's own comparative method, which is itself frequently beset with equally vague notions of just what it is that is being compared! For the Symbolists, then, only occasional inklings of insight are in the offing. Then again, if in retrospect anyone would want to proclaim all the writers we have examined an homogeneous 'school'—call it what you will—, that would be fine. As for Lévi-Strauss, we can but strive to 'translate with the least poor rendering possible' (L-S 1963c: 634) his very complex code for thinking into a version which will hopefully be more accessible to understanding, or at least to appreciation—but ideally to both.

The crucial point is that we should not think of Symbolism as some thing which in any historical sense 'gave rise to' or 'yielded' another thing, now labeled Lévi-Straussian structuralism. I do not claim that Lévi-Strauss conscientiously picked up tenets of Symbolism and elaborated them into his structuralism. One could, however, nurse the suspicion that he did just that; for he has read many Symbolists' works, as evidenced by the following: he has joined in an analysis of a poem by Baudelaire, which he already knew by heart (personal communication); he makes occasional allusions to Rimbaud; he surprises many anthropologists by talking about poetry; he idolizes Rousseau; and he borrowed from Proust one of the best known titles in French literature. But it would make no difference if Lévi-Strauss had never heard of a Symbolist poet, Rousseau, Proust, etc. In fact, from one point of view, the less direct influence that we found between our two -isms, the more interesting would be the discernment of any analogies; since these would clearly be cases of independent invention, the similarity of which would have to be either mere coincidence or a function of something other than each other (for example, a function of *l'esprit humain*!). And the more analogies we found, the less it would look like coincidence.

Lack of interest in 'historical seepage' explanations is not unusual in anthropology. Often this attitude is necessitated by the nature of the data; for example, in a paper on psycho-analysis and the seventeenth century Iroquois, Wallace observes:

> However, the data raise questions of both theoretical and historical interest: for we find here a 'primitive' people actively using a theory of the mind similar in many essentials to that expressed by Sigmund Freud and his intellectual heirs in Western European cultural tradition of two centuries later. It is at least an interesting case of independent invention (for I see no evidence of Iroquois dream theory having influenced Freud, directly or indirectly) (Wallace: 172).

This same sort of quest for cross-temporal, cross-cultural, 'primitive' to 'sophisticate' parallelisms has become almost a trade-mark of Lévi-Strauss, and one of his more controversial features. For example, he finds in South American myth a theory that coincides with Rousseau's in attributing man's downfall (from conceptualizing perfection) to the development of a neolithic economy, with the dire consequences of population expansion and disproportionately large family groups; and Lévi-Strauss concludes:

> . . . the diversity of the approaches which led Rousseau consciously, and South American Indians unconsciously, to make the same speculations on a very distant past without a doubt proves nothing about this past, but it proves a great deal about man (L-S 1967a: 260; my trans.).

In these examples Wallace and Lévi-Strauss perform kindred intellectual feats: both argue on the evidence of the texts at hand that similarities appear between the way certain pre-literates and certain Western theorists have, to put it vaguely, looked at things. But then notice how they diverge. For Wallace brings up the 'psychic unity of mankind' only after he first wonders 'what (if any) common sociocultural forces can be found to explain the existence of such similar psychological theories in two such different societies as Vienna and Iroquoia?' (1967: 172). Regardless of whether this latter question could ever in any terms be answered, it should be noted that concerning Rousseau and the South Americans Lévi-Strauss fails even to ask it. This decided refusal to distinguish between 'sociocultural forces' and ideology as isolable and causal variables has provoked extensive criticisms from British scholars regarding problems in verifying Lévi-Strauss' findings or making predictions from them.[2]

For now we should observe that in the above example Lévi-Strauss considers the important fact to be the complex analogy he can draw between Rousseau and native. Furthermore, the following train of thought is suggested: if from two sources of data so extremely separated by time and space, the one existing on a conscious, the other on an unconscious level, we can extract such complex analogies, then we are more likely to be learning something about the way man thinks in general than about chance convergences of causal chains, such as (in the Rousseau-South America case above) that frustrated family life leads to pessimism over demography, or the like. The more independent sources we can find that reveal a similar complex analogy, the more we can assume that these fairly homologous analogies might be fruitfully examined to discover essential features of the way man organizes his thoughts. Briefly and controversially, proceeding to study any *differences* among the members of that set of similar analogies yields as residue the *structure* (i.e. the relationship between those differences) of that set, a structure which can then be deemed somehow basic to human thinking. Finally and ideally, when we have gone through this procedure for all generally recurring systematic analogies, we can place the derived structures together, determine their differences, and come out with a final structure of the structures, which will be a translation of that *esprit humain* lying behind everything we have been studying from the

[2] See, for example, (Maybury-Lewis 1969), (Shankman 1969), (Burridge 1967), and (Leach 1970). See also (Buchler and Selby: ch. V–VI) for a review of empiricist objections to Lévi-Strauss' approach to kinship.

start, as well as behind the analytic devices we have been using to study it—hence the necessary circularity of Lévi-Strauss' quest. And in the face of this admitted circularity, the only aim can be to take more and more recurring, multi-leveled analogies into account, revealing ever more adequate structures for these repeating modes of human expression, refining the models, but never achieving conclusive representation of anything. For:

> What is called the progress of the human mind [*l'esprit humain*], and in any case, the progress of scientific knowledge, could never have consisted in and will never consist in anything other than . . . proceeding towards regroupings, than defining members and discovering new resources, in the midst of a totality that is closed and complementary with itself (L-S 1950: xlviii; my trans.).

The above digression—for now premature and evasive—is intended to begin justifying two limits of the present study. First, I consider it worthwhile to demonstrate complex analogies between the ways experience is organized (as manifested to me in some mythical, poetical, ethnological, and critical texts I have gathered) by peoples as different as 'primitives,' some late nineteenth century poets, one twentieth century anthropologist, and others.[3] The final aim remains, of course, to explicate and complement the views of Lévi-Strauss. I know these peoples only through my orderings of 'texts' purporting to be written by or about them or recorded from them—which is to say, my encounter with them is itself a 'text' (for you to encounter). I do not think that any analogies I present could be shown to be false, considering the sources utilized. Someone else might be able to discern some still more complex analogies or to extend the analogies I discern; or he might discover inaccuracies in the

---

[3] As always in this book, those people are most ideally 'primitive' who (1) do not have any writing, (2) do not employ 'history' (i.e. linear sequence in the absence of a present-oriented response) as their primary mode of conceptually organizing events, and (3) live in communities restricted in size to 'face to face' relations. None of these characteristics is pejorative—to the contrary! (see L-S 1954a).

texts I have used. However, as should later be clear, he could not properly refute my analogies either by saying that he had visited these people (be they natives, or critics, or anthropologists, or poets), so that he somehow *really* knew them, or by saying that the creators of these texts had no such thing in mind. On the other hand, someone might simply not be interested in the suggestion that Proust literally orders his existence more as some ethnographers suggest the Sioux do, than as, say, Voltaire does. After all, one would argue, how could this be so, since Proust had read Voltaire, while he had certainly not read a Sioux? Our hypothetical someone might not be satisfied unless he could know *why* the analogy exists; but on this point I can only offer an occasional suggestion. The final aim here is analogy.

The second limit of this study arises from what I consider to be the basic 'take-off' point of Lévi-Strauss' structuralism. Like the *sociologie* of Durkheim and Mauss and the various brands of structural linguistics of Saussure, Jakobson, etc., Lévi-Strauss *starts* with the *fact* that different cultures possess different 'texts' that seem somehow similar. For example, in one famous case:

> With myth, everything becomes possible. But on the other hand, this apparent arbitrariness is belied by the astounding similarity between myths collected in widely different regions. Therefore the problem: If the content of a myth is contingent, how are we going to explain the fact that myths throughout the world are so similar? (L-S 1963b: 208).

Again, this use of 'text' is my own. I call a 'text' any body of data in any sorts of units—sounds played, phones uttered, acts effected, colors applied, sentences writ, stars contemplated, geographical features surveyed, etc.—which smacks of systematization, *given an observer*. From such units systematically apprehended are derived music, speech, actions, paintings, paragraphs, constellations, maps, etc. respectively. Thus, in my usage a 'text' could be composed of persons (categorically defined) interrelated in specified ways, just as well as of notes, words, graphics; the important point is that it be observed from without, with an inkling as to its systematic basis. Briefly then, 'texts' are derived sensory systems. And from here we can see that there is really no ambiguity involved between this usage and the general notion of a text as some body of written language. For, the written book or poem only comes into being through the reader's systematic apprehension of its principles of order—i.e. critically. The fact of experience is that something out there (words on a page, people in a hut) seems systematic, and I encode it by relating it to other systems (texts in their own right) at my disposal. This is as much Proust as it is Lévi-Strauss. And 'text' is better than 'system' because it keeps the sensory basis in mind. Moreover, if we stay precisely at the analytic level where items of experience are systematically apprehended (to be communicated in some sensory terms), we can avoid problems about 'things in themselves' versus 'ideas of things' and other weighty philosophical issues. In sum, then, the notion of 'text' is one way of establishing a basic analytic premise: systematic sensory input is received from somewhere, wherever that might be. Or, as communication theory would have it: there *is* message. But I prefer 'text' to 'message' when it comes to myth and literature and other cultural productions, because it can underscore the complexity and creativity of the message sent—be it a poem or a culture.

The fact to be stressed is so simple as to be easily forgotten: Lévi-Strauss takes it as given that such texts exist across cultures. He does not question *how* it could be that the texts exist, asserting rather that this latter question cannot possibly be answered by analysis, since our analytic tool—language—is itself such a text and therefore assumes its own existence. Thus, we are not concerned with how it is that language, for example, *is*—language being but one variety of evidence that systematic thought takes place. Rather, after the manner of Saussure, we observe that language happens, phenomenologically. Moreover, it seems to happen somewhat differently over here from the way it happens over there, but still strikingly similarly. And the problem becomes one of discovering the basis of its translatability.

Many observers of Lévi-Strauss, especially non-anthropologists, appear to forget this absolutely essential starting point of his approach to studying man. They claim he is erecting a peculiarly pessimistic, impoverishing, and mechanized view of what men do. While we shall later address ourselves directly to this charge, let this much be remembered: as often acknowledged by himself, Lévi-Strauss would not have the first thing to say unless men were out there myth making, painting, marrying, exchanging goods—unless men were making exchanges among themselves and between themselves and features of their experience, unless they were stating themselves and those features all *in terms of* one another—i.e. unless they were creating 'texts.'

Thus I approach Lévi-Strauss almost solely in the light of his aim to confront the fact that texts exist across cultures and that men seem potentially capable of *understanding* texts other than their own, and of understanding themselves in terms of those. I am less concerned with the sources of Lévi-Strauss' analytic than with the coherence of the body of principles guiding it. It is this coherence that I propose to elucidate with the help of certain Symbolist works. To this end, the vast array of other -isms and fields that have either been noted by Lévi-Strauss as a source of his ideas or adduced by critics as foundations for his structuralism require little mention. I would argue that Lévi-Strauss generally makes it clear just what elements he is borrowing from another field of endeavor or another theorist in order to point out his own synthesis. Rather than worrying over any very casual allusions by Lévi-Strauss to some theorist or theory (which allusions may not coincide with my own views) I will treat such allusions as no more than intriguing hints—some useful, others not—for helping to follow what Lévi-Strauss is saying about what we *can* say about texts.[4] Often these hints seem elucidatory and memorable. For example, in one instance he argues that neither social life nor organic life can be justified by any 'functional value.' He suggests that

[4] Harris (1968: Ch. 18) illustrates this sort of worry. He evaluates Lévi-Strauss' work against how true it is to his own conception of Marxist theory and doctrine rather than evaluating the work in its own right.

maintaining the opposite view would lead us either into a meaningless tautology or into 'an anthropological come-back to eighteenth century Providentialism, where culture would play in relation to man the same utopian tutelary part which was attributed to nature by the author of *Paul et Virginie*. . . .' A footnote provides the necessary clarification:

In his *Etudes de la Nature* (1784) Bernardin de Saint Pierre suggested that Nature devised melon ribs to make the fruit easier to divide on the family table, and that it made fleas black so that they could more easily be caught on white skin (L-S 1944a: 17).

Most likely few experts on Bernardin de Saint Pierre would appreciate so piecemeal a use of his work; yet, it is very helpful to me, a non-expert.

Because of its textual approach, this book will afford little satisfaction to critics of Lévi-Strauss who seek an 'independent source of verification' outside of 'texts' themselves. Lévi-Strauss has argued heroically that no sorts of 'things'—whether people, objects, sounds, colors, events, ideas, etc.—can be shown to be any more immanently ordered or orderable than any other sorts of 'things.' Thus it is no more true that one sort of ordering (say, of people) can better 'explain' another sort of ordering (say, of ideas)—as have argued some empiricists—than is the contrary. Nor do orderings-of-objects (e.g. economics) 'explain' orderings-of-events (e.g. history); nor vice versa, and so forth. Attributing primacy to any one sort of ordering seems to be a matter of taste, in light of cross-cultural evidence which reveals that 'societies' can exist with very different relative degrees of ordering of all these sorts. However, the cross-cultural or comparative viewpoint also provides the only sort of 'independent source of verification' left to us in this sea of relativity—namely, the chance to discover empirically various instances of similar types of ordering. Thus, while one cannot escape from a dialectic between 'text' and 'text' and 'text' . . ., one can gradually reduce the field of inquiry by comparison. As most recently and forcefully stated by Lévi-Strauss:

This validation at a distance, by myths issuing from populations which are very diverse and separated from each other,
and by figures full of imagery from our own popular language . . . appears to us like a mode of ethnographic proof,
which is not unworthy of those utilized by more advanced
sciences (L-S 1968: 11; my trans.).

This stance appears to me to accord not only with modern
science, but with modern criticism as well. I accept it and will
try to clarify it without apologies. On the other hand, I do
apologize for the maze of imprecise, abstract terms which
have already characterized and will continue to characterize
this study—terms such as 'classifications,' 'systems,' 'classificatory systems,' 'organization,' 'orderings,' 'relationships,' 'relations,' 'taxonomies,' 'sets,' 'paradigmatic sets,' not to mention
'structures'! I probably could not always use all of these terms
precisely and consistently, even if it seemed essential to do so.
For most of them are distinguished by nuances of analysis,
such as whether one is proceeding from a 'text' to something
underlying it ('underlying' is deliberately vague here), or from
that something underlying it to the text; or whether one is
talking about the 'things' in a system, or about the principles
that systematically relate (or constitute!) those things. And
this list could be indefinitely extended; for structuralism is
intimately involved with fundamental issues in epistemology
as well as cognition. Nevertheless, I will banter about these
terms, and bandy them about, occasionally rendering them more
precise, but frequently leaving their definition to context. While
this laxity is surely at times a fault, any other recourse would
be self-stultifying, and nothing, to put it simply, would get
said.[5]

[5] However, I do try to use two such terms consistently, although both
remain vague. The terms are 'domain' and 'order.' A 'domain' is an
area of interest which seems to be fairly circumscribed on the part of
the people or author being studied. For example, two American domains
might be 'home' and 'work'; two Baudelairian domains might be 'women'
and 'language.' It is always debatable as to whether the level of contrast is suitable. (Some would thus call 'domains' emic, as opposed to
etic 'orders,' but I question the linguistic analogy.) 'Orders' are simply

In conclusion, besides explicating Lévi-Strauss and cross-clarifying his work and Symbolism, I should like—after a fashion—to offer a *demonstration* of these ways of thinking, of organizing the 'odds and ends' from texts experienced or experience 'texted'. The result of this work should retrospectively add up to at least a superficial illustration of that 'wild thinking' which Lévi-Strauss finds most perfectly revealed by varieties of preliterate myths. From the loose odds and ends of ideas in the first chapter, there should finally issue more orderly systems of analogies between structuralism and 'Symbolism.' It is also hoped that to any reader of the present work, Lévi-Strauss' *Mythologiques* might come as less of a jolt.

The most direct path to these ends would perhaps lie in following Santayana's example, when he acknowledges his debt to writers both living and dead by omitting 'any reference to them in the footnotes or in the text, in order that the air of controversy might be avoided, and the reader might be enabled to compare what is said more directly with the reality of his own experience' (Santayana: Preface). But such a policy, while laudably 'experiential,' would hardly be scholarly. I have tried to strike a middle path (between personal experience and scholarship) by using a reference system which allows exact documentation yet minimum interference with your experience of the argument. Students of the humanities might disapprove of this system, since it omits specific reference to the titles of individual poems or essays that are familiar parts of an author's corpus. Furthermore, I generally cite works from the sources where I have encountered them—e.g. some Baudelaire from here, some from there, a bit from elsewhere. What I have resisted is rearranging my references in order to imply that I have experienced them as a coherent corpus (i.e. in a scholarly fashion), when I have really met them—and will continue to meet them—in bits and pieces, odds and ends. The only scholarly order of this book is the order of the book itself. The book is essentially an arrangement of its textual references, which were

fairly circumscribed areas of interest imposed by the analyzer on the data of the people or person studied—e.g. economics, religion, personality, biography.

happened upon, more or less methodically, among its list of sources. Any fuller reference system would obscure the *way* this book—a process of discovery, ordered in the throes of retrospect—came to be.

As it stands, then, I should like the book to provide exercise in an attitude of mind, making of it a contrived invitation to distill and *construct* significance, as do Lévi-Strauss, many natives, Rousseau, Mallarmé, Proust. . . . But that remains to be seen.

I

Surface Affinities

CONTENTS AND INTERESTS SHARED
BY LÉVI-STRAUSS AND SYMBOLISTS

Mais c'est quelque chose: l'ordre mis dans des idées, là où il n'y en avait aucun (Mauss: 372).

By definition, therefore, anthropology is less subject matter than a bond between subject matters, and the anthropologist will forever find himself translating from one realm to another (Wolf: 13).

We begin in a deliberately negative fashion by considering a few traits common to Lévi-Strauss and Symbolism which, as we proceed, should prove of less and less interest. This procedure runs the risk of raising certain issues long ago happily laid to rest; but we must start somewhere. And the purpose of this procedure is not to make any original observations, but rather to arrive rapidly at an idea of what sort of comparative approach 'structuralism' advocates, by first dispensing with varieties of bases for analytic comparison which Lévi-Strauss himself has taken pains to refute. Only now structuralism, itself a *method of* comparison, is one of the things being compared.

Thus, our aim is to attain an approach to Lévi-Strauss' structuralism, as set in relief by Symbolism, which follows many of the tenets of both these varieties of creative criticism. One of the difficulties in achieving this aim stems from the peculiar nature of Lévi-Strauss' work. The major part of his writings consists in analytic anthropologizing at its headiest. Yet he couples with this program a lyric unity of vision concerning how his approach to society-as-communication illuminates the foundations of human experience-as-conceived. This universal-prone lyricism, together with the unquestionable appeal of certain subjects he studies—incest, totemism, ribald mythology—has provoked a welter of secondary literature purporting to explicate the nature of Lévi-Strauss' effort. Much of this literature is intended for readers who lack the background or will to wade through the endless analysis, in order to see what it is all 'really' about. But Lévi-Strauss repeatedly insists that it is all really about just that: endless analysis. Thus, if we heed his own words, we must approach Lévi-Strauss principally as a concerted and programmatic investigator of colorful empirical phenomena, and secondarily as an occasional contemplator of the human condition. For he is most basically the former and rather incidentally the latter—whence the difficulty.

Recent efforts to explain the 'rise of structuralism' as a new intellectual vogue afford many superficial statements about Lévi-Strauss upon which we can draw to suggest some of his least interesting (least structural?) affinities with Symbolism. For example, there is the observation that Lévi-Strauss' analytically useful distance from his data reflects a *froideur*, an aloofness from the peoples he analyzes. While I would contest the characterization, let us grant it for the moment, in order to show how in tune Lévi-Strauss would be with Mallarmé's note of advice:

O poets, you have always been prideful; be more, become disdainful (Mallarmé 1945: 260; my trans.).

Supposing such a parallel to be accurate, the question becomes one of just what it could tell us about either Lévi-Strauss or Symbolism. First, we might simply accept the statement, 'Both Lévi-Strauss and the Symbolists stand aloof.' And by condemning this stance, we would have a means of dispensing with their theories, claiming to have 'explained' them in terms of a 'causal' sentiment. Or, even if we did not condemn the stance but merely adduced it as something underlying their work, we would be contradicting basic tenets in both our -isms. For Symbolists, especially Proust, argued endlessly that an artist's

work must be confronted independently of the character of
its creator.[1] And structuralism maintains that aspects of social
systems which exist cross-culturally cannot be explained by
individual-based sentiment.[2] On the other hand, we might go
beyond this apparent aloofness and bring into the picture various other matters extrinsic to the bodies of ideas themselves.
For example, we could point to the analogy between current
characteristics of structuralism and Valéry's description of Symbolists (here referring specifically to the band that formed
around Mallarmé) as a youthful group which found in the
interrelationship of the arts a discipline and an unequivocal
truth: 'There came very near to being established a sort of
religion . . .' (Valéry: 1273; my trans.). Then, if we considered
as intrinsically worthless either youths, or synthetic arts, or
cults, we could eliminate Symbolism or structuralism (not to
mention the present synthesis!) from our list of notable en-
deavors. Or we might assemble various other features extrinsic
to the specific approaches to human expression of, say, structuralism, and follow the lead of those critics who see it as the
last gasp of bourgeois intellectualism.[3] However, I would dis-
miss all such studies as attempts to avoid having to understand
these bodies of ideas about 'texts' in their own terms. And, I
would argue (even at the risk of sounding bourgeois) that this
latter brand of understanding ranks first in modern criticism.
Finally, for anyone anxious to write off either Symbolism or
structuralism (in their guise as popular movements) as somehow just too 'French' and therefore not warranting serious concern, it should be observed that a very acute remark made about
one applies equally well to the other:

[1] Some people, who miss the very point they are criticizing in the act
thereof, 'explain' this tenet's existence by observing that since Symbolists
were generally recluse and/or perverted anyway, they had to make such
an assertion.
[2] For an extensive discussion of this very complex issue in structural
theory see (Needham 1962) and (Schneider 1965a).
[3] See, for example, (Lefebvre 1966). Abel (1970) discusses Sartre's views
on this issue.

C

Symbolism was not French; it happened in Paris (Balakian: 9).

It is to be hoped that appreciation for such keen parataxis would do away with criticism of the sort contained in remarks such as, '. . . Lévi-Strauss may be more French than anthropologist' (Sahlins: 131)—with not so much as a suggestion of any basis for contrasting the two categories designated. It must be asked: what specifically is it that an anthropologist by definition should be that a *philosophe* inherently is not, or vice versa? For in the absence of this information the French-*versus*-anthropologist remark just cited is meaningless.[4] Any brand of social theory deserves serious critical appraisal, but especially one so concerned with the logical status of its own statements as structuralism.

From these remarks in a few of the many hasty reviews of Lévi-Strauss' work, we turn to several affinities which are more intrinsic to the subject matter of the subjects of this study; yet the affinities remain superficial. Lévi-Strauss asserts: '. . . I must throw myself into the water if I am to plumb the depths' (L-S 1961b: 396). And Baudelaire cries:

Hombre libre, toujours tu chériras la mer!
La mer est ton miroir . . .

. . . .

Tu te plais à plonger au sein de ton image . . .
(Baudelaire 1961: 21–2).

O Man, so long as you are free you will cherish the sea!
The sea is your looking glass . . .

. . . .

4 Indeed, in precise contradiction of Sahlin's remark, Scholte has constructively offered the following insight: 'Returning to its first premises, structural anthropology becomes, in the final analysis, a scientific verification of the rationalist philosopher's intuitive notion of dialectics by pointing to the empirical and social manifestations of this notion in ethnographic fact' (Scholte 1970: 113).

You love to plunge into the depths of your own image . . .
(Scarfe trans.: 151).

This similar imagery is minimally interesting; and it would be
no more so, even given copious annotated examples showing
similar existential voids evoked in aquatic terms. *The Savage
Mind* offers the following observation:

It is only forms and not contents which can be common. If
there are common contents the reason must be sought either
in the objective properties of particular nature or artificial
entities or in diffusion and borrowing, in either case, that
is, outside the mind (L-S 1966a: 65).

If one adheres to this view, even more striking mutual metaphors leave us relatively unimpressed. For example, Lévi-
Strauss' concern with preliterate ideas of a 'true mythical ana-
tomy' and 'the picture of the uterine world,' calls to mind
imagery favored by Baudelaire, for instance his 'Géante':

J'eusse aimé vivre auprès d'une jeune géante
Comme aux pieds d'une reine un chat voluptueux.

. . . .

Parcourir à loisir ses magnifiques formes;
Ramper sur le versant de ses genoux énormes,

. . . .

Dormir nonchalamment à l'ombre de ses seins,
Comme un hameau paisible au pied d'une montagne.
(Baudelaire 1961: 26)

I would fain have lived with some young giantess,
Like a voluptuous cat at the feet of a queen.

. . . .

I would have loved to explore her limbs at my leisure;
To climb the slope of her tremendous knees

. . . .

> To fall trustfully asleep in the shadow of her breasts,
> Like a quiet hamlet at some mountain's foot.
>
> (Scarfe trans.: 25–6)

Yet this shared attraction to mother earth figures is no more indicative of similar *ways* of thinking—popular psychoanalysis notwithstanding—than the water symbolism.

Apart from the contents typical of the natives he studies, the anthropologist's own analytic concepts could be construed to suggest Symbolist metaphors: in digressing from an explanation of a fundamental theory, he realizes that 'it may be disturbing to some to have women conceived as mere parts of a meaningful system' (L-S 1963b: 61). One might argue (but I doubt he would) that Lévi-Strauss' aside has a Baudelairian flavor, insofar as the poet likewise employs the female as an essential *object* in his systematic dream worlds; yet this kind of analogy again offers little other than a curiosity. Finally, any similarity between Lévi-Strauss' treatment of the myth of the pregnant boy (see L-S 1963b: 234ff.) and Baudelaire's and Rimbaud's continuation of the Romantic tendency to confuse the sexes is only superficial. For—and here is the point—taken as metaphors all of these examples are mere coincidences of common content and reveal no significant similarities between natives and Symbolists. Independent occurrences of substantive images or 'symbols' tell us no more about man in general than that he always lives in the material world. Moreover, Lévi-Strauss argues that the failure of most earlier comparative studies— whether dealing with kinship, ritual, religion, or whatever— resulted from their attempt to compare *different* men on the basis of similar contents or images discovered among them. This criticism applies to everyone from late nineteenth century evolutionists and diffusionists, through Jung, down to some present-day phenomenologists.[5] Lévi-Strauss' contrary view is that for them to be of structural (universally logical, which is to say

[5] See especially (L-S 1963a) and 'The Structural Study of Myth' (L-S 1963b: Ch. XI). In this vein Percy S. Cohen (1969) offers a useful review and assessment of approaches to myth from Frazer and Tylor on down to Lévi-Strauss.

comparative) interest, it would have to be shown that the mutual metaphors are the end results of more basic and prior *processes* of thinking. These processes themselves occur in the act of overcoming a dilemma on one level of ordered experience by transferring the terms of the dilemma to another level.

An example is needed. In what follows we sketch a move from a superficial common content found in two texts to what we can call a more complex analogy. The common content involves an expressed dislike; one of the texts is a statement by Lévi-Strauss, the other text is a description of his hero by Marcel Proust. While the analytic procedures to be employed could be designated, among other things, 'structural,' we should not as yet even be thinking about those kinds of deterministic 'structures' that would be the ultimate aim of Lévi-Strauss' human science. For while one could theoretically reach these final structures by starting anywhere—e.g. with a comparison of Proust and Lévi-Strauss—there are definitely more suitable levels—namely collective and unconscious ones (see chs. II, III)—at which one can begin, thereby saving himself considerable time and work!

Both Lévi-Strauss and the narrator in Proust's *Remembrance of Things Past* take occasion to lodge a complaint against live drama. Lévi-Strauss considers himself incapable even of carrying on a discussion about it, because he is 'allergic to the theatre' (L-S in Charbonnier: 90; my trans.). Similarly, in one of the opening scenes of *Within a Budding Grove* Proust's narrator relates the story of the first live performance he ever attended, which resulted in bitter disappointment. Here then lies an affinity between Lévi-Strauss' opinions and those of a Symbolist hero, at least during a stage of the latter's development: both find something lacking in an artistic production built up out of real people. If no more were said, we would be left with just another surface trait, which in general terms would convey only this: given an experiential category, live theater, persons could be either anti, pro, or indifferent to it; it so happens that Lévi-Strauss and Proust's young narrator both fall in the first group. But if we look back at Lévi-Strauss and Proust, we find that this similar attitude stems from complex and interrelated notions about aesthetic experience and that these notions in turn point to many other features of their thinking.

Lévi-Strauss goes on to explain the basis of his allergy: 'When I go to the theater, I always have the impression that I have mistakenly burst in on the downstairs neighbors . . .' (L-S in Charbonnier: 90; my trans.). Moreover, in the theater 'it is flesh and blood men and women walking on the stage, whereas I ask of art to let me escape from the society of men in order to introduce me into another society' (p. 91). Parallel considerations are to be found in Proust. His narrator's first disappointment comes when he realizes that the spectator-situation, which he had so elaborately and monumentally pre-figured in his own imagination, is in fact comprised of ordinary program rattling, throat clearing, misapplauding mankind. Then enters Berma, the actress who plays the role of Phaedra, and she is just as life-like, just as inadequate for translating the verses of Racine into a performance as the audience is to hear them. Her physical reality and the near normality of the tempo can only interfere with the narrator's conception of *Phèdre*.

> . . . in vain might I strain towards Berma eyes, ears, mind, so as not to let one morsel escape me of the reasons which she would furnish for my admiring her. . . . I could not even . . . distinguish in her diction and in her playing intelligent intonations, beautiful gestures. I listened to her as though I were reading *Phèdre*, or as though Phaedra herself had at that moment uttered the words that I was hearing, without its appearing that Berma's talent had added anything at all to them. I could have wished, so as to be able to explore them fully . . . to immobilize for a time before my senses every intonation of the artist's voice, every expression of her features. . . . But how short their duration was! (Proust, 1956b: 27).

Thus behind their rejection of live drama we find between our two subjects a more complex analogy having to do with their values of aesthetic experience. For both of them, any artistic work, as a translation into other terms (colors, words, gestures) of some item from experience, must never too nearly re-produce that experience. A tragedy about a woman must not be too like a woman in tragedy—this a common aesthetic principle.[6] In other words, the simple common trait of being anti-theater is for both Lévi-Strauss and the young narrator indicative of a whole system of ideas, wherein what signifies (e.g. a Tragic Actress) must not be too like what is signified (a tragic woman), but there still must be a discernible connection between the two.[7]

In light of this principle, a potential source of conflict lies in the theater, where real people are portrayed by real people, as opposed to being portrayed by paint, thread, sentences, etc., in portraits, tapestries, biographies, respectively. That critical aspect of artistic expression, the components of which must be semi-alienated from what they represent, is thus contradicted in theatrical 'arts.' The contradiction is acknowledged by asserting dislike for or disappointment in the theater. And in Lévi-Strauss' case what is essentially a contradiction on the level of the intellect is finally resolved by figuratively shifting its terms to a physiological one, i.e. his *allergy* to the theater—a perfect 'structural' solution!

Once having detected this more complex analogy which interrelates different levels of our subjects' thinking, the next move is to refer back to the 'ethnography'—to the writings of Proust and of Lévi-Strauss—to see if statements of the analogy can be located elsewhere and perhaps in different terms. As it turns out, Lévi-Strauss' thinking is virtually fraught with analogous images of the following kind: one set of information (message) is encoded in multiple representations made out of different sorts of elements. It is this generalized notion which enables him

[6] Proust's narrator eventually surmounts this problem by learning to keep his imagination working *during* performances in order to monumentalize the mundane elements involved. Even in the scene discussed, the audience's applause later effects a re-monumentalization (one type of distancing) of the spectacle.

[7] For Lévi-Strauss this latter point is true of art but not of the language of speech (see ch. II).

to write in the same breath about linguistics, art criticism, opera, mathematics, genetic theory, and all bearing on *la pensée sauvage*. In Proust as well, interrelations of alternative representations of the same 'data' pervade his entire effort, as is so clearly and early highlighted when his narrator's grandmother advocates photographs of *paintings* of architectural works of art over just photographs of same (Proust 1956a: 55–6). Moreover, this same way of thinking forms the very crux of Proust; for out of the data of any 'one' experience can be built a representation both in his voluntary memory and in his involuntary memory, the latter becoming accessible only during certain privileged moments. Relating the two sorts of memory texts is the critical task.

This prefigurative discussion of Lévi-Strauss and Proust has, I hope, brought out several points through both its content and its form. In moving away from the original surface affinity, we have merely looked into the texts for more general ways of conceiving of and ordering experiences which might 'explain' the common content (their dislike of theater) by interrelating it with other contents. There is nothing especially 'French structural' about this operation; it is quite common in twentieth century criticism among, for example, literary New Critics. Probably the only peculiarly Lévi-Straussian turn in the example came when his conflict was figuratively resolved by shifting from statements on the 'level' of intellect to one on the level of physiology, or psychosomatics, depending on what you think of allergies. For now, suffice it to note that in his 'structuralism' Lévi-Strauss observes canons of certain modern criticism (and ethnography): namely, that a critic's goal is to consider as many levels and aspects of a work as he can, in seeking the most economic logic behind the work as a whole, none of this necessarily bearing any relation to the creators' intent.[8] The form of our discussion of Lévi-Strauss and Proust became more

---

[8] However, it might be misleading to talk here about 'the work as a whole.' For while Lévi-Strauss takes into consideration all the aspects of a work (e.g. a myth, a kinship system) he can, he selects for analysis only those aspects germane to definite lines of comparison which steer his inquiries.

'structural' only insofar as it became more commensurate with these general critical goals which structuralism shares. The content of the discussion in fact became more suggestive of a structuralist outlook, as it came to imply how all experience can be understood as a series of variant 'texts'—such as a tragic woman, perceptions of her, verses about her, memories concerning her, reveries over her, songs invoking her (the 'she' is, of course, only posited thanks to the 'texts')—each of which is more or less, but always imperfectly, translatable into the others. A discussion would become more distinctively 'structural' only as it came to bear less on the contents of such texts and more on the principles of their inter-translatability. For example, an actress might translate her daily self into a tragic heroine (one variant content) by *retarding* her *gestures* and *quickening* her now-poetic *speech* flow. The inverse translation into a comic character (another variant content) might be effected by quickening the gestures and retarding, perhaps until silence, the speech flow (one need only think of Charlie Chaplin). The emphasized terms pertain to the features of the actress' 'structure' (i.e. relationships among differences across her various 'orders'); all we need now is empirical verification.

Having alluded to schools of criticism, we can continue this initial catalogue of common interests by noting that other Symbolists followed Baudelaire's lead in writing literary criticism as well as poetry. In his analytic works which offer generalizations about the laws that govern artistic phenomena, Baudelaire illustrates how 'criticism is like art itself in that the relation of the critic to a work of art is much the same as the relation of the artist to nature' (Hyslop: 11). Baudelaire went so far as to deny any fast distinction between the creative function and the critical one; as Guy Michaud synthesizes:

> . . . in effect, for Baudelaire, inspiration and consciousness (or rather as he says, 'surnaturalism and irony') are not opposed, as for the Romantics, but complementary. Two things are necessary: . . . the subjective and intuitive vision; and then irony, the critical spirit, labor on oneself and on the work (Michaud: 77; my trans.).

The Symbolists' compounded notion of a poet as one who orders experience (nature) aesthetically and who, in his capacity as critic, orders orderings of experience (poems) aesthetically is relevent to Lévi-Strauss. For the anthropologist views native myths as the ordering or classification of man in nature (and vice versa) and his analytic procedures as the ordering of those classifications. In general:

> ... the demand for organization is a need common to art and science and ... in consequence 'taxonomy, which is ordering par excellence, has eminent aesthetic value' (L-S 1966a: 13).

Thus, at first glance the role of Symbolist poet would appear to include both the native (poet) and the anthropologist (critic or theorist). However, there is surely more critic in the native and poet in the anthropologist than this formula suggests. And in fact we find that other 'structuralist' thinkers have deemed their tasks as much poetical as critical: witness Peter Caws' citation of a statement by structuralist literary critic, Roland Barthes: 'The book is a world. . . . The critic confronted by the book is subject to the same conditions of utterance as the writer confronted by the world' (Caws: 89). Nor is this by any means a new viewpoint. Barthes himself, for one, detects it in Proust, whose narrator 'is employed systematically to explore the signs he has received and thus to understand, in a single motion, world and Book, the Book as world, and the world as Book' (Barthes: 151; my trans.). Oscar Wilde also expressed the viewpoint openly:

> *Ernest*　But is criticism really a creative art?
> *Gilbert*　Why should it not be? It works with materials, and puts them into a form that is at once new and delightful. What more can one say of poetry? Indeed, I would call criticism a creation within a creation (Wilde: 365).

Indeed, 'Wilde sounds like an ancestral Northrop Frye or Roland Barthes' (Ellmann in Wilde: x). Thus, recalling my surmise that there have always and everywhere been 'Symbolists,' we can now say the same for 'structuralists' (in nineteenth century England, no less) and henceforth happily forget about problems of original sources.

The difficulty thus becomes one of remaining 'true' to the text on some level. Wallace Fowlie addresses this issue in his review of French literary criticism, when he contrasts with Taine's goal of objectivity *les impressionistes*, who 'preferred to analyze their own feelings about a work of art. Their criticism was the result of an encounter between a text and themselves as readers. The most resolute of these critics would confess that criticism is a way of speaking about themselves' (Fowlie 1968: 12). To anticipate somewhat, we must beware that the alternatives of 'speaking about the text' *or* 'speaking about oneself' do not exhaust the possibilities; the alternatives, in fact, misrepresent them. For the analyzer can 'speak about himself in terms of the text' *and* 'speak about the text in terms of himself.' In other words, what one *really* speaks about is always the encounter of the two. At any rate categories such as nature as perceived (world), more or less creative organizer, and more or less creative analyzer are crucial 'odds and ends,' to be further pieced together later. For the time being we might simply suggest that for Symbolism and Lévi-Strauss' structuralism all these varieties of human expression—creating texts, retrospectively analyzing them, indeed perceiving nature itself—stem from the faculty of analogy; and

. . . savage thought can be defined as analogical thought (L-S 1966a: 263).

Likewise, as Vanor remarks concerning Symbolism:

It is above all the literature of metaphors and analogies; it seeks the possible affinities among the heteroclite phenomena of appearance. Hence those frequent expressions over which artless persons are amazed and which evoke the sound of a color, the color of a note, the fragrance of a thought (Vanor 1889 cited in Michaud; my trans.).

One thing at least is certain. Lévi-Strauss has attained a reputation for creative insight probably unparalleled in recent anthropology. Edmund Leach applauds the way he 'puts familiar facts together in unfamiliar ways and thereby provokes thoughts about fundamentals' (Leach 1965a: 26). We shall ignore for the moment how, if pushed a little further, this manner of complimenting an anthropologist *qua* empirical scientist slips into a derogatory gear. Let us just acknowledge that there is nothing intrinsically contradictory between being creative and imaginative and being scientific (i.e. true to the empirical data). And how much more this is so, if the data itself happens to be creative and imaginative! Furthermore, we should note the mounting sense of some similarity between the roles of the ethnologist (anthropologist) and the poet. Georges Bataille, in his review of Lévi-Strauss' *Tristes Tropiques*, surmises that 'the evocation of a society whose norms are not our own inevitably introduces the dimension of poetry, which is perhaps *the dimension of man* . . .' (Bataille: 100; my trans.). Elsewhere Baudelaire appreciates how 'the poet enjoys this incomparable privilege, in that he is able on will to be himself and others' (Baudelaire 1951: 288; my trans.). It appears, then, that the Symbolist poet is really an ethnologist *chez soi*, at least if we concur with Merleau-Ponty on Mauss and Lévi-Strauss:

> Ethnology is not a speciality defined by a particular object, 'primitive societies.' It is a way of thinking, the way which imposes itself when the object is 'different' [*autre*] and requires us to transform ourselves (Merleau-Ponty 1964a: 120).

Moreover, we shall see that *qua* poets both ethnologists and Symbolists, not to mention many preliterates, appear rather dispassionate and intellectual, all joining Baudelaire in assuming 'the character of a sage or seer, rather than of a bard' (Balakian: 47).

An at first glance especially superficial affinity is the strikingly non-academic quality of works issuing from both our -isms. In the eyes of Baudelaire, the poet, 'every phenomenon in man's environment is (potentially at least) raw material for a meta-phor or a poetic image' (Lehmann: 265–6). The writer is thereby brought in line with Lévi-Strauss' primitive symbol makers who attach significance to the most outlandish things, as do the analyzers themselves: Baudelaire, the critic, can meander creatively around a subject as trivial as facial make-up, while Lévi-Strauss is renowned for digressions into hitherto un-explored areas, such as the logic of race horse names. Clifford Geertz lauds the latter as 'triumphs of self parody. They are exercises in "depth interpretation" far-fetched enough to make even a psychoanalyst blush. It is all terribly ingenious' (Geertz: 30). It is all also crucial to the universalistic aspirations of Lévi-Strauss, who, rather than expecting particular reified 'societies' (France, England, etc.) to reveal a structure, an-nounces the following:

> . . . I compare . . . structures which I seek where they may be found, and not elsewhere: in other words, in the kinship system, political ideology, mythology, ritual, art, code of etiquette, and—why not?—cooking (L-S 1963b: 85).

Yet the fact that he seeks structures where they may be found is not to say that they may be found equally well anywhere. In fact, Lévi-Strauss has been concerned with outlining definite privileged areas of human thought and deed which display more endurance through time and therefore more ready access to the structural foundations of experience. He contends that these areas most likely exist in activities that are just on the verge of consciousness, being thereby relatively protected from self-conscious change when men seek to differentiate them-selves from or assimilate themselves to other men. Take, for example, these elements in our heritage:

> The position of a man's hand during urination, the prefer-ence for washing in flowing water or stagnant water, still with us in the habit of turning off or leaving on a lavatory faucet to let the water flow, etc., just so many examples of an archeology of bodily habits which in modern Europe (and

even more so elsewhere) would provide the cultural historian with knowledge as precious as prehistory or philology (L-S 1950: xiv; my trans.).

In Baudelaire's case it should be noted in passing that the seemingly trivial concerns reflect an assumption that 'the idea of beauty which man creates for himself imprints itself on his whole attire, . . . even ends by subtly penetrating the very features of his face. Man ends by looking like his ideal self' (Baudelaire 1964: 2).

A crucial common interest, to be acknowledged only briefly for the moment, is the attention given to language in its own right. Symbolist poets regard their poems as conscious constructs out of the *material* that is language: 'Writers associated with Symbolism claimed from the new field of experience not disorder but order. . . . How this architecture is produced, what actually happens when a sensation is raised by attention to the level of imagination, is the province of language, the concrete imaginative expression' (Lehmann: 85, 88). Mallarmé viewed the World's vowels and diphthongs as flesh, its consonants as a skeleton, all to be delicately dissected (see Mallarmé 1945:901). Moreover, Baudelaire, who was perhaps more deeply concerned with tying language to something greater than itself—to the mysteries of dreams and a transcendental significance of symbols—considered himself 'architecte de mes féeries'; and an architect counters chaos.[9] This de-romanticized, yet elevated, idea of poetry as a careful construct which, nevertheless, represents much more than a mere linguistic trick is central to these authors and their followers: 'The real achievement . . . of Symbolist aesthetic is to have set on foot a movement towards the proper observation of the *distinctive facts* of poetry' (Lehmann:

[9] In fact some critics feel that the whole mystic side of Baudelaire has been misjudged. Paul Arnold observes: 'There has been much discussion about the mystical experiences of Charles Baudelaire. But is the word itself not inappropriate? . . . was he not thinking more of the syntheses and of the relationships between the arts themselves, as Jean Pommier has already very well explained it?' (Arnold: 41).

Scarfe translates 'architecte de mes féeries' from 'Rêve parisien' as 'The architect of my wonderland' (Scarfe: 214).

175). Those facts, as we shall see, have to do with the power and wonder of orderly language formation in and of itself.

Analogously, departing from a keen interest in language—in what is done with it and in how to explain it—Lévi-Strauss has gone on to re-evaluate the distinctive facts of other areas of systematic thought in his studies of primitive mythology and totemic classification. Many earlier students of myth and totemism had explained them or explained them away by calling them a function of everything from ignorance, to utilitarian ends, to psychological 'needs,' to social charters, to idealized imagery. Lévi-Strauss argues that systematic representations from experience cannot be 'explained' by such reductionist arguments—any more than language can. In parallel fashion Baudelaire took the lead in shifting away from ideas that poetry is a derivation of something less than itself, but something more real or more respectable—e.g. a Romantic urge, a humanitarian ideal—to ideas of the primacy of a logically constructed 'poem world.' And his lead carried on in poetry to Mallarmé and in prose to Proust. Lévi-Strauss, then, encompasses at a second remove developments in the way these writers came to look at their art, as he attributes to various areas of human systematic expression the same sort of autonomy and totality. (Myth for myth's sake!) Such is the program launched by his controversial suggestion that:

> . . . the material out of which language is built is of the same type as the material out of which the whole culture is built: logical relations, oppositions, correlations, and the like (L-S 1963b: 68–9).

Structural anthropology's field of study is the totality of comparable thought. Granted, Lévi-Strauss focuses on preliterate, mythical thought, which most obviously 'acts as a liberator by its protest against the idea that anything can be meaningless' (L-S 1966a: 22). But this specialty is really not much of a restriction: 'We reject, in effect, the too hasty opinions on what is mythic and what is not, and we claim under our usage every manifestation of the mental or social

activity of the populations studied . . .' (L-S 1964a: 12). On
the Symbolists' side we find such people as Mallarmé, this
'servant of a poetry that claimed a transcendent place in the
universe and whose value was postulated as the only reality
accessible to mankind' (Hartley: ix). The tendency toward
universalization common to Symbolism and structuralism has
provoked similar accusations—narcissism and solipsism, respectively (this respective order reflects his opponents' acknowledgement that Lévi-Strauss at least does not create *all*
his own data). Lévi-Strauss has fanned the fire by welcoming
Ricoeur's label of 'Kantism without a transcendental subject':
'In letting itself be guided by the search for mental constraints,
our problematic rejoins that of Kantism' (L-S 1964a: 19, 18;
my trans.). While problems with different idealist labels provide one of our central themes, for the moment let us note a
standard sort of generalization: (1) 'Idealism makes the world a
construction of our own minds' and (2) 'its aim is mathematical
explanation and abstraction' (Gauss: 11). One's initial inclina-
tion would be to deem both our -isms idealisms—Symbolism
principally under rubric (1) and structuralism under rubric (2).
One major goal of this study will be to discourage this inclina-
tion. However, we can at once with Uitti (1961: 27) appreciate how some Symbolist works loom as a reaction against
literary Naturalism (i.e. Realism, which 'assumes the world
as given and its aim is description and observation' [Gauss:
11]). And structuralism can be seen as an effort to escape the
empiricist restraints of the anthropological functionalism which
is locally restricted in collecting instances and generalizing them
in a formula. Émile Durkheim and Marcel Mauss, the two
direct precursors of Lévi-Strauss offer the following observation:

> Aristotle was the first to proclaim the existence and the
> reality of specific differences, to show that the means was
> cause, and that there was no direct passage from one genus
> to another. Plato had far less sense of this distinction and
> this hierarchical organization, since for him genera were
> in a way homogeneous and could be reduced to each other
> by dialectic (Durkheim and Mauss: 5).

Given this view, it can hardly be disputed that both our Symbolists and Lévi-Strauss—as well as the preliterates he describes—stand side by side in the Platonic camp. The crucial question becomes whether 'nature' (i.e. facts 'on the ground') does likewise.

The final 'odd' of this initial toss of the dice is a warning. Lévi-Strauss' works provide the reader with a unique experience, because of the author's apparent fluctuation between extremely rigorous scholarship and ponderous, yet playful, rumination; this fluctuation stimulates reactions ranging from sheer delight to firm disapproval. An example of the latter is found in a piece entitled 'Anthropology's Pope' (*TLS* 1968: 445–7), the author of which opines:

. . . but it should not need arguing that scholars ought rather to demand the more sober, inconspicuous, and enduring accomplishments of clarity, exactitude, and validity (p. 447).

Without informing us if and by whom, in his opinion, whatever sorts of validity he has in mind have been achieved in anthropology, he deals the final blow:

. . . the image of this luminary that forms on the dazzled retina of the mind seems at times to assume, perturbingly, less of a resemblance to Marcel Mauss than to Marshall McLuhan (p. 447).

Now, here we have an interesting opposition indeed. Unfortunately, the author fails to elaborate just why this alliterative juxtaposition of two theorists dealing in human communication gives reason for dispensing with Lévi-Strauss. I fail to see anything grossly contradictory between Mauss and McLuhan, the difference being rather one of the degree of close inspection of data, Mauss' specialization in preliterate groups and his efforts to articulate a locus of unconscious process; and on all these counts I would place Lévi-Strauss with his teacher. But the point is this: if opponents such as the one quoted above, or

D

some of the colleagues he cites, merely complain that Lévi-Strauss *seems* too wildly speculative in relation to his periods of sobriety, but cannot even among themselves decide *when* he is being *which*, then this fact might go further toward telling us something about anthropology or about the nature of the phenomena it studies, than toward providing a basis for dispensing with one of the discipline's luminaries.

To conclude, the difficulty in ascertaining when Lévi-Strauss is *sérieux* (does he himself know?) is a critical point in appreciating him.[10] And what the dissenter fails to recognize is that colorful speculation can be wonderfully, indeed empirically, documented. Take the noted example of the title, *La Pensée sauvage* (*The Savage Mind*), already singled out as a 'spectacularly untranslatable pun' (Geertz: 31)—which is no overstatement. For, on the first level '*La Pensée sauvage*' designates both the subject matter of 'primitive thought' and the 'wild pansy' illustrated on the book's cover—a rather weak *double entendre*. However, the central thesis of the work is that native categories of plants and animals are logically transformable into abstract concepts; and in this light the pun becomes a masterful microcosm of the entire work, as the meaning of 'flower' graduates into that of 'thought' (or vice versa), whether in present understanding or in the word's etymological history. The empirical documentation for this fanciful flight comes in the work's appendix; it presents data from folklore demonstrating that such a metaphorical transformation between levels *really* occurred, as revealed by the personified legends that once surrounded the flower.[11] The pun is even more ingenious when one realizes that the clear-cut distinction between the natives' concrete and abstract concepts is only an analytic device: totemic categories are just as simultaneously 'natural' and 'social' as '*pensée*' is 'pansy' and 'thought.' Yet,

[10] For an extensive analysis of what it means in France to be *sérieux*, and in order to gain a little ethnographic insight on Lévi-Strauss himself, although he was born in Belgium, see (Wylie: 119–23).

[11] This appendix is omitted in the English translation. It was apparently thought that the data's significance would be lost without the titular pun and cover illustration. For the original see (L-S 1962a).

the pun is not exhausted; for a second theme in the work is that 'primitive thought' is a general, universal aspect of conceptualization, present in even (especially?) the most sophisticated analytic processes, for instance, *La Pensée sauvage*. Thus, the title can serve not only as *referent* to subject and *label* for flora, but also as *label* for that which is wrapped up in the book jacket. *La Pensée sauvage* is not only *about* the title but *is* the title—idealized, classified, and labeled, just like the illustrated *pensée*.

As a general rule I would recommend careful scrutiny of all titles in Lévi-Strauss' works. But I would recommend even more careful scrutiny of the works themselves. Commentators should not dwell on his contrived cleverness, whether condemning or commending it, at the cost of neglecting Lévi-Strauss' immense corpus of work—some dozen tomes containing a unified and programmatic cross-cultural analytic of man's classificatory activities.

II

Structural Analysis

A VIEW FROM BAUDELAIRE'S 'LES CHATS'

On this opportunity, this chance of for once detaching oneself from the implacable process, life itself depends. Farewell to savages, then, farewell to journeying! And instead, during the brief intervals in which humanity can bear to interrupt its hive-like labours, let us grasp the essence of what our species has been and still is, beyond thought and beneath society: an essence that may be vouchsafed to us in a mineral more beautiful than any work of Man; in the scent, more subtly evolved than our books, that lingers in the heart of a lily; or in the wink of an eye, heavy with patience, serenity, and mutual forgiveness, that sometimes, through an involuntary understanding, one can exchange with a cat (L-S 1961b: 398).

Granting that it may be overingenious to argue that . . . (Brooks: 86).

'In poetic works the linguist discerns structures which present a striking analogy with those that the analysis of myths reveals to the ethnologist' (Jakobson and L-S 1962b: 1; my trans.).[1] So Lévi-Strauss observes, and then indicates that a poetic work, considered in isolation, contains in itself a set of ordered variants, the variants being stacked, as it were, thanks to the poem's multiple levels—phonological, phonetic, syntactic, prosodic, semantic, etc. (p. 1). On the other hand myth, which by his definition occurs in many cultures with different languages, can only be analyzed in terms of its semantics; therefore, to obtain a suitable set of variants for analysis one must compare versions of a myth from several cultures. We should

---

[1] All translations from this article are my own. An English translation by Katie Furness-Lane has recently appeared in Michael Lane (1970: 202–21).

at once note that these statements do not necessarily oppose
poetic works to myth. In fact, there is no reason not to think
that 'a myth,' when recounted in its native language, might
occur in poetic forms affording a text of more simultaneous
'stacked' variants, than would any translation of its semantics
alone. But to be a 'myth' in Lévi-Strauss' sense, some similar
text—accounting for some aspect of man's relation to his natural
surroundings, such as how he has come to eat what he eats,
marry whom he marries, be where he is, etc.—would have to be
reported from several different cultures. And since these cultures can have different languages, any basis for their all having
a similar text would have to stem from the semantics of the
thing, i.e. from whatever in the text is translatable, since that
is all that would have been borrowed across languages. Thus,
with respect to any one culture a single text of this sort is a
telling of 'a myth,' but only the whole set of variants of that
text is a 'myth' in the larger, cross-cultural sense. Finally, since
to compare myths from many different cultures, we generally
translate them into a different language anyway—our own—
we may as well start with what must be assumed to have been
translatable in the first place! All this is necessarily circular,
and we shall be taking up the matter again.

Roman Jakobson and Lévi-Strauss set directly about providing a structural analysis of Baudelaire's 'Les Chats.' In the
article they offer no preliminary explanation or justification of
their approach, appearing rather to tackle all units of language—in particular of poetic language—as they come and to
note how frequently the units occur and in what order. One is
reminded of a passage from *The Savage Mind* in which the anthropologist generalizes:

> . . . since scientific explanation is always the discovery of an
> 'arrangement,' any attempt of this type, even one inspired by
> non-scientific principles, can hit on true arrangements. This
> is even to be foreseen if one grants that the number of struc-
> tures is by definition finite: the 'structuring' has an intrinsic
> effectiveness of its own whatever the principles and methods
> which suggested it.

For even a heterogeneous and arbitrary classification preserves the richness and diversity of the collection of facts it makes (L-S 1966a: 12, 16).

In a not unkindred spirit Jakobson and Lévi-Strauss explore the gamut of classes and categories in this example of Baudelaire's language:

Les amoureux fervents et les savants austères
Aiment également, dans leur mûre saison,
Les chats puissants et doux, orgueil de la maison,
Qui comme eux sont frileux et comme eux sédentaires.

Amis de la science et de la volupté,
Ils cherchent le silence et l'horreur des ténèbres;
L'Érèbe les eût pris pour ses coursiers funèbres
S'ils pouvaient au servage incliner leur fierté.

Ils prennent en songeant les nobles attitudes
Des grands sphinx allongés au fond des solitudes,
Qui semblent s'endormir dans un rêve sans fin;

Leurs reins féconds sont pleins d'étincelles magiques,
Et des parcelles d'or, ainsi qu'un sable fin,
Étoilent vaguement leurs prunelles mystiques.

Here is my word-oriented translation to which the remainder of the chapter will refer:

The fervent lovers and the austere scholars (scientists)
Love equally, in their ripe season,
The powerful and mild cats, pride of the house,
Who like them are cold-natured and like them sedentary.

Friends of science and of voluptuousness
They seek the silence and the horror of darkness;
Erebus would have taken them for its funereal steeds
If they could have to servitude inclined their arrogance.

They assume in musing noble attitudes
Of grand sphinxes stretched out in the depths of solitudes,
Who seem to fall asleep in a dream without end;

Their fecund loins are full of magic sparks,
And particles of gold, like unto a fine sand,
Star-stud vaguely their mystic pupils.

Anything goes as a basis of organization: rhyme distribution, masculine and feminine rhymes, grammatical categories (e.g. gender, case), sentence structure, syntactic parallelism, semantic aspects (animate, inanimate), homophony, internal rhymes, rhymes in assonance, roots of words, verb tenses, identical phonemes, nasal vowels, liquid consonants, human categories, paronomastic links, rhymed suffixes, timbre, metaphoric function, metonymic function. . . . A delineation is made not only of such individual elements, but also of their combinations, for example: noun-plural-feminine-long units as opposed to noun-singular-masculine-short ones. Similar units are isolated and set in opposition to each other until 'some connections are established, and something which resembles an order appears behind the chaos' (L-S 1964a: 11; my trans.). The poem is confronted in the same way as one might approach a foreign text, (ideally) knowing nothing about it other than the language out of which it is composed. The sort of extreme into which such a procedure can fall is illustrated by paragraphs like the following:

The cats, *chats*, named in the sonnet's title, figure by name in the text only a single time—in the first proposition, where they serve as direct object: *The lovers . . . and the scholars . . . Love . . . The cats.* Not only does the word 'cats' fail to reappear in the course of the poem, but even the initial hushing sibilant /ʃ/ comes back but in a single word: /ilʃɛrʃə/. The hushing sibilant designates, with reduplication, the first action of the felines. This voiceless hushing sibilant, associated with the name of the sonnet's heroes, is carefully avoided in what follows (p. 13).

The authors provide here some precious perusals on the phonetic level, especially in so formally singling out the twofold /ʃ/. But it must be admitted that there is an abundance of pronouns in the poem's latter half, which avoid the necessity of repeating 'cats.'

Only later in the article is the motive for this tedious fragmentation revealed, when the authors suggest: 'Let us try to show how the different levels where we positioned ourselves are cross-checked, how they are completed or combined' (p. 17). Then they proceed to relate thematically (or, as suggested by Lévi-Strauss' introduction, purely semantically) the patterns which appear behind the chaos of the statistical breakdown of formal and lexical elements. In effect, the patterns suggest a series of non-concurrent orderings of the entire poem, each of which can be persuasively 'authenticated,' depending on which formal and lexical units of the poetic language one chooses as a basis for dividing the work. All these patterns are outlined with no concern over what Baudelaire might have had in mind. Occasionally another poem in his *Fleurs du Mal* is mentioned, if it affords a clue for detecting an additional signification for this or that element; likewise, Baudelairian scholars can provide helpful clues. But the sole purpose in utilizing these external sources is to help amass the richest possible repertoire of conceivably interrelatable significant features of the language in this (for our purposes) independent text.

The aim in this chapter is to consider carefully this structural analysis, in order to understand precisely what makes it 'structural.' We are talking about a limited field of data: the data are largely the poem on page 40. While the following discussion will no doubt be slow going, our efforts should be rewarded in achieving a concrete point of reference that will facilitate many arguments in later, brisker chapters.

Two principal ways of organizing 'Les Chats'—which is to say, two modes of organization underlying the poem as a linguistic formation on the page—are described in the following passage:

The sonnet's ternary division implies an antinomy between

the stanza units with two rhymes and those with three. This division is counterbalanced by a dichotomy which partitions the work into two sets of stanzas, that is to say into a pair of quatrains and a pair of tercets. This binary principle, itself supported in turn by the text's grammatical organization, also implies an antinomy, this time between the first section with four rhymes and the second with three, and between the first two subdivisions or four-line stanzas and the last two three-line stanzas. It is on the tension between these two *modes d'agencement*, and between their symmetrical and dissymmetrical elements that the entire composition of the whole work is based (p. 7).

The first of these *modes d'agencement*—the tripartite division—is the standard one which is formally supported by the rhyme scheme and the sentence periods. Here we find the traditional sonnet thematic structure of two stanzas of descriptive tension, followed by the final intensified movement of resolution. First of all, the two quatrains 'view . . . the cats from without, one in the passivity to which the lovers and the scholars are especially sensitive, the other in the activity perceived by the powers of Erebus' (p. 17). In contrast are the last six lines which 'overcome this opposition by acknowledging in the cats a passivity which is actively assumed, and interpreted no longer from without, but from within' (p. 17).

A moment's pause to review what Lévi-Strauss and Jakobson have done might be helpful; Clifford Geertz describes the method:

> . . . these schemas, or structures . . . can then be related to one another—i.e., reduced to a more general, and 'deeper' structure embracing them both. They are shown to be mutually derivable from each other by logical operations— inversion, transposition, substitution: all sorts of systematic permutations . . . (Geertz: 30).

To be more precise, one would probably designate the mappable *forms* of the text its schemata, its *structures* being the set of principles which can translate the materials of one schema into those of the other schemata. Of course, these structures can themselves be diagrammed or mapped, thus making them appear more like 'things' underlying the text than 'ways' (or operations) which make it work. All of these terms necessarily shift about according to the point of view. For example, in what follows we can consider that there are three schemata (quatrain, quatrain, two tercets) each of whose elements must be translated into the others. Or, in the larger context, all three of these can be designated one schema, whose contents must be related to those of the poem's other formal mappings (to be treated later in the analysis). In the case of the poem, then, the authors have so far discerned a set of formal schemata—the most obvious ones: quatrain, quatrain, two tercets—and have shown their contents to be systematically interrelated by the following logical operations: A passive cat is inverted into an active cat, both viewed from without; the viewpoint is transposed to within, as the previous opposition (conflict between active and passive) is resolved by the substitution of an actively assumed passivity, with the cat now no longer viewed from without, but viewing from within. Thus, what has happened on this level through these schemata can be stated *structurally*—and not *formally*, since we are, after all, talking about relationships of *contents*. It is not the stated or implied contents, such as cats, position described, viewer, but their altering relationships which count.

The poem's second *mode d'agencement*—the 'binary principle' (two quatrains and two tercets) is more complex, owing to the various possible ways of logically associating its components. A noticeable syntactic parallelism would suggest linking the first quatrain to the first tercet, since in both stanzas there are subordinate clauses introduced by 'who,' each of which 'embraces the last line of the stanza and is attached to a masculine plural substantive, which serves as a complement in the principal propositions (*The cats, Of . . . sphinxes*)' (p. 8). On the other hand, viewing the subjects and objects of the work in terms of animate versus inanimate yields three different ways of 'corresponding' quatrains and tercets: the fact that the subjects of the first and third stanzas designate only animate beings, as opposed to the inanimate subjects predominating in the other two, suggests an arrangement of 'horizontal correspondences'; the inanimate nature of the grammatical objects of the two tercets groups them in opposition to the tendency in the two quatrains toward animate direct objects, thus providing 'vertical correspondences'; finally, we derive a set of 'diagonal correspondences,' which oppose the exterior stanzas, where the subjects and objects belong to the same class (animate or inanimate), to the interior stanzas showing reversed classes for these parts of speech (p. 8). The authors later extend the bases for these sets of relationships, first amalgamating the horizontal and vertical correspondences in explaining how one can oppose 'the two tercets taken together to the quatrains taken together, bringing to light a tight relation between the first quatrain and the first tercet, and between the second quatrain and the second tercet.' In effect:

(1) The two quatrains taken together are opposed to the two tercets taken together in the sense that the latter eliminate the observer's point of view (*lovers, scholars, powers of Erebus*), and situate the being of the cats outside all spatial and temporal limits;

(2) The first quatrain introduced these spatio-temporal limits (*house, season*); the first tercet abolishes them (*in the depths of solitudes, dream without end*);

(3) The second quatrain defines the cats as a function of the darkness where they position themselves, the second tercet as a function of the light that they radiate (*sparks, stars*) (p. 18).

Then they point out that underlying the diagonally opposed groups is the fact that the cats function as complement in the first and last stanzas and as subject in the other two. Furthermore, the latter formal distribution has striking semantic correlations:

The point of departure of the first quatrain is furnished by the proximity, in the same house, of the cats with the scholars or the lovers. A double resemblance issues from this contiguity (*like them, like them*). In the final tercet also, a relation of contiguity develops even unto resemblance: but, whereas in the first quatrain the metonymic relationship between the house's feline and human inhabitants establishes their metaphoric relationship, in the last tercet this situation is found, in a way, interiorized: the relationship of contiguity depends on synecdoche rather than on metonymy proper. The parts of the cat's body (*loins, pupils*) prepare for a metaphoric evocation of the cosmic, astral cat, which is accompanied by the passage from precision to imprecision (*equally— vaguely*). Between the interior stanzas, the analogy rests on relationships of equivalence, the one rejected by the second quatrain (cats and *funereal steeds*), the other accepted by the first tercet (cats and *sphinxes*); this leads, in the first case, to a refusal of contiguity (between the cats and Erebus) and, in the second case, to the establishment of the cats *in the depths of solitudes*. One sees, then, that inversely from the preceding case, the passage is made from a relation of equivalence, a reinforced form of resemblance (thus a metaphoric function), to relations of contiguity (thus metonymic) whether negative or positive (p. 18).

We shall return to Jakobson's fundamental idea of metonymy and metaphor as modes of language usage. At present I want only to indicate that through their discussion of these first two *modes d'agencement* the authors have carried out a program such as that described by Lévi-Strauss in *Structural Anthropology* for comparing systems from different orders of experience at different levels of conscious awareness:

. . . The question is not to substitute one particular content for another or to reduce one to the other, but, rather, to discover whether the formal properties present homologies, and what kinds of homologies; contradictions, and what kind of contradictions; or dialectical relationships that may be expressed as transformations (L-S 1963b: 85–6).

At the risk of some repetition, it must be stressed that *every-thing* has 'orders' containing potential systems: 'a culture' has language, economics, religion, kinship, etc. (none of which is necessarily distinct); 'a language' has syntax, poetics, phonetics, semantics, etc., 'a word' has phonetics, semantics, graphics, etc. A fine summary by Sheffler helps us appreciate the import of this observation:

> In Lévi-Strauss' view, no society or social system can ever be grasped as a whole. Each society must be seen as composed of diverse and perhaps only more or less interdependent 'orders' of relationships between persons, or between persons and objects, or between objects as conceived by persons . . . each order must have the same ultimate structures as all others.[2] Because of this we may, again, find that each order is but a conditioned variant of some other, the conditioning variables being the kinds of materials involved and the 'dialectical' rules governing the number of possible permutations or variations . . . this possibility of viewing 'orders' . . . as conditioned variants of one another applies cross-culturally as well as within the boundaries of a single society (Scheffler: 71).

In the present article the authors have treated Baudelaire's poem as a world composed of things (formal elements, real referents) that are held together in logically consistent ways across 'orders.' They have assumed the poem is extraordinarily systematic and somehow suggestive of sets of taxonomic principles, dialectically interrelated.

There is more. Thorough as the above two *modes d'agence-ment* might seem, 'neither the dichotomous division nor the partition into three stanzas results in an equilibrium of the isometric parts' (p. 9). That is to say, there are many other formal elements which fail to mesh with either stanza grouping,

[2] Consider Merleau-Ponty's rhetorical question: 'Society itself is a structure of structures: how could there be absolutely no relationship between the linguistic system, the economic system, and the kinship system it employs?' (Merleau-Ponty 1964a: 118).

other formal elements which contradict the degrees of white paper intervening between the poem's lines. The authors, there-fore, posit a third arrangement of the work: 'The middle couplet (lines 7–8) and two isometric groups, which is to say the six lines preceding and the six following the couplet. One has thus a sort of distich [a two-line unit] between two sestets' (p. 10). Among the distinctive grammatical features of the distich are its proper noun, singular number, subjunctive and conditional verbs, pronominal direct object, lack of an epithet for the agent, and the order inanimate-animate. While the en-suing sestet is the standard sonnet unit composed of the two tercets, the preceding six lines are unified by, among other things, 'a reiterative trait: a symmetrical pair of coordinated terms, linked by the same conjunction *and* . . ., binary *détermi-nants*, forming a chiasmus with the binary *déterminés* in the following line—*the silence and the horror of darkness*—which puts an end to these binary constructions' (p. 12). Along with the cementing task of the rhymes in the series of adjectives, 'a double etymological figure linking the beginnings of three lines—*The lovers-Love-Friends*—contributes to the unification of this six line "half-tone stanza" ' (p. 12). Finally, in justifying the sestet-distich-sestet division, the authors allow for the possibility of viewing the special nature of lines 7–8 as only part of a general feature of the second quatrain, all four lines of which appear isolated and elevated from the rest of the poem by several criteria: by peculiarities in its combinations of rhyme, gender and speech parts; by emphases in its 'phonic texture'; and by the fact that 'all the sonnet's rhymes, except those of the quatrain in question, present one or several identical phonemes which precede, immediately or at some distance, the tonic syllable, ordinarily supplied with a supporting consonant' (p. 11).

On the semantic level the authors see this central couplet arrangement (and the accompanying special status of the en-tire second stanza) as a means of opening up the closed 'systems of equivalences' offered by the two prior stanza-based group-ings. A progressive dynamic from beginning to end is suggested, which comes nearer to positing what the poem might mean to the poet than does the rest of the analysis.[3] Briefly, we have here 'the stages of a progression, from the order of the real (first sestet) to that of the surreal (second sestet). This passage is operated across the distich, which for an instant, through the accumulation of semantic and formal processes, transports the reader into a doubly unreal universe, since the distich shares with the first sestet its exteriorized character, while anticipating the mythological resonance of the second sestet' (p. 19).

Finally, we come to two general features of the poem which in retrospect seem to have persisted as an undercurrent throughout all its possible divisions: first, the importance of grammatical number; second, the relationship between rhyme classes and the poet's choice of grammatical categories (p. 11). The first of these features ties in with the theme of immeasurables being projected into infinities, as in those 'final transfigurations: dilation of the cats into time and space, constriction of time and space into the person of the cats' (p. 20). The second feature bears on Baudelaire's alleged preoccupation with womanhood. In particular we find 'this motif of vacillation between male and female,' in which the aspects of 'femininity' and 'super-virility' join together:

All the sonnet's characters belong to the masculine gender, but *the cats* and their alter ego *the grand sphinxes*, partake in an androgynous nature. The same ambiguity is underscored all through the sonnet by the paradoxical choice of feminine substantives for so-called masculine rhymes. Of the poem's initial constellation, formed by the lovers and the scholars, the cats, through their mediation, facilitate the elimination of the woman, leaving face to face—if indeed not confounded—'the poet of the Cats', liberated from 'well restrained' love, and the universe, delivered from the austerity of the scholar (p. 21).

This, then, is the final stage of the sort of 'structural' analysis

[3] This part of the analysis resembles Kenneth Burke's 'dramatistic' symbolic action approach to poetry; see, for example, his study of Keats (Burke 1962: 447–63).

that Jakobson has developed for poetry and that Lévi-Strauss draws on in his analyses of myth.[4] As we have seen, it is noted that in a text there are many different levels on which information can be conveyed. In forms of poetry this is all the more so, due to conventions of rhyme, meter, stanza divisions, etc. For with such conventions equivalences can be implied *en route*, thereby achieving an intensification of the statement of conflict with which the text is concerned. Any information lodged in similar conventions implies some sort of equivalence—i.e. a metaphorical relationship—which through the course of the poem can be played upon by being affirmed, refuted, or left ambiguous. And it is in light of these implied equivalences that a poem can be called a series of classifications.

With this in mind a structural analysis makes two assumptions. First, it assumes maximum systematization of all elements on all levels; that is, it assumes that the elements are interrelated in such a way that if one were changed it would cause significations to shift throughout the text. This assumption of maximum systematization across *all* levels could then be qualified, depending on the end sought in any one analysis. For example, if one wanted to reconstruct how Baudelaire consciously constructed his works, one would be obliged to consider only those levels of this text that were specifically treated in other texts of his which describe how he wrote a poem. The second assumption of the structural approach involves its major analytic device, namely: 'binary oppositions—that dialectical chasm between plus and minus' (Geertz: 29). The basic units in terms of which the poem is explored are these simplest types of contrasted pairs: plural/singular, long/short, animate/inanimate, masculine/feminine, absence/presence of anything; as well as oppositions stated in the poem's contents: interior/exterior, inhabited area/desert, earth/heavens, etc. Only after statements of such contrasts have been sought throughout the text on all its levels do the authors opt in the end for a particular fundamental contrast which appears to be the most pervasive one. They find this in the opposed sets of female-sensuality/ male-logic. It is this contrast, then, which appears most fre-

[4] See especially Jakobson's influential article (1960).

quently on various levels, both formal and semantic, of the poem. And it is the contradiction implied in this contrast that is resolved by means of transformations across levels of the various oppositions: e.g. plural nouns referring to sex-specific, earth-bound animate creatures are transformed eventually into the image of a single, hermaphroditic cosmic cat, no longer known through our eyes, but through whose eyes we know. If the poem could be said to be 'about' something, it would be this conflict. But for our purposes it is less important to remember what the poem is about than how it effects multiple, interrelated levels of signification. For this is its 'mythic' aspect.[5]

In an interesting article Michael Riffaterre seeks to refute much of Jakobson and Lévi-Strauss' analysis (Riffaterre 1966). I think many of his criticisms come from certain mistaken suppositions about the authors' goals in their article. For example, under his rubric 'the irrelevance of grammar,' Riffaterre observes: 'But there is no telling which of these systems of correspondences contribute to the poetry of the text. And there is much to be said about the systems that do not' (p. 206). By 'poetry of the text' he seems to mean some sort of basis for a reader's sensitive response; and his observation is doubtless true. Only some of the 'structures' detected by Jakobson and Lévi-Strauss would

---

[5] If the reader is beginning to wonder what such imaginative poetic convolutions can possibly have to do with preliterate 'texts,' let me simply cite prematurely the English translation of a summary in the opening chapter of Lévi-Strauss' multi-volume *Mythologiques* on South and North American Indians: 'Let us agree then to summarize the myth as follows: A violation of the bonds of marriage (the murder of the incestuous wife, which deprives a child of his mother), aggravated by a sacrilegious act— another form of excess—(the interment of the woman, thus denying her an aquatic burial, the precondition of reincarnation) leads to the disjunction of the two poles; heaven (child) and earth (father). The agent, whose double misdeed banishes him from the society of men (which is an 'aquatic' society, like the society of souls whose name it bears), re-establishes communication between heaven and earth by creating water; and having established his abode in the land of souls (since he and his companion became the heroes Bakororo and Itubore, the chiefs of the two villages of the beyond), he re-establishes communication between the dead and the living by making the latter acquainted with bodily ornaments and adornments, which are both emblems of the society of men and spiritual flesh in the community of souls (L-S 1969b: 58–9).

E

be operative in a given reader's response; nor do the authors assert the contrary. Yet, I imagine they might take anyone to task who would claim to be able to demonstrate *the* basis of 'the poetry of the text'—is it a statistical question, an individual and subjective one? Riffaterre asserts simply that 'no segmentation can be pertinent that yields, indifferently, units which *are* part of the poetic structure, and neutral ones that are not' (p. 209). Yet he fails to demonstrate that this admittedly worthy goal is also a feasible one. I would argue that Riffaterre almost at once shows that he himself cannot distinguish between poetic and neutral units. *I* know he cannot distinguish them because he deems 'neutral' a structural feature which to me is always 'poetic' when I read French poetry. It comes when Riffaterre criticizes Jakobson and Lévi-Strauss where they 'take literally the technical meaning of *feminine* as used in metrics and grammar and endow the formal feminine categories with esthetic and even ethical values' (p. 209). Now, regardless of the reasons—embedded in some distant linguistic past—for rhymes and substantives being designated 'masculine' or 'feminine,' whenever I read French poetry I am sensitive to the admittedly superficial potential device of playing off gender and rhyme type against associations with the two 'real' sexes. This rather coarse brand of sensitivity can more than likely be attributed to my foreignness.

All Jakobson and Lévi-Strauss imply is that a poet could easily take this *bricolage* attitude to his own language and construct contrasts and correspondences out of different varieties of linguistic elements bearing the same names. What is more, such a procedure sounds to me very 'Symbolist'-like. We might even go so far as to observe that most Symbolists were in intimate contact with languages other than French (usually English). We could even declare a foundation of Symbolism to be that tendency to assume a naïve (from-the-outside-looking-in) stance in regards to one's own language, in order to confer significance where others know habit alone. Furthermore, besides playing on language-habits such as gender or rhyme type, as a general rule when Symbolists submitted to 'poetic convention,' they did so in a fashion which indicated their awareness of the convention as such (and as such, something to be questioned, if not challenged). Indeed, insofar as their attitude toward linguistic materials is concerned, our Symbolists display several characteristics included by Lévi-Strauss in his image of the *bricoleur* which is central to his work. He evokes a type of intellectual do-it-yourselfer to illustrate the principles involved when logical arrangements are derived from concrete (sensory) elements:

> The 'bricoleur' is adept at performing a large number of diverse tasks; but, unlike the engineer, he does not subordinate each of them to the availability of raw materials and tools conceived and procured for the purpose of the project. His universe of instruments is closed and the rules of his game are always to make do with 'whatever is at hand'....
> The elements which the 'bricoleur' collects and uses are 'preconstrained' like the constitutive units of myth, the possible combinations of which are restricted by the fact that they are drawn from the language where they already possess a sense which sets a limit on their freedom of manoeuvre ...
> (L-S 1966a: 17, 19).

It is in this spirit that a poet might tinker with gender and rhyme types.

Finally, in order to refute the pervasive hermaphroditic contradiction, Riffaterre offers proof that 'cat' does not *necessarily* imply 'woman' for Baudelaire (a fact, we should note, never claimed by the authors). He summarizes:

> Of course, Baudelaire is perfectly capable of perceiving the cat in the woman, the woman in the cat. He occasionally uses the one as a metaphor of the other. But not always. Whatever the role of cat in his private erotic imagery, it was not such as to make him write *chat* instinctively when he meant *femme* ... (p. 237).

However, Jakobson and Lévi-Strauss show no concern whatsoever for either the poet's intentions or his 'instinct.' As Lévi-Strauss has observed:

> Most often in every sort of creation or discovery, the manner in which the one achieving it has become conscious of it or formulated it to himself is very much different from the objective result he has obtained (L-S in Charbonnier; my trans.).

They are demonstrating a method for discovering a text's structural potential, most of which is self-contained, but which can be occasionally clarified by hints from exterior sources of data. The fact, which Riffaterre acknowledges, that Baudelaire *sometimes* appears to relate cats and femininity points to *one* way of interrelating multiple features of the poem. There are other ways; there might be better ways; there are no incontestably final ways, unless one places specific restrictions on the aims of the analysis, for instance, the demand that any distinctive feature found in 'Les Chats' must occur consistently throughout Baudelaire's *Fleurs du mal*. However, this would clearly limit us to a structural analysis of ' "Les Chats" in terms of *Les Fleurs du mal*' rather than a full analysis of 'Les Chats.' It all depends on which and how many 'texts' are to be stacked.

This brief sketch of a controversial article may provide a sense of the sorts of concerns which predominate in a structuralist approach. It is crucial for our purposes to note the authors' lack of concern for relating the text to anything other than itself. Their very silence on this count, the very single-mindedness of an article composed almost completely of method, underscores how no extrinsic data is regarded as somehow more relevant, more 'explanatory' than the text itself.

For us the problem becomes one of pondering Lévi-Strauss' role in this matter, given his reservations over applying a structuralist approach to literary works. These reservations have been strongly affirmed:

> The fundamental vice of any literary criticism with structuralist pretensions comes from its amounting too often to a play

of mirrors, wherein it becomes impossible to distinguish the object from its symbolic reverberation in the consciousness of the subject. The work studied and the analyzer's thoughts reflect themselves in each other, and we are denied any means of discerning what is simply received from the former and what the latter puts there. One is thus trapped in a reciprocal relativism which can afford subjectively certain charms; but we do not see what type of external evidence it could be referred to.

. . . one never knows during the unfolding of a pseudo-dialogue between the critic and the work, if the former is a faithful observer, or the unconscious animator of a production whose spectacle he is providing for himself, and whose audience will always be wondering if the text is emitted by flesh and blood characters or if it is bestowed on puppets which the critic himself has invented through a ventriloquial skilfulness (L-S 1965a: 126–8; my trans.).

There is a striking similarity between these remarks by Lévi-Strauss concerning unverifiable structural analysis of literature and many criticisms leveled against his own myth studies (see Yalman's comments below, ch. III, and Leach 1965c and 1970). Clearly there is somewhere a failure to communicate: Lévi-Strauss thinks his analyses are validated by some kind of independent source; whereas many of his critics accuse him of 'mere' literary achievements of the sort he here condemns. To anticipate later discussion a little, the misunderstanding must have to do with the continental category of the 'social.'

In chapter III we will discuss at length just why a literary text is not suitable for ultimate structural analysis. At present the nagging problem is the anthropologist's interest in 'Les Chats.' Why has he joined in an exploration of a single poem in a particular language, when he is primarily interested in myths which must persist because of some embodied, universal logical pattern, since they occur among different groups and in different linguistic forms? One reason might be that Jakobson has treated many doubtless unconscious linguistic features in the poem; this is one source of independent data that Lévi-Strauss feels can render structuralism in literature more sound. However, there remains the fact that only one text is presented, and considerable attention is paid to what must be conscious creative processes of the poet. A clue to the reason for Lévi-Strauss' interest in analyzing the poem can be gleaned from an observation made by Mary Douglas:

> After reading the analysis [of 'Les Chats'], we perceive the poem's unity, economy, and completeness, and its tremendous range of implication.
>
> When the lemon-squeezer technique is applied to poetry it has a high rate of extraction and the meaning flows out in rich cupfuls. Furthermore, what is extracted is not a surprise—we can see that it was there all the time. Unfortunately, something goes wrong when the technique is applied to myth: the machine seems to spring a leak. Instead of more and richer depths of understanding, we get a surprise, a totally new theme, and often a paltry one at that (Douglas: 62–3).

These comments, although cast in a negative vein, lead us to appreciate that two variations on a single interest can be traced in Lévi-Strauss' work: on the more scientific side, he seeks out universal structures of human logic, which can only be discovered by maintaining a distant outsider's viewpoint over multiple cross-cultural texts in order to detect their differences (see L-S 1963b: 328); *and*, on the humanistic side, he celebrates the complexity of the systems of classification which serve as his field of inquiry. The cupfuls of meaning wrung from 'Les Chats' result from the fact that the analyzers, knowing French, can manipulate the myriad of formal and lexical elements in seeking clues to patterns and can thereby suggest the marvelous density of a certain author's single concatenation of systems.

This same sort of celebration could likewise center on any single mythic text, provided one knew its language. In this respect it is interesting to compare 'Les Chats' with a typical Lévi-Straussian approach to 'society-texts.' Take, for example his brief analysis of several Australian tribes (L-S 1966a: 87).

To detect a transformational richness on a par with 'Les Chats,' it is necessary to stack all of the Aranda, the Arabanna, and the Warramunga. Only then do we get a fully stated, semantic-behavioral transformation across space and time of 'earth marked as sacred' becoming 'earth marked as social' which is comparable to the French poem's 'cat marked as sedentary' becoming 'cat marked as active.' This contrasting degree of richness comes not from any difference intrinsic to the data, but from a difference in point of view: in Australia we are outsiders (ethnologists), and in the poem we are insiders (*chez nous*, or at least ethnographers).

On the other hand the paltry results mentioned by Mary Douglas are forthcoming when that first motive to discover universal logical patterns prevails; this is the essentially *comparative* motive behind those tactics concisely described by Edmund Leach:

> According to Lévi-Strauss the best method of ascertaining the 'meaning' of a myth is to assemble together all the variant forms in which it has been recorded regardless of their date or source. What we are looking for is the fundamental essence, and this essence, according to Lévi-Strauss, is a matter of logical structure that will persist throughout all the diversities of form by which the myth story has been perpetuated. A comparison of the different versions of a single myth complex will reveal this common structural nexus ... (Leach 1965b: 576).

Jakobson and Lévi-Strauss could have viewed the poem solely with this end in mind, perhaps first translating it out of French. But then a cross-cultural, comparative scope would have been necessary to suggest units of opposition from which to derive structures. One might conclude, then, that the authors have utilized formal elements in an example of a classificatory system in order to reveal a potentially demonstrable 'fundamental contradiction'—the result being female-lust/male-reason, or the myth of the mental hermaphrodite. To fulfil the tendency toward universalization, they would next be obliged to treat many cultures' versions of such hermaphrodite myths (perhaps couched in other terms), to see if common logical transformations do occur. But we would still, alas, not necessarily and demonstrably be in the foremost realm of the 'social.'

Thus, there are at least two levels on which Baudelaire's work may be appreciated. As a poem it offers an example of a more basic form of knowledge and can be analyzed as such:

> . . . just so should the work of the painter, the poet, and the composer and the myths and symbols of primitive Man seem to us: if not as a superior form of knowledge, at any rate as the most fundamental form of knowledge, and the only one that we all have in common; knowledge in the scientific sense is merely the sharpened edge of this other knowledge (L-S 1961b: 127).

But on this level of truly 'common knowledge,' the translatable aspects alone would be interesting. The attention paid to the poet's *procedures* reflects Lévi-Strauss' concern with poetry as an example of one of the *approaches*—that of art—typical of varieties of human thought described as *la pensée sauvage*. However, we shall later see that the Symbolists' own notion of their 'art' brings it more in line with Lévi-Strauss' concept of myth than of art. It will then be evident how some of Baudelaire's and other Symbolists' procedures represent a kind of mythic operator implicit—though not in the form of a consciously contriving individual—in Lévi-Strauss' work. Poems such as the one in question, with no specifically referential subject matter, suggest prime models of human classificatory behavior—that patterning of conceptualization, that basis of translatability underlying a universal 'mental harmony.' In this light the poet is analogous to a myth-maker; but insofar as the poet might be intentionally constructing classifications (interrelating metaphoric associations), his role would parallel that of the anthropologist. If Lévi-Strauss 'undoes' into certain structures what a poet has at least partially systematically 'done,' (i.e. structured), then some mutual outlook can be assumed to exist between the analyzed and the analyzer, and we can check back into their 'ethnographies' to verify the assumption.

It is proposed, then, that Baudelaire can serve the anthropologist as a sort of straw Everyman. The poet's work is a straw man example for illustrating the worth of the analyzer's methods, because the poet and the analyzer share similar 'reality worlds.' Indeed, certain of Baudelaire's poems are credited with foreshadowing that sort of 'indirect statement' which was later fully elaborated by Mallarmé. With this indirect statement Baudelaire introduces the 'sine qua non of Symbolist writing': 'He leads us to a new definition of poetry: *the poem becomes an enigma*' (Balakian: 49). However, Baudelaire is also an Everyman, since his arrangement-making processes are no less indicative of general human ones simply because he might be more aware of them. (The same can, in fact be said for the processes of Lévi-Strauss; and he himself demonstrates a sparkling awareness of the fact that he is simultaneously doing what he is studying—that he is organizing the phenomena of organizing the phenomena of . . .). Thus, Everyman is a straw man. He must be insofar as he is 'natural Man.' To advance Baudelaire's poem as an archetype of *methods* by which man conceptually structures his world of sensory experience is far from being a self-evident proposal. Indeed, it offends our common sense, unless we keep in mind that in the case of man such methods occur outside conscious awareness.

In sum, the Symbolist poem on the page is in one sense a standard 'hunting ground' for those logical structures of fundamental essence. But, in another sense it is a set of program notes which reflect on a near-surface level the types of logical processes which maintain any interrelated body of semantic fields. The Symbolists synthesize the sort of orders of experience which Lévi-Strauss assumes as 'real' and which lie behind his analyses. He seeks to demonstrate the universality of the kinds of arrangements they fabricate (they too, of course, consider their poems to be reflections of the 'universal'). One might finally say that Lévi-Strauss' interest in 'Les Chats' can be attributed to his notion of a poem as an instance of highly formalized, inter-order operations of transformations that are qualitatively analogous to such operations in general. A poem, however—due to its density and conventions—enables emphasis to be cast on the operations as such. Some poems of some Symbolists are straw man examples to demonstrate this notion, because their idea of what they were creating is perfectly in tune with it.

Finally, let me digress here to appreciate the personal appeal 'Les Chats' might have for Lévi-Strauss. Recalling the poem's two line 'modulation'—in which the goal is to resolve the opposition between the work's metaphoric and metonymic functions—brings to mind a passage in *The Savage Mind*. Here Lévi-Strauss deems science an approach to organizing experience that is metonymical in nature ('it replaces one thing by another thing, an effect by its cause'), while art is an approach of a metaphorical order (L-S 1966a: 24–5). (For now we will accept the statement in *Tristes Tropiques* that groups myth with art.) The goal of Baudelaire's distich and, as later shown, of the entire poem, could then be restated as the resolution of the opposition between science and art or myth, which resolution is in certain ways precisely the aim of Lévi-Strauss. This vein of interpretation of the sonnet is continued by noting that 'the solution brought about by the final sestet consists in transferring this opposition to the very heart of metonymy, while expressing it through metaphoric means':

> . . . Each of the two tercets proposes an inverse image of the cats. In the first tercet, the cats primitively enclosed in the house are, so to speak, extravasated from it in order to expand themselves spatially and temporally into the infinite deserts and the dream without end. The movement proceeds from the inside towards the outside, from the recluse cats towards cats in liberty. In the second tercet, the suppression of boundaries is found interiorized through the cats' attainment of cosmic proportions, since they contain in certain parts of their body (*loins* and *pupils*) the sands of the desert and stars of the sky. In both cases the transformation is operated with the help of metaphoric procedures (Jakobson and L-S 1962b: 19).

Lévi-Strauss himself would seem to set about resolving the oppositions in exactly the inverse fashion, i.e. by transferring the opposition to the heart of metaphor (art), while expressing it in the metonymic means of his analyses. His work moves from the universal of cosmic statements of art and myths to the closed units of analytic statements. But while it is, indeed, highly satisfying to explain Lévi-Strauss' attraction to 'Les Chats' by means of such a structural inversion, the explanation will not do. For we shall see that myths (as well as some art) are not simply metaphorical, any more than Lévi-Strauss' analyses are purely scientific in the sense of technical (metonymical). That combination of metonym and metaphor—realizing the one by means of the other—which characterizes Baudelaire's poem likewise typifies myth; and the anthropologist's studies are analogous to the latter. It's all a matter of sensory logic.

III

Poetic Everyman

BY WAY OF THE MODERN POEM (AND LANGUAGE) TO REGAIN A SENSE OF MYTH

Between this postulated matter and the postulated thinker, the curtain of phenomena swings, partly dependent on both (Wild: 89).

The antinomy between mind and body, word and deed, speech and silence, overcome. Everything is only a metaphor; there is only poetry (N. O. Brown: 266).

Various Symbolists shared a sense of the primacy of poetic language, as reflected in the words of Jules de Gaultier:

> It would be a seductive hypothesis to imagine that . . . poetry was the primitive form of language, and that men subsequently substituted for it a more abstract idiom, with whose help they erected general ideas, scientific and philosophical systems (in Lehmann: 145; my trans.).

Similarly it has been proposed that Mallarmé's 'theory of the suggestiveness of words comes from a belief that a primitive language, half-forgotten, half living exists in each man. It is a language possessing extraordinary affinities with music and dreams' (Fowlie 1962: 264). A similar notion is found in Lévi-Strauss' concern over various forms in poetic language which can be taken for marks of residual categories like those found in myths and rites—'remains of methods of observation and reflection which were (and no doubt still are) precisely adapted to discoveries of a certain type: those which nature authorized from the starting point of a speculative organization and exploitation of the sensible world in sensible terms' (L-S 1966a: 16). Thus a poem—at an even further remove than preliterate societies' myths—could offer vestiges of inter-order classifications 'distorted by discrepancies that bear the unmistakable stamp of time elapsed. A cracked bell, alone surviving the work of time, will never give forth the ring of bygone harmonies' (L-S 1963b: 117).

But there is a less primordial, a less esoteric side to these matters, as suggested by Lévi-Strauss when he observes that 'an institution can be archaic because it has lost its reason for existing or on the contrary because this reason for existing is so fundamental that its transformation has been neither possible nor necessary' (L-S 1964c: 45). The problems that intrigued Symbolists concerning the primal symbolization processes of language are the very problems dealt with by Lévi-Strauss. He is interested in classificatory systems built on taxonomic principles; and the principles derive from processes which he takes to be the foundation of systematic thought. The passage quoted from *Tristes Tropiques* (on p. 58) indicates that Lévi-Strauss, who first won fame from his studies of exchange systems and structures in diverse marriage practices, attaches special significance to myth, music, and poetry. A production in these fields strikes him as unbound, 'free to abandon itself to its creative spontaneity':

> . . . *l'esprit*, delivered over to a tête-à-tête with itself and escaping from the obligation to compose with objects, is itself in a way found reduced to imitating itself as object. . . . it thus confirms its nature of a thing among things . . . if *l'esprit humain* appears determined even unto its myths, then *a fortiori* it must be so everywhere (L-S 1964a: 18; my trans.).

In proclaiming art and myth the best areas of study for discovering organizing principles, Lévi-Strauss is in no way singling them out as qualitatively different from other fields of experience. Unlike the Symbolists, whose goal was to 'establish art as an autonomous branch of human activity' (Lehmann: 30) (albeit the only meaningful branch), Lévi-Strauss views all persisting human activity as artistic activity, which is to say, order-creating activity. Or to be more exact, such activity is the extrapolation of data from one level of experience by means of its arrangement on another level:

> . . . The essence of aesthetic transposition, let us say of aesthetic promotion, is to introduce onto the plane of the *signifiant* something which does not exist under this mode or under this aspect in its uncultured state (L-S in Charbonnier: 130; my trans.).

The advantage in concentrating on myth, music, painting, and poetry is that such productions—which, after all, are just as empirically a 'real' part of experience as is 'behavior'—illustrate taxonomic activities less easily distorted by change. This is true simply because neither concepts, nor colors, nor notes, nor sounds—i.e. the units ordered in these enduring fields— exist in any simple direct relationship with the concrete facts of existence. Nor do these units suddenly die off or discover means of increasing their numbers alarmingly. On the other hand, both the latter tendencies plague orderings composed of units ('objects') of human beings. Thus, when one tries to study the latter kind of ordering—generally designated 'kinship'—he is repeatedly frustrated by 'texts' that are imperfect. They are partial remains showing only portions of the more complete systematic thinking which must have generated them. And since preliterate societies lack historical documents, there is no way to discover a record of a more perfect kinship 'text' that more accurately corresponds to any systematic thought. Lévi-Strauss argues that kinship is no more intrinsically an orderly domain than is another—witness, for example, the Eskimos who, like Americans, as far as we know lack fully systematic, categorical people-to-people relations (see e.g. L-S 1963a: 12). He concludes that other areas of orderly productions might yield better records of how men in general make of their experience a systematic place.[1] Finally, when Lévi-Strauss describes artistic works as the 'national park' of modern, science-oriented societies, i.e. 'zones in which savage thought, like savage species, is relatively protected' (L-S 1966a: 219), he is referring to their resistance to the disharmonizing effects of diachrony, which tend to reduce multiple significations to univocal ones.

Perhaps his view can be clarified by a lengthy consideration of Lévi-Strauss' use of structural linguistics, first the ideas of Ferdinand de Saussure and then of Roman Jakobson, in his approach to all cultural 'texts,' linguistic and otherwise. While the Symbolists will tend to fade into the background, they shall be with us in spirit. For much of our discussion harbors vestiges of their ideas on the primacy of relations between objects over the objects themselves. Moreover, we shall be continuously sensing the sort of value that they placed on 'indirect statement,' which, as far as systematic signification goes, strives for flexible becoming rather than having become.

The analytic notions of synchrony and diachrony are involved in Saussure's basic distinction between *langue* and *parole*. To oversimplify, *parole* is the body of specific utterances of a language, none of which is ever exactly reproduced through time. *Langue* is the structure underlying those utterances, the system (grammar) which yields to them the quality of communicability: 'It is the whole set of linguistic habits which allow an individual to understand and to be understood' (Saussure: 77). Excerpts from a crucial publication in the development of structural linguistics should relate these concepts to the problem of synchrony and diachrony:

> The best way to distinguish the essence and the character of a language [*langue*] is the synchronic analysis of current facts, which alone offer complete materials that one can sense directly (Prazsky ... 1929: 7; my trans.).

From the *parole* (current facts) of any community of speakers

[1] It is interesting to compare the two editions of *The Elementary Structures of Kinship* (L-S 1949 and 1969a) to appreciate better the force of Lévi-Strauss' having arrived at this conclusion.

at a given time, we can abstract a *langue* which is their basis of communicating. (Of course, such abstraction requires our having achieved some sort of comparative viewpoint in order to isolate units of *langue* by detecting how one *parole* is different from some other *parole*—most likely an earlier variant of the current *parole*.) The 'synchronic viewpoint' of this *langue* is 'the true and only reality to the community of speakers' (Saussure: 90). Yet note that already we are imposing synchrony where there is none—namely, inter-individually. And Saussure offers this corrective: 'the term *synchronic* is really not precise enough; it should be replaced by another—rather long to be sure—*idiosynchronic*' (p. 90). But even at this individual level 'synchrony' is an analytic conceit; for the *parole* is never duplicated, and the basis of any individual's *langue* (our analytic construct) is undergoing constant change. As Lévi-Strauss has observed, then:

> This is precisely what is expressed in Saussure's distinction between *langue* and *parole*, one being the structural side of language, the other the statistical aspect of it, *langue* belonging to a reversible time, *parole* being non-reversible (L-S 1963b: 209).

To continue:

> The conception of language [*langue*] as a functional system consists in viewing equally in the study some past states of language, whether it is a matter of reconstructing them or of noticing their evolution. . . .
> Linguistic changes often aim at the system, its stabilization, its reconstruction, etc. Thus, the diachronic approach not only does not exclude the notions of system and of function, but exactly to the contrary, not taking these notions into account renders it incomplete.
> On the other hand, synchronic description is no more able to totally exclude the notion of evolution, for even in a sector viewed synchronically there exists a consciousness of the stage in the process of disappearing, of the present stage,

and of the stage being formed. The stylistic elements that feel like archaisms, and in the second place the distinction between productive and non-productive forms, are facts of diachrony that cannot be eliminated from synchronic linguistics (Prazsky ... 1929: 7–8; my trans.).

Here then, it is all a matter of *langue*; and the point to note is that while a single *langue* can always be analytically posited for one time and place, that *langue* inevitably derived from a somewhat different one, of which fact evidence persists.

Lévi-Strauss' concept of 'structure' is to myth and other 'texts' as Saussure's *langue* is to language. Synchronically, the structure is a set of logical relationships among the myth's oppositions, i.e. among its constituent units, which are derived from the differences found in different versions of the myth. (From this stance a poem can be approached in the same structural fashion, although the constituent units must be derived through insight, guesswork, inspiration, etc.). Diachronically, the structure is the set of relationships—transpositions, inversions, and so forth—among as many synchronic structures (i.e. among their differences, their contrasts) as past studies make available to be derived: the structure, so to speak, of the structures. A diachronic perspective can, of course, facilitate any one synchronic analysis by suggesting types of constituent units or relationships. In other words a diachronic viewpoint is one variety of comparative viewpoint. However, as in the case of language, each synchronic segment reveals an awareness of stages of structures both passing and in the process of formulation. Moreover, Lévi-Strauss states:

Whether the myth is re-created by the individual or borrowed from tradition, it derives from its sources—individual or collective (between which interpretations and exchanges constantly occur)—only the stock of representations with which it operates. But the structure remains the same, and through it the symbolic function is fulfilled (L-S 1963b: 203).

The constant structure here referred to is the diachronic

F

structure, the structure of the structures, which in its ultimate
form serves as 'the complete range of unconscious possibilities,'
the 'logical framework for historical developments,' (L-S 1963b:
23). It is this ultimate form that a perfect structural analysis
would unearth. One hardly need point out that this diachronic
viewpoint, derived from comparing different versions of a production, is difficult to bring to bear on modern poems, which
most often are approached in their guise of independent texts
achieved by individuals. A single poem is clearly relevant to
diachrony only as a vestige (in the forms of poetic language)
of some wistfully hypothetical, primal, perfect classificatory
moment, when all was order: rhyme *and* reason.

Related to the idea of more perfected, antecedent systems of
experience-ordering is Lévi-Strauss' point about decreasing
'motivation' of the systems. The phenomena noted is that in time
an informant is less and less able to tell you why—or it is
less apparent to the observer why—this element of the native's
existence is related to that element in such and such a way.
Lévi-Strauss contrasts this diachronic characteristic of preliterate logical networks to Saussure's view of language:

> For Saussure . . . language moves from arbitrariness to moti-
> vation. The systems we have been considering . . . go from
> motivation to arbitrariness: conceptual schemes (at the limit,
> simply binary opposition) are constantly broken open to
> introduce elements taken from elsewhere; and there is no
> doubt that these additions often entail modification of the
> system (L-S 1966a: 156–7).

Thus, poetic language presents itself as vestiges of some ultimately 'motivated' conceptual ordering (perhaps we could
replace 'motivated' with 'sensible' in all connotations of the
latter term). But unlike any single documentation of one mem-
ber in a mythic series, the poem cannot readily be treated as
just one version in continuous but changing orderings of experience—which latter for Lévi-Strauss should reveal a diachronic structure persisting even as 'motivation' decreases and
as 'the systematic appearance is . . . disturbed or temporarily

put in abeyance' from time to time (L-S 1966a: 157). Indeed, as we saw with 'Les Chats,' a single poem on a page can provide an area of relief from problems of diachrony—a chance to pause and celebrate undisturbed classificatory potential.

This whole question of 'motivation' arises only in the light of Saussure's assertion of the fundamental 'arbitrariness' of language. And Lévi-Strauss' understanding of this matter is crucial to his entire program of research, as ours of his is to ours! Saussure begins with a sense of two realms ('levels'-to-be): (1) as yet undifferentiated sound (more precisely 'sound image'), which will yield members of the set of *signifiers*; (2) as yet undifferentiated conceptual matter, which will yield members of the set of the *signified*. These two realms cannot be demonstrated to be intrinsically related. But the *fact* of their systematic relationship is *language*, which is composed of units called 'signs.' Thus,

> . . . THE LINGUISTIC UNIT IS A DOUBLE ENTITY, ONE FORMED
> BY THE ASSOCIATING OF TWO TERMS (Saussure: 65; my
> capitals).

Of these two terms, one belongs to the now distinct sound-image level of experience, and the other belongs to the conceptual level. But these two levels are *nothing* until being connected by a 'sign'—which is in fact no more than their state of connection—because there is no other 'level' in terms of which to understand (to encode) the other 'level' until they are related, or more precisely *arbitrarily* related. In light of the above then,

> Linguistic signs, though basically psychological, are not abstractions; associations which bear the stamp of collective approval—and which added together constitute language—are realities that have their seat in the brain (Saussure: 15).

This statement is extremely important. For it implies a tone of this sort: if, then, *anything* is not abstract (i.e. is concrete), it must be the 'sign'; and if 'signs' (which are, after all, merely a state of connectedness) can *be* any*where*, they must be in the brain. Surely this is how Lévi-Strauss means to say that 'structures' are *real* and that they exist in the brain.

Now, what is meant by the arbitrariness of the sign? Most simply, it means that there is no 'motivation,' no natural connection between the signifier and the signified (see Saussure: 69). Lévi-Strauss has commended Jakobson and Benveniste for their reconsideration of Saussure's thinking, as they emphasize how this 'arbitrariness' might be self-defeating as soon as it is achieved. For once a system of signs is posited, motivation can begin to accrue:

> To simplify my argument, I will say that the linguistic sign is arbitrary *a priori*, but ceases to be arbitrary *a posteriori*. . . .
> . . . it is in no way certain that these phonemic options, which are arbitrary in relation to the *designatum*, do not, once the choice has been made, imperceptibly affect, perhaps not the general meaning of words, but their position within a semantic environment. This *a posteriori* influence works on two levels, the phonemic and the lexical (L-S 1963b: 90–1).

However, back at the *a priori* level, where arbitrariness still holds, it is intriguing to note that there really could not even conceivably exist such a signifier-signified natural connection (a connection 'in nature'), since before the fact of the connection there is no*thing* to connect:

> Neither are thoughts given material form nor are sounds transformed into mental entities; the somewhat mysterious fact is rather that 'thought-sound' implies division, and that language works out its units while taking shape between two shapeless masses (Saussure: 112).

We might here foreshadow Proust's similar conclusion regarding the locus not of language, but of the conceptualization of experience lived, as pointed out by Moss: 'Nothing exists until it is connected by memory to a former experience; the connection between two nonrealities gives them an existence' (Moss: 110). We are witnessing the death of dualism.

But the arbitrariness underlying language is more pervasive still. Apart from the essential arbitrariness of any conceivable signifier-signified connection, once given a system of such links, it is far from determined just what unit on one level is referred to by a unit on the other level. A comparative viewpoint affords ready proof of this fact, through the observation that 'the difference in value between *sheep* and *mouton* is due to the fact that *sheep* has beside it a second term [*mutton*] while the French word does not' (Saussure: 116). Thus, we come to the remarkable conclusion:

> Instead of pre-existing ideas then, we find in all the foregoing examples *values* emanating from the system. When they are said to correspond to concepts, it is understood that the concepts are purely differential and defined not by their positive content but negatively by their relations with the other terms of the system. Their most precise characteristic is in being what the others are not (Saussure: 117).

And so, meaning becomes a system; a change of one unit on one level reverberates throughout the language: take away 'mutton,' and 'sheep' is something you serve on the table, causing it to be no longer associated with 'cow,' insofar as the latter contrasts with 'beef' . . . and so on through the paradigmatic sets.

In Saussure, then, Lévi-Strauss discovers the notion of how a *system* can be composed of socially contracted *relationships* or connections (rather than things) between 'levels,' whose substantive content is of secondary interest. He adds to this another corrective to Saussure suggested by later linguists. This involves the concept of the phonetic model, which demonstrates that Saussure was in part wrong about the signifier (the auditory unit) when he said: '(a) it represents a span, and (b) the span is measurable in a single dimension; it is a line' (Saussure: 70). Rather, the auditory unit is delimited by a stacked set (a bundle) of distinctive features. And the whole series of distinctive features exists in principle as a set of binary oppositions (voiced/unvoiced, open/closed, front/back, etc.) which, through various combinations of the oppositions' different sides, should generate the entire acoustic array known to human language. Thus, not only can complex systems take shape out of 'shapeless masses,' but any one unit in a system can contain multiple features—relatable to other features—simultaneously. That is to say, a panoply of features can lurk within some apparently unitary thing (such as a vowel-thing or a consonant-thing). Hence came Lévi-Strauss' famous article on the structural study of myth (1963b: ch. XI) with its bundles of distinctive features built out of differences.

Jakobson has greatly influenced Lévi-Strauss' thought, particularly in his concepts of metonymy and metaphor. For example, in discussing 'species' Lévi-Strauss states:

> Each system is therefore defined with reference to two axes, one horizontal and one vertical, which correspond up to a point with Saussure's distinction between syntagmatic and associative relations. But 'totemic' thought, unlike speech, has this in common with mythical and poetical thought that, as Jakobson has established for the latter, the principle of equivalence acts on both planes (L-S 1966a: 149).

Jakobson observes that all language events involve two psychological processes—selection and combination—both of which are normally always present, but in varying degrees (Jakobson and Halle 1956). In any linguistic production certain elements have been *selected* from a sort of 'metaphorical pool'—a substitution set, theoretically composed of elements 'linked by various degrees of similarity, which fluctuate between the equivalence of synonyms and the common core of antonyms' (p. 61). The selected elements are *combined* in a context wherein their status is one of contiguity. Thus, from one viewpoint the speaker selects certain elements from a *langue* level 'metaphorical pool' and places them in contiguity as an instance of *parole*. (And all the elements that could be conceivably substituted for each other in the same position in a given instance on the level of *parole* constitute a paradigmatic set). Moreover, from another viewpoint different forms of linguistic contiguity might be selected and still convey the same message. Thus, one might say, I think, that there exists on the level of *langue* a sort of 'metaphorical pool' of metonymy.

Putting this in more recent terminology, we could say that any 'message' is derived from a 'code' composed of alternative associations (metaphoric function) and of alternative connections (metonymic function). Finally, it should be noted in passing that such choice-potential of more or less analogous metonymical associations is greatly increased if one extends his scope from 'speech' to 'communication events.' For example, Lévi-Strauss describes native social groups as having 'the choice of several synthetic procedures to assure the transmission of the message: nomenclature, emblems, modes of behavior, prohibitions, etc., used either alone or together' (L-S 1966a: 150). As a single *procedure* each of these choices is syntactic (metonymic), but as an element in the set of choices it pertains to the metaphoric function. 'Metaphor . . . is not a later embellishment of language but is one of its fundamental modes' (L-S 1963a: 102). To this point we shall return.

We need to consider two aspects of Lévi-Strauss' use of metaphor and metonymy: first, insofar as they are mental functions involved in the *formation* of structures in any order (kinship, myth, etc.); and then, insofar as they (especially metaphor) are bases of any 'code' by which we can move from a structure in one analytically determined order to a structure in another order, i.e. by which we can *maintain* the interrelationship of those orders. Again I follow Lévi-Strauss' definition of codes as 'means of fixing significations by transposing them into terms of other significations' (L-S 1966a: 172), remembering that 'signification' here refers to Saussure's *value* (i.e. the contracted association of one particular sound-image unit with one particular concept unit—but more generally and beyond language, the contracted association of any two different kinds of units). I then touch on some of the ways Lévi-Strauss handles what might be called crystallizations of man's metaphoric function—'metaphors' in the usual sense. And finally, we consider Lévi-Strauss' own use of the word 'semantic' and briefly ponder

where all this leaves us in respect to 'meaning.' Still another
mid-stream epigram should suggest the general tenor of what
follows. It indicates how far removed we are from any referential definition of meaning, no matter what the order of experience; Lévi-Strauss here refers to the nature of objects in
works of art:

> Exactly like words in language: in themselves, objects have
> a very blurred meaning [*sens*], almost empty; they really only
> take on meaning in a context. A word like 'flower' or 'stone'
> designates an infinity of very vague objects, and the word only
> takes on full meaning in the interior of a sentence (L-S in
> Charbonnier: 101; my trans.).

He justifies this Mallarméan viewpoint precisely in the way
Saussure would have: 'Thus *time* and *temps* cannot mean the
same thing in French and English, if only because English also
has the term *weather*, which French lacks' (L-S 1963b: 93).

We have pondered the place of metaphor and metonymy in
language. But for Lévi-Strauss the metaphoric function and the
metonymic are presupposed in any 'text' of systematic thought,
whether conscious or unconscious; and both functions are
crucial in determining through analysis the structure of anything that has resulted from systematic thought. Metaphor
is a means toward association, a means of connecting 'things,'
whether objects-to-objects, relations-to-relations, levels-to-levels,
domains-to-domains, objects-to-domains, people-to-birds, people-
to-people, etc. The justification for the connection is the *similarity* that is sensed to exist between the things. Metonomy is a
means of connecting things by the notion of their juxtaposition,
whether temporal or spatial. For example, a table is spatially
related to a chair by metonymy, a 'Gesundheit!' temporally to
a sneeze; synecdochic metonymies can be spatial or temporal.
In other words if I say 'knife' and you respond 'fork,' you
have effected a metonymic association; however, if your response
is 'sword,' the association is metaphoric. The critical conclusion
is that metonymy and metaphor are principles which underlie
any lexical substitution set in language; but they are also the

logical prerequisites for the formation of any system out of any elements. Thus, it is not quite true, as has been maintained, that 'Lévi-Strauss, like all good rationalists, starts with a *tabula rasa*' (Goddard: 410). The *tabula* is indeed devoid of *things*, but at least two *principles* are present, although not to be accounted for.

For Lévi-Strauss these two principles are *a prioris* of any system. Whether the units of the system are the sounds of language, the people of kinship, or the animal, bodily, geographic (etc.) imagery of myth, those units can never stand related in a system unless the principles are already assumed. In fact, for any level of 'social discourse,'[2] these principles must already be there before we begin thinking of them. He demonstrates this dramatically in the opening chapters of *The Elementary Structures of Kinship*. Yet, the priority of metaphor (association by a sensed likeness) and metonymy (association of unlikes by juxtaposition) can equally well be demonstrated in any example of a simplest system, i.e. in a binary opposition. To illustrate this point, let us ponder an opposition which underlies many kinship structures. The opposition is WE/THEY, and the statement of this opposition is a rule that WE must marry out (see L-S 1969a: ch. III–IV). Robert Murphy summarizes the matter well:

> In plainer language, the basic 'we-they' distinction within human society is set by the rules of incest coupled with the laws of reciprocity. Among the latter rules or norms, those regarding the preference for marriage with one or another, or both, cross-cousins are the most elementary means of guaranteeing that he who gives a woman in marriage will have the expectation of getting one back as a wife (Murphy 1970: 166–7).

We assume a universe so divided: WE necessarily in relation with THEY, and that is all; but already metonymy and metaphor pervade. The WE is metonymically related to the THEY by

---

[2] To appreciate this usage of 'discourse' see (L-S 1963c: 640).

juxtaposition. Both WE and THEY are each related metonymically to the totality WE/THEY (part to whole). Moreover,
from this level any further differentiated categories within WE
or THEY will be metaphorically related, because they will be
alike, i.e. WEs, not THEYs, or THEYs, not WEs. But, if we
drop our point of view a degree and look back to the level
above, these further differentiated WEs becomes metonymically
related to the whole WE, 'spatially' because they are parts of
it, and 'temporally' because they derived from it. But all these
subdivisions of WE are metaphorically interrelated among themselves by similarity: all are WEs. And so on. Thus, metonymy
and metaphor are given in any system and of any structure
analytically derived from its variants. They are essential to a
system's being and to its further formations or elaborations.
Finally, it should be noted how binary opposition stands in relation to systems in general, just as dual organization stands in
relation to social structure. Both are the logically simplest examples of something that can indeed be more complex. Thus,
if something is true of binary opposition, it must hold for systems
in general—hence the opposition's utility as a tool of investigation (see L-S 1944a, 1969a: ch. I–IV).

It must be stressed that what we are talking about here is
absolutely crucial in Lévi-Strauss' work. It is the socio-logic—
originated by Durkheim, concretely articulated by Mauss, expanded through linguistics—that serves as the core of Lévi-
Strauss' every concern. He observes that logically there can be
no communicative-systems without the two 'functions' we are
calling metaphoric and metonymic (again, metaphor = sensed
identity; metonymy=conceived difference plus *necessary* interrelationship). In the domain of 'kinship' which derives communicative-systems out of categories of people, this socio-logic
can be most clearly seen in what Lévi-Strauss calls the 'atom
of kinship' (L-S 1963b: 72), which is the simplest concrete
embodiment of the basic requirements for conceiving of people-
communicative-systems. Here is the atom: a brother is identified
with his sister whose future offspring require an impregnator
other than the brother. In *a priori* terms this situation is known
as the incest taboo. Given a potential impregnator in the same

position, the simplest solution is for the two males to exchange sisters. But observe that in this most basic of concrete ideal constructs, a minimum of two groups (two brother-sister identities) is required, both of which *conceive* of the *other* group as different but as that to which it necessarily must relate itself. Thus, the fact of the *social* is just as paradoxical—and just as unapproachable through behaviorist notions—as the fact of *language,* when one ponders their necessary conditions (on language see below). These, then, are the minimal dimensions of communicating man. Systems as conceived or acted in terms of—whatever sorts of elements constitute them—can disregard biology, historical 'fact,' needs, drives, etc.; but the systems cannot ignore these basic principles of their own composition. Man is Social Man. Social Man is classifying or communicating Man, who fundamentally must needs elaborate categorical distinctions and equivalences amongst the features selected from his experience. That is not necessarily all there is to Man, but it covers a lot, especially in what pertains to the zone of cross-cultural contact and comparison.

On a still grander scale, we find ourselves confronting Nature/Culture. For what have we been discussing here, if not that very passage between Nature and Culture which is Lévi-Strauss' most general concern? Are not the metonymic and metaphoric functions the very processes by which *rule* is imposed, by which the 'natural order' is disrupted and re-arranged into something new, something unnatural, something cultural? Yes. Culture itself, as opposed to natural order, is a function of these two functions. For culture or 'society' subsumes a sensed identity or solidarity (metaphoric function) with *others,* together with a notion of differentiation but necessary interrelatableness (metonymic function)—both of which are contained in the essential cultural fact, namely *reciprocity* as manifested in positive exchange. Moreover, as Jean Pouillon has it:

> It is a matter of repeating an endeavor whose significance is determined *a priori* by the double relationship of man with other men and of man with nature, a positive relationship of exchange in the one case, a negative relationship of

detachment in the other case; repeating the endeavor, nothing more, because everything which truly matters is situated at the beginning, in the initial movement by which man founds the reign of culture (Pouillon 1956: 169; my trans.).

Pouillon is here, however, slanting matters toward the modern West. For basically the positive exchange is not just between men and men, who find themselves ever more alienated from the natural surroundings. On the contrary, men are likewise alienated from men and in positive reciprocation with natural elements —whence the significance of 'totemism,' house pets, and senti-mental zoo keepers. Men are just as capable of associating themselves with animals, plants or things as they are with each other. While this imposition of rule is most generally recognized in its guise of non-random distribution of sexual rights as stated by the 'incest taboo,' it is equally characteristic of all areas of 'human' endeavor.[3] For example, what we might desig-nate the 'raw taboo' achieves various systematic relationships between men and natural items—relations that might otherwise be absent. For another example, the 'vocal noise taboo' *means* that there is a systematic potential in sounds. All of these ex-amples are illustrations of 'passages from nature to culture,' i.e. of precipitating interrelatable constituent units (disconti-nuities) out of a prior, continuous data source. The systems thereby rendered possible are what is particularly human—and inexplicable in any utilitarian or 'natural-cause' terms—about man.

Thus, we can follow Leach half-way when he states:

This analogy [between matrimonial exchange as a system of communication between social groups, and cooking as a sys-tem of communication between Man and Nature] is not preposterous. Human brains devised styles of cooking and human brains devised rules of marriage—the two codes of

[3] On the sensed identity *plus* necessary interrelationship of differents and how this is 'stated' by the incest taboo, see (L-S 1969a; chs. I–IV and 1956). On zoo keepers see (L-S 1966a: 38).

thought may well link up. But Lévi-Strauss has not tried to show that they in fact link up ... (Leach 1967b: 10).

But the latter half of this statement is misdirected. For it is not a matter of 'two codes of thought'; rather what we have here is one code of thought applied to two different orders of units. In marriage the units are men and men (set into relationship by means of women), and in cooking the units are men and plants, animals and utensils (by means of fire). Leach's mistake comes in assuming that men are necessarily Man and that plants and animals are Nature. Lévi-Strauss' concepts are much more operational than this; for Nature is ultimately anything random and Leach's Man (actually Culture) is anything regulated. And even Man can be very natural, for example, if he copulates regardlessly, randomly.[3a]

Finally, Lévi-Strauss has apologized (1966a: 247n) for describing such a Nature-Culture passage too much like an historical genesis, as in the ringing conclusion to the introduction of *The Elementary Structures of Kinship*:

The prohibition of incest is where nature transcends itself. It sparks the formation of a new and more complex type of structure and is superimposed upon the simpler structure of physical life through integration, just as these themselves are superimposed upon the simpler structures of animal life. It brings about and is in itself the advent of a new order (1969a: 25).

For whether such a single moment ever occurred is beyond our

[3a] Lévi-Strauss does employ a more commonsensical nature/culture opposition in his approach to 'totemism': '. . . when I make loose usage of the term totemism, I never refer to a past or present institution but to a classificatory device whereby discrete elements of the external world are associated with discrete elements of the social world' (L-S 1963d: 7). Of course in terms of the grander rationalist Nature/Culture opposition, any discrete elements are 'culture' as opposed to undifferentiated continuity (call it 'nature'). It is this grand opposition which Lévi-Strauss employs to stress the relative autonomy and systematic quality of all man's efforts toward classification, from kinship to myth.

knowledge. What is far more important is that the passage
occurs repeatedly, daily and on multiple levels in different areas
of effort, whenever discontinuous units are derived in systematic
interrelationship from experience. For example,

> . . . art constitutes, at its highest point, culture's taking
> possession of nature, which is the characteristic type of the
> phenomena studied by ethnologists (L-S in Charbonnier: 115;
> my trans.).

And the only remaining point to be added should really come
as no surprise. Any genesis of constituent units has to take place
in *two* places *at once*, if the units are to become systematic, i.e.
interrelatable, exchangeable, communicable. This fact is most
obvious in the case of language:

> You know that it is the *vexata quaestio* par excellence and
> that philosophers have for a very long time run up against
> this contradiction—namely, that language has not always
> existed, but that on the other hand we do not understand
> how it could have originated. Since for language to arise it
> is not sufficient for someone to invent discourse; it is more-
> over necessary that he who is opposite understand what is
> being undertaken to be said to him (L-S in Charbonnier:
> 160; my trans.).

The point, then, is simply this: 'Structuralism postulates that
in achieving this passage from nature to culture, man obeys
laws he does not invent' (Gramont: 30). Thus, it is maintained
that the basis of communication, the assimilation of the *other*
into ourselves, is extra-individual and the formation of that
basis is Nature *becoming* Culture. In the complex phrasing of
Lévi-Strauss:

> Exchange is not a complex edifice, constructed out of obliga-
> tions to give, receive and return, with the help of an affective
> and mystic cement. It is a synthesis immediately given to, and
> by, symbolic thought which, in exchange as in every other

form of communication, overcomes its inherent contradiction of perceiving things as the elements of the dialogue, simultaneously under the relation of self and of others, and destined by nature to pass from the one to the other (L-S 1950; xlvi; my trans.).[4]

As Merleau-Ponty concludes: 'If the symbolic function outstrips what is given, there is inevitably something confused in the whole order of the culture it sustains. The antithesis between nature and culture is no longer sharp and clear' (1964a: 123).

Returning more specifically to metonymy and metaphor proper, we must consider how Lévi-Strauss regards metaphor as a means of maintaining the interrelationship of different structures, how metaphor helps constitute 'codes.' This aspect of the language function corresponds exactly to what we have already discussed; but—our viewpoint has changed. Now we accept the fact that systems on analytically different levels have been formed: beyond the theoretical limiting case of simple binary opposition have arisen whole complexes of cross-cutting, interrelatable conceptual categories. But the balanced growth of *pensée sauvage*, always in dialectic with '*réalité concrète*,' can wherever it takes root become disheveled.[5] Such thought formulates categories only to have the *réalité concrète* half of the dialectic drop out, due to demographic trends, natural catastrophes, and so forth. But the metaphoric function is constant, always at hand to attempt to reinstate equilibrium.[6] It is that same mental process, which is prior to any system, that is activated to restore systematic relationships—inter-level correspondences—where others see none. This is the stage in the metaphoric process that Lévi-Strauss seems to have in mind, when he says:

---

[4] Or in a translation of Merleau-Ponty's paraphrase, '. . . the exchange would not be an effect of society but society itself in act' (Merleau-Ponty 1964a: 116).

[5] *Réalité concrète* ('the concrete reality of empirical observation') as distinct from *réalité* is discussed briefly by Lévi-Strauss in (Tax: 115).

[6] This matter is treated at some length in (L-S 1966a: 67ff.).

The effectiveness of symbols would consist precisely in this 'inductive property,' by which formally homologous structures built out of different materials at different levels of life— organic processes, unconscious mind, rational thought—are related to one another. Poetic metaphor provides a familiar example of this inductive process, but as a rule it does not transcend the unconscious level. Thus we note the significance of Rimbaud's intuition that metaphor can change the world (L-S 1963b: 201–2).

In a later work he goes on to clarify this vein of thought:

> . . . thanks to myths, one discovers that metaphor rests on the intuition of logical relationships between one domain and other domains, into whose ensemble metaphor reintegrates then the first domain, notwithstanding that reflexive thinking which is intent on separating the domains. Far from being added to language in the manner of an embellishment, every metaphor purifies language and restores it to its primary nature, through obliterating momentarily one of the innumerable synecdoches out of which discourse is made (L-S 1964a: 345; my trans.).

What is the same in the *a priori* metaphor and the maintaining metaphor is the process itself: association due to sensed likeness. And the results of this constant process are at more or less of a remove from the hypothetical state posited by Lévi-Strauss, when he suggests that 'for the sake of argument, we suppose an initial point at which the set of systems was precisely adjusted' (L-S 1966a: 68)—this being an analytic device frequently used. In sum, 'All the world's a stage' is at a far further remove from such an assumed point than:

> A relative by marriage is an elephant's hip (L-S 1969a: epigraph).

The latter example of metaphor is actually the starting point for Lévi-Strauss' opus on kinship. It is effective as such for the following reason: from our analytic, word-oriented point of view, the metaphor appears absurd, or if not that at least of far too wide an angle for serious consideration. But our reaction stems from our own notions of metaphors as referential statements. Lévi-Strauss would argue instead that the epigram in question reflects a categorical equivalence: 'affine-things' are not like 'elephant-hip-things'; rather, both of these items of experience for the people in question fall into the same category (i.e. are metaphorically associated) but from our point of view at different levels—one social (affine), the other natural (elephant). The significations of one level are metaphorically associated ('coded') by means of metonymy (juxtaposition in the epigram) to the significations of another level, and with no direction or priority implied. (And for the metaphor to 'make sense' we would have to discern further codings: for example, that a blood relative is an elephant's back—thereby making blood relatives elevated and unitary in relation to the lower and multiple relatives by marriage; or the like.) The code is closed and circular; and since in this instance the code uses real things to interrelate natural categories and social ones, it might change if all elephants or all in-laws die off. Finally, we should note that Lévi-Strauss frequently leads into his works by means of such off-key metaphorical statements. For example, all of *Du Miel aux cendres* (1966b) is generated from a few clichéed metaphors about honey and tobacco, which turn out to occur significantly throughout the Old and New Worlds and to provide means of transposition from the natural and social orders of imagery to supernatural and imaginary ones, thanks to the very disparate distinctive features marked by each of these two substances. Moreover, as Lévi-Strauss himself builds codes between systems on different levels, he feels free to drop metaphors in order to hint at what he is about. As we have seen in the *pensée sauvage* example (see ch. I), he likes to illustrate *en route* the process he is describing, in order no doubt to give the reader a chance to try his own significance-constructing out of disparate elements, before it is—or in case it is not—done neatly for him. Thus, while the *goal* of Lévi-Strauss' structuralism is eventually to get down to the *sine qua non*s of systematic

G

productions, we shall later see that its satisfaction lies in the getting there, in the suggestive discovery of inter-order correspondences.

We turn now to a brief consideration of how all the above relates to various issues in semantics. First, what does the term 'semantic' mean to Lévi-Strauss? A quick semantic study of Lévi-Strauss' '*sémantique*' has revealed the following: the word frequently appears in discussions of the domains of art and language and always against a Saussurian background; the general framework of these discussions is suggested by the following:

> The essence of language—as Ferdinand de Saussure so clearly branded it—is to be a system of signs without material relations with that which it is their mission to signify. If art were a complete imitation of the object, it would no longer have the character of the sign. So indeed, it seems to me, we can conceive of art as a significant system, or as an ensemble of significant systems, but one which always remains half-way between language and object (L-S in Charbonnier: 115–16; my trans.).

Elsewhere in the same work Lévi-Strauss commends cubism because 'it rediscovers art's semantic verity, for its essential ambition is to signify, and no longer only to represent' (pp. 79–80). Moreover, he states that a work's semantic function tends to disappear both when individualization increases and when imitation takes precedence over signification (pp. 66, 128). On the individualization side of things, what we find is that an expressive function overrides any semantic one. And in extreme cases such as concrete music or abstract painting, the whole work is made 'outside any semantic rule,' with only an occasional signification surging out from the work, and then only by chance.

Thus in art and language an element has relatively greater semantic value (meaning) the more it displays Saussurian-type signification, i.e. the more it relates distinguishable units in one system to distinguishable units in other systems (in this case not just sound systems and concept systems). Hypothetically, 'sheer' imitation would be non-semantic, because the representation of the object or concept would be the object or concept itself, and not an encoding in other units (e.g. paint, phones) of that object or concept (see L-S 1966a: ch. I). Likewise, any supposedly sheer expression would be non-semantic, not because some intrinsic relation between the code and the encoded is necessary or possible (although a sensed relation prevails in art), but because for any signification to be effected in the first place, *multiple* systems of signs on different levels—such as sound-images, graphics, concepts, etc.—must already be agreed upon (socially contracted). Sheer expression would not be based on any such contract. And so it is that in language, art, or anything else, communicability lies somewhere between reproduction and randomness; therefore, communicability cannot be exact, yet neither can it be absent.

From this position we can better understand Lévi-Strauss' use of 'semantic' throughout *The Savage Mind* and elsewhere, with all the talk of 'semantic levels,' 'semantic position,' 'semantic loads,' etc. (L-S 1966a: 52, 56, 64). For example, when he speaks of the complexity of the semantic position of bees in a certain culture, he has in mind the diverse aspects which are marked—sex, animateness, honey manufacturing and so forth—and which through the application of metaphoric or metonymic principles enables 'bees' to point to various systematized domains simultaneously. Finally, such semantic richness (always based on arbitrary positioning) is characteristic of myths in general, these being but worlds of interrelated, multilevel significations initially constructed—as is language—out of the arbitrary.

The most obvious implication of this is that the sorts of systems most interesting to Lévi-Strauss are not founded on any referential meaning, but rather on an operational and contextual one. Any view of meaning which might be labeled 'referential'[7] could never be more than a secondary theory, belatedly superimposed on the foundation of systematically

[7] Stephen Ullmann (1967) provides a very clear and literary account of this sort of theory.

interrelated, multi-level structures. Such a view would appear to relate to the discovery of writing, which aways implies hierarchy —i.e. the state wherein one element of society feels itself superior to certain elements of the culture and therefore in a position to use them as things: people so used are slaves to the elite; units of language so used are equivalents of 'things' (predecessors of referential words, I would suppose) which are likewise sources of power to incipient elite classes.[8] In Lévi-Strauss' overall view, writing, which makes of language a thing removed, and its logical concomitant hierarchy, which makes of people things removed, eventually lead (not historically but tendentiously) to 'science' as contrasted to 'myth.' And 'science' (we should say 'technology') makes of experience itself something removed, something composed of units with one-to-one referents in reality, units to be 'used.' But the sorts of systems Lévi-Strauss studies and the stage at which he studies them are least 'interrupted' by referential meaning, as he seeks to expose the operational bedrock of human culture.[9]

Perhaps then, to gain a clearer semantic perspective on Lévi-Strauss' work, it would be best if we directly compared his notions of metaphor and semantics to an operational theory of meaning, such as that explicated by John Lyons' *Introduction to Theoretical Linguistics* (1968). But a difference in predominant interest must first be noted. Lyons, in part drawing on the tradition of transformational grammar studies, is most concerned with how an existing language operates; he can start

---

[8] In light of the *Times Literary Supplement* article cited in this study (on p. 35), I should note that this is Lévi-Strauss at his most McLuhanesque. To trace the complex and provocative argument concerning the function of 'alienation' in man's capacity to symbolize and subsequently to *use* symbols, see (L-S in Charbonnier: chs. II, III, IX, XI), (L-S 1969a: chs. XXVIII, XXIX), (L-S 1963c), (L-S 1952), and (L-S 1966a: ch. IV). Then compare (McLuhan: *passim*). See also (Goody 1968: Introduction and ch. I).

[9] Compare Wheelwright's notion of 'steno-language': 'In steno-language the basic elements are easy to identify: they are the *term*—which is non-assertorial: it simply means, but does not declare; and the *proposition*—which is an assertorial relation between terms' (Wheelwright: 97); also: 'Myth . . . arises in an age before steno-language has been evolved to any marked extent' (p. 97).

with intuitively correct utterances in that (usually his own) language. Lévi-Strauss is concerned with the principles of formation of all cultural systems, of which language is but the clearest example. Lyons, then, considers a 'language' as somehow isolable, self-contained, at least for analytic purposes. But, while Lévi-Strauss can isolate language as a particular level, he never considers it as being self-contained, but always as being just as interrelated with systems on other levels as they are with it—at least in those preliterate situations that he generally examines.

If we keep this difference in mind, Lévi-Strauss and Lyons can be put on common ground in terms of the latter's 'having meaning' formula. For Lévi-Strauss would certainly agree with Lyons' general Saussurian position that ' "the meaning" of a given phonological unit is simply its difference from every other phonological unit (if there are any) that might have occurred in the same context' (Lyons: 419). Moreover, I think he would follow Lyons' assertion that '*any* linguistic element which occurs in an utterance has meaning only if it is not completely determined ("obligatory") in that context' (p. 418). Now certainly, in Lévi-Strauss' view any element that is completely determined in a system has no meaning, since—as we have seen with 'sheer imitation' in art—it could point to no other system in terms of which it itself could be encoded. But an element that might appear 'obligatory' in the context of the utterance alone, can perhaps been seen as a bundle of diacriticals in the whole context in which the utterance would normally be made. And it is this 'whole context' composed of many cross-cutting paradigmatic sets, and not just the linguistic paradigmatic set, that would be of interest to Lévi-Strauss.

As an example consider the utterance 'Bees make honey,' on the level of the words which comprise it. In Lyons' terms 'bees' would have no meaning, since in the context of the utterance no other word could be substituted for it. I think that at this level Lévi-Strauss would agree, but he would never stop, or rather start, there. He would start by extracting 'Bees make honey' out of some fuller context, e.g. the mythic variant of a certain society. And then 'bees' would break down into

many more marked features than just 'honey making,' such as
'striped, not solid,' 'venomous, not sweet,' etc.—each of which
would point to a system in its own right on some level in some
terms. Thus, Lévi-Strauss could not in the end accept Lyons'
formula which states that 'the *less* probable a particular element
is, the *more* meaning it has in that context' (p. 415), simply
because he would never accept the operational restrictions
Lyons places on 'context.'

In other words Lévi-Strauss does not start with utterances;
he starts with 'texts'—myths, kinship, cultures. One might argue
that the 'bees' in 'Bees make honey' has no meaning by limiting
his analysis to linguistic matters and to paradigmatic sets in the
area of 'language' (in our simplified example the paradigmatic
set is limited to word contents on the level of 'bees'). I think
that Lévi-Strauss would consider this imposition of a limit as a
misrepresentation of how meaning is generated by codes among
systems—or at least by those bedrock codes among bedrock systems that he studies. (So as not to forget the Symbolists, it
should be suggested that such a semantic bedrock was precisely
what many of them were after.) In refusing this sort of operational restriction Lévi-Strauss opens up the potential of
metonomy and metaphor as processes underlying codes, both his
natives' and his own. Because he proceeds with the notion of
multiple paradigmatic sets on multiple levels (simultaneously)
in mind, any systems he studies appear to have meaning which
is on the one hand incredibly rich and extendible, but on the
other hand disturbingly arbitrary. The *process* is all that is left,
and that is the way Lévi-Strauss leaves it. He is far from the
first to observe the sort of operational basis of signification that
characterizes various preliterate phenomena; Radcliffe-Brown,
for example, noted it clearly:

When I was beginning my work in Australia in 1910, a
native said to me, '*Bungurdi* (kangaroo) [is] my *kadja* (elder
brother).' This simple sentence of three words gives the clue
to an understanding of Australian totemism. The speaker did
not mean that individuals of the kangaroo species are his
brothers. He meant that to the kangaroo species, conceived

as an entity, he stood in a social relation analogous to that in which a man stands to his elder brother in the kinship system. I am sorry that there is not time on this occasion to expound this thesis more fully (1965: 169).

But with Lévi-Strauss the thesis is not only expounded; it is called upon to clarify the nature of that very research which was a prerequisite of its derivation—as savage thinking comes to provide the perspective which brings into focus the operations involved in scientific (comparativist) inquiry.

Concerning Lévi-Strauss' refusal to limit context or to impose set bounds on some domain, Dell Hymes observes how 'slippage back and forth between individual systems, and any and all systems, as context for structural relevance, recurs in his work . . .' (Hymes: 45).[10] We have seen above how this slippage is a vital aspect in his comparative studies, since the content of any particular category of indigenous thought cannot be assumed to remain constant across cultures. Thus, to trace the significations of 'bees,' the analyzer cannot restrict his inquiry to a people's insect lore, since 'bees' might be *person*ified or otherwise encoded in an endless number of ways. Or, in our other example, to continue tracing the significance of women in Baudelaire's semantic universe, we would have to trace out everything he says about cats. In this light, then, I should think that Lévi-Strauss could not follow Goodenough in the following optimistic assertion:

Since then, semantic analyses of kinship terminologies have considerably expanded and revised our list of criteria. We can now envision the possibility of arriving at an exhaustive and systematic account of these criteria, similar to the exhaustive and systematic account of the phonetic or acoustical criteria used in the formation of the various phonemes of the world's many languages (Goodenough 1969: 332).

[10] See also Sturtevant's review of developments in ethnoscience (1964) and Tyler's *Cognitive Anthropology* (1969) to appreciate how the new ethnographers have pursued some of the same problems that Lévi-Strauss confronts.

Goodenough here assumes that there is some good cross-cultural way of restricting and closing the category of 'kinship,' as there is presumed to be in the case of 'phonetic system.' But can this be assumed?[11] One is perhaps on safer ground with phonetic systems, for it seems that man's vocal apparatus can do only a few things. (However, the ground is still not altogether safe; as Paul Kay has warned: '. . . there is probably much less agreement right now within linguistics on the general outlines of universal Phonetics than many anthropologists imagine' [1970: 25]). Yet many linguists do argue that the phenomena of human vocal sound can be exhaustively described by means of a set of contrastive pairs, this yielding the units for building a phonetic *system* that only requires some conceptual system to be coded to. But can 'kinship' be restricted and bound in the same way, in face of the evidence that biologically-true genealogy need not affect how 'kinship' relations are defined or enacted? This is a matter of current debate in anthropology (see, for example, Goodenough 1970). In one work (L-S 1949) Lévi-Strauss said kinship could be so restricted, but only by defining 'kinship' in a very limited sense as some number of groups exchanging sisters for brides, which *exchange* is grounded in that fundamental socio-logic we discussed earlier. By this definition alone could a sufficiently limited number of contrasts be set apart to make of 'kinship' a viable comparative operator. But since that work—and especially as of *La pensée sauvage*— he has ceased to utilize any such restricted operator in preference to a mythic operator, which by definition is wide open to inter-relating all culturally defined domains in all analytically imposed orders, limited only by the logical possibilities of discovering other systematic domains which—like phonetics—might be in-trinsically (naturally) limited as to possible sets of contrasts. It has been suggested, for example, that 'cooking' might be such a domain (see L-S 1965b and 1964a). While this sugges-tion has been challenged (in Shankman 1969), it remains true that all known cultures 'cook' (de-naturalize their food through heat). Moreover, cooking systems, whether or not as rigidly re-

[11] This same question is posed at length in Schneider's arguments against componential analysis (see Schneider 1965b, 1969).

stricted as phonetic systems, appear more naturally bound than 'religion' or 'kinship' or many other orders that have been utilized to effect cross-cultural comparisons. Yet, in the end Lévi-Strauss declares all semantic domains unboundable, always open to new significations. Thus, unlike Goodenough, he expects no exhaustive accounts. It is probably this (conservative?) position of Lévi-Strauss which sets his work apart from many studies in ethnoscience. For not only does he argue that 'it is vain to try to isolate privileged semantic levels within myths' (1964a: 347), he also deems the same to be true of analysis— making it myth-like.

Before laying linguistics *per se* to rest, we might attempt a summary conclusion of Lévi-Strauss' interest in the subject. He has repeatedly acknowledged his indebtedness to particular linguists for demonstrating how systems deal with relationships and not things and how they can operate with amazing efficiency on unconscious levels. In fact, the assumed locus of grammar is the illustration par excellence that 'the unconscious would thus be the mediating term between myself and others' (L-S 1950: xxxi; my trans.). More generally still, however, modern linguistics suggests definite limitations of and directions for types of explanations in human sciences. Perhaps Ruwet has hit the most general mark with the following observation:

> Since its first steps, then, theoretical linguistics has recognized the existence of this fundamental duality between process and system—which is to be found under various names: *parole/langue* (Saussure), message/code (Jakobson), usage/ schema (Hjelmslev), and, for Lévi-Strauss, the order of events and the order of structure—a duality which corresponds to the opposition between the lived and the conceived (Ruwet: 567; my trans.).

'Ce texte a de quoi nous plaire . . .' (L-S 1966b: 13), and should be kept in memory to be especially recalled when we come to Proust.

In our sally into some basic issues within traditional, twentieth century linguistics, we alluded to one or two features of myth that seem to bear little on modern poems. In effect, since the latter are presented as individual and more or less alert creations, all those basic French *sociologie* problems concerning the collective nature of the unconscious appear irrelevant. A quotation from Jakobson concerning patently communal forms of communication places us squarely before the issues at hand:

> It is particularly noteworthy that the alleged 'strict limits for variations' lose their compulsion in secret jargons and in verbal plays—private or semi-private—as well as in personal poetic experiments or invented languages. Propp's trailblazing discovery . . . has revealed the rigid structural laws which govern all the fairy tales of Russian (and any other) oral tradition and admit but a severely limited number of compositional models. These restrictive laws, however, find no application to such individual creations as Andersen's or Hoffmann's fairy stories. To a considerable degree, the rigor of general laws is due to the circumstance that both language and folklore demand a collective consensus and obey a subliminal communal censorship (Jakobson 1970).[12]

According to this view, the more any phenomena or 'texts' are subject to this 'subliminal communal censorship,' the more they should disclose some extra-individual basis for their inter-individual occurrence. This manner of thinking has been with us at least since Durkheim's declaration of the autonomy of the 'social.' Lévi-Strauss credits Mauss both with discovering how to ground the 'social' in ethnographic fact through his concept of 'exchange' and with discerning its true locus to be the unconscious. Then Lévi-Strauss goes on to synthesize these ideas

[12] For Lévi-Strauss' views on Propp's discovery, see (L-S 1960b). Elsewhere Lévi-Strauss forewarns us that his own exemplary comments on the Greek Oedipus myth are misplaced (see L-S 1963b: 217), because—like Andersen's fairy stories—that myth in its Greek dramatic forms has become individual-creator-specific and biased toward definite dramatic and social *uses*. One observer describes this development as immediacy becoming literature: '. . . the original matter of myth has been transmuted and given values of dramatic form by later philosophic interpretation' (*TLS* 1967: 521).

with findings in linguistics. Through the summary insight of
Evans-Pritchard we can appreciate how pre-ordained this move
might now seem. Evans-Pritchard is discussing here Durkheim's
category of 'religion':

> It is true, of course, and Durkheim would certainly not have
> contested it, that religion is thought, felt, and willed by indi-
> viduals—society has no mind to experience these functions—
> and as such it is a phenomenon of individual psychology, a
> subjective phenomenon, and can be studied accordingly. But
> it is none the less a social and objective phenomenon which
> is independent of individual minds, and it is as such that
> the sociologist studies it. What gives it objectivity are three
> characteristics. Firstly, it is transmitted from one generation
> to another, so if in one sense it is in the individual, in another
> it is outside him, in that it was there before he was born and
> will be there after he is dead. He acquires it as he acquires
> his language, by being born into a particular society. Secondly,
> it is, at any rate in a closed society, general. Everyone has
> the same sort of religious beliefs and practices, and their
> generality, or collectivity, gives them an objectivity which
> places them over and above the psychological experience of
> any individual, or indeed of all individuals. Thirdly, it is
> obligatory. Apart from positive and negative sanctions, the
> mere fact that religion is general means, again in a closed
> society, that it is obligatory, for even if there is no coercion
> a man has no option but to accept what everybody gives
> assent to, because he has no choice, any more than of what
> language he speaks (Evans-Pritchard: 54–55).

Thus, clearly 'religion'—and to this we can add 'myth'—can
be approached as portions of the 'social discourse' of a closed
community. Evans-Pritchard proceeds to clarify how this fact
points straight back to a prior concern in this chapter:

> *Language is a good example of what Durkheim was driving at.*
> It is traditional, general, and obligatory; it has a history and
> structure and function of which those who speak it are quite

unaware; and, though individuals may have contributed to
it, it is certainly not the product of any individual's mind.
It is a collective, autonomous, and objective phenomenon
(p. 55; my emphasis).

Lévi-Strauss' main achievements consist in having followed
through on the observation underlined above. Moreover, insofar
as this is the case, what Tiryakian emphasizes about Durkheim's
program applies equally to that of his 'inconstant disciple' (L-S
1963b: dedication):

> Durkheim's positivism is grounded in accepting social facts
> as *sui generis* phenomena of intersubjective consciousness,
> as products of social interaction, which cannot properly be
> understood if reduced to a lower order of phenomena (physi-
> cal or organic). They must be approached *naïvely*, that is,
> without preconceptions as to their nature or functions; this
> implies a suspension of the causal framework within which
> the positivism of the physical sciences operates (Tiryakian:
> 680).

In this light it can be seen how criticisms such as those of Marvin
Harris concerning *The Elementary Structures of Kinship* are
very much beside the point. Harris tells us:

> Given Lévi-Strauss' intellectual pedigree, it is not surprising
> that at several critical junctures, equivocation and ambiguity
> overwhelm the often brilliant and always ingenious explica-
> tion. At the very outset, for example, there is the question of
> the function of reciprocity. On the one hand, following Durk-
> heim's master strategy and Mauss' specific suggestion, we
> encounter the theme that reciprocity is the ancient and con-
> tinuing condition for social solidarity in groups larger than
> the nuclear family. But what are the reasons for having
> socially solidary units larger than the nuclear family? Evi-
> dently if the gift of women brings people closer together,
> fathers and sons would benefit from such an exchange
> (Harris: 490).

It is discouraging that Harris could accuse Lévi-Strauss of ambiguity on this fundamental point, when Lévi-Strauss went through six chapters (I–VI) to establish the view that reciprocity *cannot* be explained in any such functional terms (see again Tiryakian above on Durkheim's 'social facts').[18]

This concept of the 'social' remains very foreign to people who regard societies as being composed of conglomerates of individuals. Edmund Leach demonstrates the difficulty:

> When [Lévi-Strauss] is talking about Man, it is the 'human mind' which becomes the creative agent responsible for the miracle of culture and this 'human mind' is an aspect of the human brain, something shared by all members of the species *homo sapiens*. But when he is talking about particular peoples, a slightly different kind of entity has to be reified. . . . The philosophical difficulty is how to move from the level of the individual to the level of the group (Leach 1965a: 16).

Any view less than a radically empiricist one must broach the problem of the communication of knowledge in the absence of a posited 'natural' relationship among things. Now, the Symbolists have been accused of enriching the 'repertory of modern civilization by only one myth, and that a renovated one—Narcissus' (Lehmann: 14). Similarly, some critics have claimed that Lévi-Strauss' 'Human Mind' is no more than his own mind, making of him a narcissist or, at best—allowing for his 'phenomenal' empirical bent—a universal solipsist. But, we can again draw upon Leach's sense of difficulty to suggest the oversimplification of such easy labels. Leach points out two directions Lévi-Strauss takes to indicate the primacy of the 'social': '. . . firstly by reifying society and treating it as an active creative entity *like* an individual, and secondly by asserting that the pure individual, the "I," has no separate existence at all' (Leach 1965a: 27). I think we will find the last part of this remark useful in defending Symbolists from any charge of simple narcissism. At any rate the denial of the 'pure individual' is of utmost importance

[18] Speaking of ambiguity, what is the 'evident benefit' Harris is here referring to—getting more people? getting potentially more yams?

to our topic. Furthermore, Lévi-Strauss can bypass all criticism in this area by insisting that, empirically, myth is a
collective phenomenon. It is the groundwork for articulating
human relationships with other humans and with the surroundings. As such it bears on Durkheim's notion of *conscience
collective* as the representation of the 'social,' here clarified by
Bohannan:

> Since, as I have interpreted Durkheim, the collective repre-
> sentation is both a thing perceived (consciously learned or
> subconsciously impressed) and a perceiving (conscious or
> subconscious) agent, one can say that it is 'perceiving.' Seen
> in this way the mass of collective representations—of 'per-
> ceivings'—becomes the *conscience collective. Conscience
> collective* is the cultural idiom of social action (Bohannan:
> 82).

Indeed, under the rubric of the 'social' the philosophical difficulty
outlined above by Leach is just the reverse: the difficulty comes
in moving from the level of the group, now basic, to the level
of the individual, now derivative. At present my point is that
an analysis of a poem highlights this problem of individual
versus group in a minimal fashion, only insofar as the poem is
language (i.e. communication) created and experienced by
social beings. The fact is that such creation and experience seem
to occur one at a time and in individuals. It is possible that
some critics use this 'modern poetry model' in their conception
of the sorts of texts that Lévi-Strauss, Jakobson, and others deem
unconscious and positively *social*, basic in communication and
thus pertinent to cognition. In fact, the latter theorists argue
that the *social* status of the texts is made possible because of
the unconscious basis of their assimilation by and in men (see
L-S 1946a).

Yet Nur Yalman considers that in Lévi-Strauss' work 'the
problem of the unconscious remains open':

> As long as one is totally immersed in myths as evidence, one
> is trapped in a play of mirrors in which one moves from
> reflection to reflection (Yalman 1967: 86).

In brief the difficulty is this: a myth can be shown to overcome a logical contradiction by transforming that contradiction into different terms for which a mediator exists (e.g. scientist/lovers→ stars/loins); resolved in a cosmic cat; this can be quite unconscious. But if one then sees the myth as *functioning* to license activity in other realms—in more 'real' realms—by eliminating the same contradiction in them, the question of conscious versus unconscious becomes very vexed. Poetry is relatively free of such difficulty. The poem as experienced (created) by the poet and experienced (read) by the reader—although no congruity between the two experiences can be proved—can, however controversially, be regarded as a world of its own. The poem can posit its particular contradictions and resolve them only insofar as it itself is concerned. And if we are to accept the implication of Yalman and many stronger implications by others, this is likewise all that Lévi-Strauss' analyses can do.

Here is the crux of the issue: when Lévi-Strauss asserts that 'mythological thought always progresses from the awareness of oppositions towards their resolution' (L-S 1963b: 224), one must ask whether the opposition is resolved *for the myth* or, in fact, *for the natives*. In *Le Cru et le cuit* the anthropologist makes one of his most scandalous assertions:

Mythic analysis does not have and cannot have as its object to show how men think. . . . Thus we do not aim to show how men think in myths, but how myths think themselves in men, and without their knowing it (L-S 1964a: 20; my trans.).

Lévi-Strauss suggests the parallel case of a grammar which in no way purports to reveal how men consciously think during speech acts. The difficulty with this parallel is that a grammar necessarily generates *all* articulate native thought (or at least, any thought that can be linguistically communicated to us for study), while myth is a particular variety of expression which (for analytic purposes) must temporarily be separated from other varieties. Again one confronts that functionalist question of how unconscious resolution in myth can be instrumental in justifying behavior in other realms.

I think that parallel problems in poetry can clarify some of the confusion here. In the experience of a poem there are at least two standard ways of arguing that some contradiction or conflict is overcome. The first way is related to the ' "romantic" conception of Romanticism according to which a work of art is the direct and immediate product of a personal experience, preferably a painful one' (Tassart 1963). This concept makes of a poem a rite of purgation, a tension valve through which the poet therapeutically objectifies some dilemma, derived from a conflict, and invites the public, insofar as they share the dilemma, to do the same. This ' "romantic" conception of Romanticism' is analogous to a functionalist conception of ritualized performances of myth, in which society vents steam. The second way a poem can overcome a contradiction is related to what I would call the 'symbolic' conception of Symbolism. It involves a passage from opposition to resolution, all taking place *within* the context of the work itself—as opposed to *within* society *by means of* the work. This is the way towards resolution evidenced in Jakobson's and Lévi-Strauss' discussion of that dynamic structure in 'Les Chats' centering on the middle couplet. It is also central to Allen Tate's well-known concept of poetic 'tension.' Tate discusses the 'achievement in poetry':

> I propose as descriptive of that achievement, the term *tension*. I am using the term not as a general metaphor, but as a special one, derived from lopping the prefixes off the logical terms *ex*tension and *in*tension. What I am saying, of course, is that the meaning of poetry is its 'tension,' the full organized body of all the extension and intension that we can find in it. The remotest figurative significance that we can derive does not invalidate the extensions of the literal statement [i.e. 'insight into . . . the human predicament'] (Tate: 82–3).

Proceeding from this view, the amount of internal potential for resolution of conflict would depend on the degree to which formal and semantic aspects of the poem invited one to move along the line extension-intension. In Tate's view it seems that all poetry presents the same potential for such resolution of

conflict. Tate, like Lévi-Strauss, speaks of 'logical contradictions,' such as (in a poem by Donne) a unitary, non-spatial
soul embodied in a spatial image or an extensive finite image
logically contradicting an intensive meaning of infinity. Furthermore, he stresses that neither element in opposition invalidates
the other: 'Intension and extension are here one, and they
enrich each other' (Tate: 84). Tate seems to feel that the contradictions are resolved in and of the fact that they are objectified in images; this puts him nearer our pressure valve point of
view: read the poem and release your repressed oppositions. But
the second way of opposition outlined above would necessitate
our moving from the initial contradiction to some new level
(whether stated or implied) of resolution. The movement would
be along *formal* paths provided expressly for this intrinsically
dynamic process—such as the paths provided by the central
couplet in 'Les Chats,' where multiple inversions occur on
different levels. To experience any effects of this process one
must contract to enter wholeheartedly into the work, thereby
agreeing to achieve a resolution in the terms its forms and meanings establish.

Where does this leave us in relation to myth's function of
overcoming contradictions? Well, on the one hand we might
be expected to recall that the public of modern poetry is a
rather special group of enthusiasts. Then, in emphasizing the
dynamic, interior conflict resolution of myth, we could confront
British empiricist objections that this cannot be related to
other realms of activity by acknowledging as much, arguing:
a native appreciates myth in the same way that a poetry lover
appreciates poetry; both can go to work in their fields (offices),
even while they are confronted by irrefutable oppositions (up/
down, life/death), thanks to the fact that they know that in
the really real realm of myth (poetry) these oppositions are
finally resolved. Or we might take a more esoteric tack by
arguing that the empiricist objections are inappropriate, since
the native actually lives the myth, because for him myth *is* the
world: geographical manifests economic manifests social manifests cosmic, and vice versa, starting anywhere. Any daily
routine would then for the natives be no more than affirmations

H

of continuously reciprocal manifestations of being. 'Real' tilling
of the soil is only part of the mythical story about soil tilling.
And life presents itself as communal poetry in motion.[14]

However, I would argue that neither the matter-of-fact nor
the very esoteric (and unverifiable) viewpoint outlined above
is that of Lévi-Strauss. To understand his viewpoint better,
let us consider together a series of his notions about myth and
totemism:

(1) Myth is a variety of 'social discourse.'
(2) Myths think themselves in men.
(3) . . . the system of totemic symbols permits the unifica-
    tion of heterogeneous semantic fields, at the cost of
    contradictions which it is the function of ritual to sur-
    mount by 'acting' them . . . (L-S 1966a: 96).

It must be cautioned that point (3) might be misleading, at
least for students of British anthropology. For the term
'function' is used in its simplest mathematical sense: a 'function'
is just a way of stating one thing in other terms which are
equivalent.[15] Therefore, in point (3) ritual 'surmounts' (not
'resolves') contradictions merely by the fact that it translates
them out of terms of *ideas* into terms of *act*, thereby justifying
each in terms of the other, without really 'solving' anything.
Thus, we can generalize: the sort of contradiction-'resolution'
(I should say 'surmounting') attained by mythic and totemic
classifications is like that interior variety we found in poetry.
By inversion, assimilation, and transposition of the units, what
is contradictory on one level is restated in different terms on
another level, and thereby authorized. And since all of this
proceeds unconsciously (i.e. outside explicit awareness), 'myths
think themselves in men.' What is amassed by the men, then, is
a 'unification of heterogeneous semantic fields.' These unified

---

[14] See, for example, Eliade's concept of *homo religiosus* in (Eliade:
1959).

[15] Note also his use of 'functionally' when Lévi-Strauss remarks of the
Cinderella legend 'that types B and C are linked functionally, i.e. that the
inversion of the sexes is accompanied by the inversion of other motifs'
(L-S 1954b: 107).

heterogeneous fields are most likely manifested in some sort of 'texts,' where formal paths can be found for moving across orders to achieve interior surmounting of contradictions. However, these unified semantic fields *also* serve as a body of 'social discourse' (itself the subject of the 'texts') which can be *referred* to by individuals, in order 'rationally' (in their terms) to overcome any contradictions they meet in 'real' experience. Thus while not expressly synthesized to serve a set purpose, myths are there to be referred to, if one is called upon to explain why something is as it is, or why he does what he does. I recently witnessed a perfect example of this usage of 'social discourse,' of this 'wild thinking':

Apollo 11 was sitting on the moon; mankind had made its giant leap. Therefore, a television news reporter was interviewing some Atlanta, Georgia high school students to gauge their reactions. Of one bright-eyed girl he soberly demanded: 'What is this going to do to your religion?' To which she sincerely replied, 'Well, I don't know; I suppose if God wants us to go to the moon and back, He'll let us, and if He doesn't, He won't.' Then the newsman slyly queried, 'What, then, if the men *don't* make it back from the moon?' And the girl pertly concluded, 'Well, I don't know; if you don't make it the first time, try, try again!' She smiled sweetly.

And so, by means of referring to a conceptual pool of 'social discourse,' still another stultifying contradiction was thwarted. A suitable 'text' from American culture—with formal paths for overcoming the technical progress *versus* Divine Will contradiction—would be found in some body of statements of the Protestant Ethic (a written 'text') or in Our Lady of the Skies Chapel at Kennedy International Airport (an architectural 'text'). Both these complex texts are thus *symbols* of the progress/Providence contradiction. And the very elements of which the symbols are composed are themselves keyed to systematic orders which enable the contradiction to be surmounted. (Compare Baudelaire's 'cat' symbol—a unity which when viewed from within is systematically composed of starry eyes [keys to mysticism], loins of sand [keys to sphinx], and so forth.) Preliterates on the other hand specialize in oral (versus

written or architectural) indices of their arrangements of elements in different orders for overcoming contradictions. Thus,
the resulting 'social discourse'—whether it is composed of mythic
and totemic entities or of the bric-à-brac of anthropomorphic
cosmologies and this-worldly clichés (c.f. example above)—can
'license' activity in the *real* realm of everyday living, but only
by affording paths for stating the activity's contradictions in
other sorts of terms. Such 'social discourse' can even maintain
pious moon-shots in the face of divine wrath. It provides a
stockpile of its own logically interrelated justifications for actions,
such as leaves Aristotelian either/or reasoning virtually power-
less as an explanatory device. Ask *any* native; and, up pops
la pensée sauvage.

However, preliterate cultures provide a fresher perspective
for us to observe this systematic interrelation of various domains.
For they present to an outside observer far fewer readily accessible elements out of which to construct systems of signification;
and their contradictions are perhaps more easily discerned. In
these 'languagely' rarified contexts the most ambitious achievements at synthesis of meaningful elements—their myths—stand
out in fuller relief. Myths are the principal 'texts' serving both
to interrelate perceived features of experience and to differentiate this experience from *other* such experiences. From this
point of view Lévi-Strauss notes the previous failure to understand the nature of myth:

> . . . what escaped them was the distinctive character of myths,
> which is precisely emphasis, resulting from the multiplication
> of one level by one or several others, and which—as in lan-
> guage—has as its function to signify signification (L-S 1964a:
> 346; my trans.).

In other words myth is meta-. Myths indicate how meaning is
to be. They can be seen by the analyzer as symbol-filled 'texts'
which articulate a people's 'social discourse.' The most critical
point to remember is that throughout these transformations
of contradicting terms, nothing is ever really *solved*. The contradiction is merely displaced, but by becoming so, it expands

a culture's store of signification. Lévi-Strauss makes this point explicitly when he credits Durkheim (1965) with sensing this fundamental property of myth in his following observation on totemic myths:

> [They] no doubt explain nothing and do no more than displace the difficulty, but by displacing it they appear at least to mitigate any logical scandal (L-S 1964a: 13; my trans.).

The final topic in this chapter—which has attempted to move dialectically from the notion of a poem to a sense of myth—involves once again metonymy and metaphor. We have already had occasion to appreciate how 'in verbal art the interaction of these two elements is especially pronounced,' and how the compulsory parallelism established by verse patterns affords a wealth of relations by similarity and by contiguity (Jakobson and Halle: 77). But in proceeding to discuss 'the various motives which determine the choice between these alternants,' Jakobson asserts:

> The primacy of the metaphoric process in the literary schools of romanticism and symbolism has been repeatedly acknowledged, but it is still insufficiently realized that it is the predominance of metonymy which underlies and actually predetermines the so-called 'realistic' trend, which belongs to an intermediary stage between the decline of romanticism and the rise of symbolism and is opposed to both. Following the path of contiguous relationships, the realistic author metonymically digresses from the plot to the atmosphere and from the characters to the setting in space and time. He is fond of synecdochic details (Jakobson and Halle: 77-8).

Later it is concluded that 'for poetry, metaphor, and for prose, metonymy is the line of least resistance, and, consequently, the study of poetical tropes is directed chiefly toward metaphor' (p. 82). The causal grouping of romanticism and symbolism under the rubric of metaphoric primacy appears to me misleading, at least in respect to our specific criteria for 'Symbolism.'

The references above to metonymic movements from plot to atmosphere and from character to space-time, and to a fondness for synecdoche—both being deemed features of the 'realistic' trend—recall crucial parts in the analysis of 'Les Chats.' While it can be argued that Baudelaire bridges Romanticism and Symbolism, he is certainly not a realist opposed to both, nor does 'Les Chats' impress one as being prose. What we have here, then, is a contradiction between form and trope—a poem which is, at least to a considerable degree, directed towards metonymy, towards the utilization of contiguity to achieve its effects. Turning to Lévi-Strauss, we can extract a means of surmounting this contradiction.

In a discussion of conceivable ways of representing a piece of lace, Lévi-Strauss opposes production to reproduction:[16]

> Science would have worked on the real scale but by means of inventing a loom, while art works on a diminished scale to produce an image homologous with the object [a miniature painting is the work in question]. The former approach is of a metonymical order, it replaces one thing by another thing, an effect by its cause, while the latter is of a metaphorical order (L-S 1966a: 24–5).

(This remark about metonymy might be confusing. We must remember that metonymy concerns syntagmatic associations in time *or* space; therefore, cause and effect—temporal juxtaposition—are as metonymical as knife and fork—spatial juxtaposition on the table.) The author later proceeds to contrast art and myth:

> In the case of works of art, the starting point is a set of one or more objects and one or more events which aesthetic creation unifies by revealing a common structure. Myths travel the same road but start from the other end. They use a structure to produce what is itself an object consisting of a

[16] In what follows, the word 'science' would be better translated as 'technology.' Think of the engineer that we have already seen opposed to the *bricoleur* (on pp. 52–3).

sct of cvcnts (for all myths tell a story). Art thus proceeds from a set (object+event) to the *discovery* of its structure. Myths start from a structure by means of which it *constructs* a set (object+event) (L-S 1966a: 26).

Lévi-Strauss' ideas about 'art' are admittedly conservative (see L-S in Charbonnier: ch. X). His 'art' as 'metaphorical order' applies only to art with a realistic bent. For from the point of view of the realistic artist, art is a metonymical *procedure* (analytic precision is required to paint a miniature or describe a real room) with a metaphorically apprehended *result*. It is more precisely the so-called realistic artist, rather than just any artist, who scientifically (technically) observes a set to discover its visual structure and represent it. Then we experience the work metaphorically, concluding that certain forms resemble certain things. Some of Baudelaire's more conservative poems fall into this category. However, a poem like 'Les Chats,' which operates through indirect statement, is altogether a different matter. Here there is no one discernible 'real' object or event serving as stimulus, not even a romantic self-reflecting lake or an harmonious evening; nor is there the striking visual imagery of a surrealistic dream sequence. Instead, words are grouped without any single and necessary direction given to what associations they should stimulate; and what results is a considerable opening up of the poem's signifying potential.[17] 'Les Chats' is, then, neither metonymic prose, describing a rcal situation, nor metaphoric romantic poetry, invoking a full and emotive image of what something is like. Lévi-Strauss' category of 'art' is here less suitable than is that of 'myth.' For in a fashion similar to myth, the Symbolist poem appears to proceed from structure to set (object+event=story). And if this is sometimes true of Baudelaire, how much more so of Mallarmé. In other words the contradictions, oppositions and interrelated

[17] Indeed, 'Professor Guiraud, who has fully investigated the associative field of the French word *chat* "cat", was able to collect about 2,000 terms which were related to it on formal or semantic grounds. By subjecting this vast material to structural and other criteria he was able to rcducc it to about 300 words which form, so to speak, the minimum associative field of the term *chat* . . .' (Ullmann: 240).

levels in 'Les Chats' appear to be prior to—or at least dialectically involved with—the poem's 'story' (i.e. that cats love to
sleep and look like sphinxes, etc.). The complex I have suggested
for realistic art—metonymical process apprehended metaphorically—would then be the inverse for both myth and the
Symbolist poem. For the latter are both metaphorical processes,
since 'the original structure is conceived of in terms of sets of
oppositions viewed as *equivalent*, even though each set can be
from different lexical categories' (L-S 1966a: 149). And their
results are apprehended metonymically (i.e. as object+event=
story-in-time-and-place). In this light not all verbal art is
equally interesting as a field of interaction of Jakobson's two
poles of language association. For example, an (hypothetically)
utterly romantic poetry would be only a metaphoric process
apprehended metaphorically (making it the complete opposite
of technology, which is similarly restricted to metonymy); while
Symbolism self-consciously follows Lévi-Strauss' 'law of mythical thought that the transformation of a metaphor is achieved in
a metonymy' (L-S 1966a: 106).

To conclude, a contrast between Romanticism and Symbolism
can also be indicated by means of Allen Tate's scale of 'tension'
which was discussed above. Tate generalizes:

> The metaphysical poet as a rationalist begins at or near the
> extensive or denoting end of the line; the romantic or Sym-
> bolist poet at the other, intensive end; and each by a strain-
> ing feat of the imagination tries to push his meanings as far
> as he can towards the opposite end, so as to occupy the en-
> tire scale (Tate: 86).

The equivalence assumed here between romantic and Symbolist
poets results from Tate's narrower views of which units of poetic
language can 'intense' and 'extense' between figurative significance and literal statement; for his discussion centers on *word*
meaning. I would counter that certain Symbolists (especially
Rimbaud and Mallarmé) do not start figuratively and stretch
toward denotation. Rather, utilizing a much fuller range of
linguistic elements, they start from both ends—with figurative

word meanings and denotative genders, vowel arrangements, graphic forms, rhyme classes, etc.—and stretch both ways simultaneously, as did the analyzers of 'Les Chats.' The following statement indicates the diminished status of metaphoric images (as opposed to the metaphoric function) in some Symbolist works:

> ... metaphors ... are also artistic structures; and if they are imbued with formal elements reminiscent of religious or mythical symbolism, these enter into their overall structure on the same terms as any other ingredients of art—color, musical form, vocabulary, rhythm, or the like—and not as any privileged class (Lehmann: 113).

The result is not unlike a preliterate myth.

Perhaps, then, the claims cited in chapter II concerning the striking analogies between structures a linguist derives from poetry and those an ethnographer finds in myth would have been less spectacularly demonstrated, had just any poem been explored. And on this note Baudelaire, the Symbolist—or rather our ideal Symbolist (for we recall: 'There is really no such thing as Shakespeare's Hamlet')—appears to be shifting from Everyman to straw man....

IV

Poetic Straw Man

SELF-AWARE SYNTHESES OF PENSÉE SAUVAGE

Il y a sans doute dans l'esprit une espèce de mécanique céleste, dont il ne faut pas être honteux, mais tirer le parti le plus glorieux, comme les médecins, de la mécanique du corps (Baudelaire 1951: 938).

According to A. G. Lehmann 'the Symbolists' definitions stand at an important turning point in the history of aesthetic consciousness'; he refers to their tendency toward observation about poetic activity: 'their importance as artists calling out for new systematic thought is exceptionally great' . . . (Lehmann: 175, 14). Baudelaire appears to head the trend with the assertion:

> What is pure art following the modern conception? It is creating a suggestive magic containing simultaneously the object and the subject, the world exterior to the artist and the artist himself (Baudelaire 1925: 119; my trans.).

'This superb formula not only characterizes much of Baudelaire's own evocative verse, but also became the basis of the poetic theory of the Symbolists' (Hyslop: 31). The desired quality of 'suggestive magic' implies that a certain degree of ambiguity was sought in a poem; but it must be remembered that ambiguity can result from references which either are vague or are precise in multiple ways. This latter brand of operational ambiguity, enabling one line of poetry to say many things, reaches a high-point in some works by Mallarmé. The Symbolist interest in simultaneously capturing subject and object, self and other, exterior items and interior sensations, can be demonstrated to derive from sundry idealist philosophical influences—from Plato's pure ideas to Schopenhauer's philosophy of the Will and transcendent Art. But for our purposes suffice it to say that their view of the poem as a suitable vehicle for embodying universal types stems from 'their assumption regarding the symbolic foundation if not of language in principle, at least of language in poetry' (Lehmann: 144).

Lévi-Strauss on the other hand de-qualifies the latter assumption and extends it precisely to 'language in principle'. He has ideas similar to the Symbolists' notions about art, but he logically and empirically extends their 'art' to include all of human 'bedrock' thought, which is something the Symbolists were only to muse about. We have already seen (on p. 82) Lévi-Strauss single out poetic metaphor as a familiar example of symbolic induction, wherein organic, unconscious mental, and rational levels of experience are interrelated. But he then added that 'as a rule it does not transcend the unconscious level' (L-S 1963b: 202). The Symbolists afford a striking exception to this rule; therein lies their significance. Highly programmed, yet highly mutable, semantic universes effecting correspondences across the orders of experience-as-conceived are the goal of native, Symbolist, and structuralist alike. They all aim to make sense out of the totality of experience in its own terms. Consider this statement by Baudelaire:

> With excellent poets, there is no metaphor, comparison, or epithet which is not an exact mathematical adaptation in the current circumstances, because these comparisons, these metaphors, and these epithets are drawn out from the inexhaustible depths of the *universal analogy*, and they cannot be drawn from elsewhere (Baudelaire 1951: 1078; my trans.).

His interest is in the act of analogizing, or more precisely of universally analogizing—which is to say, I think, communicably analogizing.

The differences in the way poet and ethnologist go about

attaining this universalistic aim reflect their different views concerning what has become of language. The Symbolists are culture bound, fairly ensconced within modern French, which offers only a stockpile of impoverished, referential words, the language itself having been over-popularized, journalized, and subjugated to goal-oriented *use*. Valéry considers this linguistic impurity to be an intrinsic one, observing that language, although so intimate a part of our soul, is nonetheless statistical in origin and purely practical in destination:

> And the problem for the poet must be to *extract from this practical instrument the means of achieving an essentially non-practical work*. . . . It is a matter, for him, of creating a world or an order of things, a system of relations, devoid of any relationship with the practical order (Valéry: 1460; my trans.).

One of the several poetic programs derived from Baudelaire was an attempt to refurbish a too practical medium in order to achieve Mallarmé's celebrated aim 'to give a purer meaning [*sens*] to the words of the tribe' (Mallarmé 1945: 189; my trans.). In contrast Lévi-Strauss' tactics for discovering universal modes of ordering different levels of experience are cross-cultural and empirical. He strives to appreciate a state of mind, a state of thought, which is logically prior to any goal-directed, univocal interest:

> This thought, Claude Lévi-Strauss has recently proposed to call 'savage,' while recalling that it is not the thought of savages, but an intellectual course in its savage state, not domesticated in expectation of a return. In particular this thought would not have ceased to be exercised in every authentic poetic creation (de Heusch: 1963: 51; my trans.).

The anthropologist finds this state of mind most perfectly represented in societies where language lacks the literate dimension which generally seduces the Western observer into assuming that language is primarily a recording tool that can divorce

events from contexts, thereby 'objectifying' them. In preliterate
groups, then, language is more obviously a system of symbols,
a source of semantic diacriticals that are differentially distributed as markers of features from experience. Moreover, tendencies to claim exclusive rights to linguistic elements, such as
in widespread customs of naming (see L-S 1966a: ch. VI),
reveal how language can be handled as a scarce commodity
ordered in a system of exchange. Thus Lévi-Strauss does not
see language as something that needs refurbishing. Rather, the
goal proclaimed for Valery's poet is just what language has.
For, as is highlighted by preliterates, language is *essentially* systematic, essentially creative of a 'world or an order of things,'
and only secondarily 'practical.' Therefore, Lévi-Strauss looks
to preliterate systems as the most ready source of general modes
of the *universal analogy.*

One becomes increasingly convinced that Symbolism and
structuralism represent similar moments in the developments
(cycles?) of two disciplines. Most obviously, in the case of our
Symbolists, 'idealist [Schopenhauer's] philosophy could be construed as an escape from the problems of origin and heredity
so completely treated by the Naturalists' (Uitti 1961: 27).
Similarly, Lévi-Strauss' structuralism is a continuation of functionalism's reaction against evolutionary aims:

> The mistake of . . . the Naturalist School was to think that
> natural phenomena are *what* myths seek to explain, when
> they are rather the *medium through which* myths try to
> explain facts which are themselves not of a natural but a
> logical order (L-S 1966a: 95).

This is true in the same way that 'Les Chats' was not trying
anecdotally to tell us something about cats *per se*, but was
employing cats to effect a shift in orders and thereby surmount
a contradiction in experience. An observation about Mallarmé's
views on poetry suggests deeper similarities between the two
'moments':

> [Mallarmé's] answer to the question 'What is the use of

poetry?' was to assert that poetry alone had any use or meaning, and his way out of the collapse of the original Romantic
concept of the poet as an 'unacknowledged legislator of mankind' was therefore both more radical and more logical than
that of his fellows (Hartley: xxiii).

To put it quite simply: 'No poet more steadfastly than Mallarmé
believed that the subject of all poems is poetry . . .' (Braun:
108; or Fowlie 1968: 19). What Mallarmé claimed for the
poem, Lévi-Strauss declares to be true of myth: more than the
functionalists' mere secondary license for any one culture's version of social life, myth appears as the record of the basis on
which the disparate elements of social life are integrated (I
would rather say 'orchestrated'). Again, myth is meta-. It
does not 'license' a society; it states the communicative stockpile in terms of which a society's being is conceived. Ultimately
it is the super-'text' that endows *sense*. It is the corpus of
sensory logic that can be manifested on the ground through
house plans, in chants or songs, through words, in acts, through
rules and taboos, etc.—and in any one society the *sense*-making
system might be represented in all, some, or, as a limiting case,
none of these forms.
   But I must be more explicit in making allusions to the same
moment in two disciplines, especially in light of my earlier
skepticism over 'historical seepage' models of 'schools of thought.'
Here all I am suggesting is the following: there are a finite
number of ways of 'explaining' the basis of varieties of texts.
Theoretically, a series of levels can be abstracted out of experience—psychological, emotional, rational, social, metaphysical, biological, humanitarian, material, ethereal, romantic,
mundane, religious, goal-oriented, and so forth—and any one
or ordered set of these levels can be designated as primary, of
which the 'text' is declared a function. Different 'schools of
thought,' then, are only the phenomenon whereby different
levels of experience come to be marked as primary. The schools
differentiate themselves from their forebears just as adolescents
do from parents or tribal groups and nation states do from
their neighbours (see Leach 1965c on L-S). And this holds for

philosophies of or theories about literature, just as much as for anthropological explanations of foreign customs.

Thus, if the present book can be said to contain a thesis, it is the following: Lévi-Strauss defines anthropology as the effort towards translating what is most strikingly and systematically *other* into terms of ourselves (and vice versa). Similarly, I would say that literary criticism (in the sense of theory) confronts a similar problem, since it too is faced with peculiarly 'exotic' and systematic texts which it must interrelate and translate into terms commensurate with everyday, habitual living (and vice versa). Therefore there most probably exist close parallels in the different ways that have been tried to incorporate literary texts and texts of other cultures—these two types of the *other*—into the familiar. For example, just as there is a Romantic view of poetry, there is a Romantic view of other cultures—generally contained, I think, within theories involving notions of animism. Moreover, people who 'make sense out of' poetry by attributing it to emotion-bound, imaginative error might be expected to regard other non-commonsensical forms of behavior in a similar fashion.

Of more particular concern to us is the parallel between Symbolism and structuralism. My ideal-type Symbolism insists that any text—painting, poem, symphony, dress style, etc.—exists in its own right and not as a function of some Romantic urge, religious awe, humanitarian motive, or propagandistic program. This, then, is an assertion about the *limits of explanation*. Lévi-Strauss' structuralism says something similar. His relegating 'cause' to *l'esprit humain* is one way of denying primacy to any of those levels of experience that we abstracted above. Note, however, that this is *not* to say the 'levels' are not there. It is this denial which makes his stance more general than that of, say, Freudian theory, Weberian theory, or Marxist theory, at least as popularly understood. But, it might be argued, does not Lévi-Strauss merely posit still another causal 'level'— namely, that of 'logic' (or aesthetic), what with all his thinking from homologies, inversions, transpositions, etc.? Yet this argument is, I think, inaccurate. For these processes are not really part of an abstractable 'level'; they are rather the things without which there could be nothing communicable on any level. They are therefore subsumed in any theories which eventually designate one particular level as primary. They are therefore, again, more general or, as Lévi-Strauss would have it, more scientific. It is in the above sense that I deem Symbolism and structuralism the same moment in two disciplines. They are similar combinations of like variables, insofar as they divide texts into a great many levels and consider all levels as equally significative and 'inter-deterministic.' In other words the two -isms are 'structurally' the same moment. Moreover, since the moment is a structural one, the two -isms did not necessarily (historically) have to occur at the particular relative points in time in which they did. Symbolism might have happened without Hugo's patriotic verses and structuralism without Levy-Bruhl's 'prelogic' formulation. And both have no doubt occurred before and they will occur again . . . with luck. To conclude, there is no 'progress' in disciplinary schools, rather just varying degrees of general applicability and completeness. But, as will be seen, this is not cause for dismay; for if it were, the structural method—which in effect implies this view—would be implicitly condemning itself.

Lehmann has stated succinctly the place of 'symbols' in the philosophy of poetry of those who actually adopted this term as their banner. A symbol was an image representing an Idea, and 'Ideas,' as understood across Schopenhauer from Plato, were 'whole classes of things' (Lehmann: 254, 58). An Idea, then, is a 'whole class in intuition,' a 'unity dissolved into multiplicity'; and 'the symbol of an Idea will be either a word or any object in the external world':

Thus in this art, the pictures of nature, the actions of men, all concrete phenomena could not themselves be manifesting themselves: you have there sensory appearances destined to represent their esoteric affinities with primordial Ideas (Lehmann: 56, 67. Moreas cited in Lehmann: 66; my trans.).

Yet, these speculations sound to me too vague and ethereal, too far removed. For our ideal Symbolist would not be just surmising about 'primordial Ideas.' He would, as a matter of fact, be programming a 'whole class in intuition' into his literary efforts. He would be constructing an indirectly stated text that could only *work* if experienced across a series of processes which are themselves like such an 'Idea' in action. Thus the unity of the class does not remain above and beyond in some Platonic realm. The unity instead *happens*, at least eventually, in our effortful experience of the literary work in which intellectually we go about piecing together, in which we *operate* the 'text.' And while these notions sound idealistic, it is a very down to earth idealism, grounded in the language of the text, where an effort is made to include all possible systems of reference simultaneously and not exclusively. In other words within a poem a 'symbol' can indeed and in fact represent a class, a multiple unity: witness once more our 'cats' of chapter II.

The most famous application of the notion of the underlying unity of a whole class is Baudelaire's doctrine of correspondences. As described in his most familiar sonnet 'Correspondances,' the 'class' in question appears as the universe of experience:

> La Nature est un temple où de vivants piliers
> Laissent parfois sortir de confuses paroles;
> L'homme y passe à travers des forêts de symboles
> Qui l'observent avec des regards familiers.
>
> Comme de longs échos qui de loin se confondent
> Dans une ténébreuse et profonde unité,
> Vaste comme la nuit et comme la clarté,
> Les parfums, les couleurs et les sons se répondent.
>
> Il est des parfums frais comme des chairs d'enfants,
> Doux comme les hautbois, verts comme les prairies,
> —Et d'autres, corrompus, riches et triomphants,
>
> Ayant l'expansion des choses infinies,
> Comme l'ambre, le musc, le benjoin et l'encens,
> Qui chantent les transports de l'esprit et des sens.
> (Baudelaire 1961: 13).

I

Nature is a temple, in which living pillars sometimes utter
a babel of words; man traverses it through forests of symbols,
that watch him with knowing eyes.

Like prolonged echoes which merge far away in an opaque,
deep oneness, as vast as darkness, as vast as light, perfumes,
sounds, and colors answer each to each.

There are perfumes fresh and cool as the bodies of children,
mellow as oboes, green as fields; and others that are perverse,
rich and triumphant,

that have the infinite expansion of infinite things—such as
amber, musk, benjamin, and incense, which chant the ecstasies
of the mind and senses.

(Scarfe trans.: 36–7).

'Correspondances' has been largely interpreted in terms of
sensory phenomena linkage—sound, color, odors—even though
the poem's last line refers to *l'esprit* as well as *les sens*. Moreover,
when *l'esprit* is taken into account, the tendency is to infer transcendental nuances. Yet Balakian has flatly stated:

There is no spirituality here, even though most translators
of Baudelaire's famous sonnet have used the English word
'spirit' to transmit the concept of 'esprit,' thereby turning
this rather sensual poem into a metaphysical one.
. . . Baudelaire clearly defined the priority he gave to the
type of imagination which is an intellectual rather than an
emotional evidence of poetic creation . . . (Balakian: 35–6).

Curiously and analogously, there has also been a tendency to
stress one side of a *sens/esprit* dichotomy in Lévi-Strauss' work.
This time, however, it is the latter term which is singled out—
and this time too not as 'spirit' but as 'mind'—by critics who
consider him too rational and too much of an intellectualist. Yet
Lévi-Strauss maintains that he aims to achieve 'a sort of *super-
rationalism* in which sense-perceptions will be integrated into

reasoning and yet lose none of their properties' (L-S 1961b: 61).
One of the major oversights on the part of many critics has been
the failure to appreciate the *sens* half of his effort. For Lévi-
Strauss has been long arguing that there is no real intrinsic basis
for distinguishing between the sensory-concrete and the intel-
lectual-abstract. At his hypothetical point of harmonious cross-
system balance, the sensory and the intellectual are one. But, as
we have noted, the harmonious balance of sensory-intellectual
(concrete-abstract) can be upset by the loss of 'motivation'
through time. Or the abstract can loom excessively, when a
person from one culture confronts another, since he is blind
(insensitive) to the sensory grounding of the systems he ab-
stracts. Thanks to the cross-cultural method this same sort of
situation can be turned into an advantageous one, wherein
long forgotten—or never consciously realized—sensory (natural)
foundations of human intellectual endeavor can be discovered.
Such is Lévi-Strauss' goal in *Mythologiques*.

His critical concern with the mutual complementarity of *sens/
esprit* explains Lévi-Strauss' dismay over the fact that some
critics have accused him of formalism. For formalism is precisely that sort of over-abstraction which would destroy the
true basis of any sort of cultural 'text.' One might receive the
impression of formalism from Lévi-Strauss' works during a
cursory page thumbing of their contents. Then their most striking feature (especially in *Mythologiques*) would be the often
elaborate schematic diagrams that summarize structural processes across time and space. But these diagrams, which are
easily ignored if bothersome, derive from a body of prose
saturated with sensory contents. What is more, Lévi-Strauss
constructs his works (once more, especially *Mythologiques*) in
a way that obliges the careful reader to experience any abstract
discussions more concrete-sensorily, and vice versa. For example,
this or that inversion or transformation is in essence another
way of saying that 'honey' becomes 'ashes,' which is another
way of saying the 'imaginary' becomes the 'supernatural,' etc.
(L-S 1966b). And a central aim of *Mythologiques* is to demonstrate in the Americas an entire world of 'social discourse,' of
interrelated semantic fields, which is at once ultimately concrete

and likewise abstract—a world we can sense through the reading of it. It is as though an empirically demonstrable Symbolist
poem were being rewritten, across two continents and several
centuries.

The disturbing problem for Baudelaire and for ensuing critics
of Symbolism (more so perhaps than for ensuing Symbolists)
was whether or not the particular links one senses between realms
are necessary or arbitrary. The difficulty results from Baudelaire's
assuming not only horizontal relations among elements of
analogies but also vertical relationships. In this philosophy of
poetry the ultimate value of 'symbols' derives from the fact
that the analogy they evoke 'is a cousinship that exists only
through a common grandparent—a transcendental entity—
"symbolized" by each cousin' (Lehmann: 213). Of course,
Lévi-Strauss in his studies of native myth is interested solely
in the horizontal relationships among analogous elements. Far
from seeking a Baudelairian universal hierarchy of symbols, he
views all symbols as keys to the universal logical process of
analogizing between analytically separate orders of experience.
Moreover, his approach leads one to infer that 'these primary
modes of thought . . . are essentially intellectual, rational,
logical, not emotional, instinctive, or mystical' (Geertz: 31).
Whether or not this inference is accurate is beside the point, as
far as any rational study—any conceived analytic of experience-
conceived—is concerned. For emotional or mystical components
cannot, by definition, be logically assimilated. This same line of
reasoning justifies emphasizing the architectonic side of Symbolist poems at the expense of considering any mystical strains
that defy description. Regardless of how far Baudelaire considered himself a transcendental seer, for the purpose of the
analysis of his works (which is not exactly to say *appreciation*
of those works) we might as well assume him to be logical,
for the sake of communication. Better a logical analysis (at
best, a logical poem) about an assumed-to-be-logical poem than
an inarticulate sigh about it (such as: 'Of course it's a great
poem—*Why?*—Well, because it, ah it, *sigh*, works!'): 'L'in-
exprimable n'existe pas' (Baudelaire 1925: 174). We can, however, still proceed to appreciate how emotion might enter into

the poem-systems for their practitioners, ideally to the point of sharing some similar emotion (see ch. V).

Finally, Lévi-Strauss' taxonomizing natives are unconsciously analogous to Baudelaire in his role of correspondence constructor. But the anthropologist, unlike that poet, would postulate no *fixed* relationships—even in the absense of a transcendental basis—between elements of experience, at least not across systems. Gerard Genette underscores this point in a discussion that stems from disputes centering on Rimbaud's 'Voyelles':

> . . . structuralism can here advance a commentary which takes into account at once the arbitrariness of each vowel-color relationship and the widespread feeling of a vocalic chromatism: it is true that no vowel naturally evokes and isolates a color; . . . but it is also true that the distribution of colors in the spectrum . . . can find its correspondence in the distribution of vowels of a given language . . . there is a spectrum of vowels as there is a spectrum of colors; the two systems evoke and attract each other, and the global homology creates the illusion of a perfect analogy, which each realizes in its fashion by an act of symbolic motivation comparable to that indicated by Lévi-Strauss in regard to totemism (Genette: 41; my trans.).

In line with this, Lévi-Strauss vigorously asserts a fundamental point to reveal the value of his empirical approach:

> The truth of the matter is that *the principle underlying a classification can never be postulated in advance*. It can only be discovered *a posteriori* by ethnographic investigation, that is, by experience (L-S 1966a: 58).

His natives establish their correspondences. Like George in Edward Albee's *Who's Afraid of Virginia Woolf?*, they *can* just decide these things (or so it first appears from the outside), but once a decision is made as to some correspondence they must follow through systematically, or meaninglessness results.

There is nothing absolutely 'natural' from the outside observer's viewpoint about corresponding pairs such as 'crane-sky; red songbird-sun; eagle-mountain; hawk-rock; bluebird-tree; hummingbird-plant; cornbeetle-earth; heron-water . . .' (L-S 1966a: 40). Indeed, other arrangements are conceivable, but the principles of generating them and their interrelationships would be the same. And as we recall from reconsiderations of Saussure's notion of 'motivation' (ch. III, p. 69ff), once a system of arrangements has been instigated, the modes for incorporating any further contents into the arrangements are restricted.

But still, the units within one relatively closed system bear no universally *fixed* connection (Saussure's *value*) with particular units in other closed systems. This is the case both across different systems within the arts—color systems, tone systems, graphic systems, etc.—and across different systems which anthropologists call 'cultures.' This lack of fixity should not disappoint us. For as Genette has noted of the vowel-color phenomenon (and as in the quotation from Lévi-Strauss on page 1 of this study), we still have left the *processes* by which such relationships can be posited, worked out and lived with. Moreover, this same absence of fixed cross-system *values* means that when the systems are *different*, there is still hope for rendering them inter-communicable. This hope is the primary motivating force of Lévi-Strauss' ethnology.

Furthermore, it is this sort of stoic resignation to establish the authenticity of channels *across* systems which render Lévi-Strauss' work 'dry' and unsatisfying to some. For example, there is the long debate between Lévi-Strauss and hermeneutist Paul Ricoeur (see Ricoeur 1963, 1964) which is summarized and, it seems to me, resolved by Ruwet when he observes:

> Each of the two perspectives has its limitations: structural analysis necessarily implies an abstraction, and thus in a sense an impoverishment; while hermeneutic interpretation, lacking distance in regards to its object, is incapable of achieving a general theory, of discerning, in its object, a transformation of other objects belonging to the same ensemble (Ruwet: 567–8; my trans.).

Thus, the only way totally to avoid dryness (sometimes mis-labeled 'formalism') in analyses such as that of Asdiwal (L-S 1967b) is not to be a comparativist, to remain ensconced within one symbol system, typically our own.[1] For it is clear that whenever one system is translated into another's terms, the latter will lack something of what went into the being of the former. This is the case whether we are translating a poem or painting into music, or vice versa, or translating another culture into our own. Nonetheless, as both Symbolists and structuralist note, the effort *towards* translation, however imperfectly achieved is sublimely worth the trouble, for it is what makes men Man.[2]

Baudelaire speaks of nature as 'an incoherent mass of materials that the artist is invited to associate and put in order'; he avows nature's *déterminant* paucity to the point of asserting: 'It is man who created line and color' (Baudelaire 1925: 15; my trans.). For the Symbolists man's basic means of establishing

---

[1] Van Esbroek (1968) treats these issues at length.

[2] This is perhaps a good place to note G. B. Milner's (1969) interesting comparison of Lévi-Strauss and Bergson. I would take issue with the following statement: 'As Lévi-Strauss describes it and analyzes it, *pensée sauvage* is distorted because the aesthetic faculty (as well as the emotions) are largely missing, for reasons, we must assume, of philosophical conviction' (Milner: 21). This comment may be misleading, as careful readers of *Tristes Tropiques* (L-S 1961b) will attest. To understand why Lévi-Strauss tends to neglect emotions as well as the sort of Bergsonian 'aesthetic faculty' discussed by Milner, we need not assume he does this by philosophical conviction. *Tristes Tropiques* informs us that he does this by reasoned resignation. That book documents how extraordinarily difficult, if not impossible, it is to render any emotional aspects of a culture translatable into terms that can be understood by even one other, much less render them universally translatable. It seems that towards the end of his article Milner loses sight of the true meaning of *pensée sauvage*, taking it to refer more to a stage of 'savage thought' rather than to the 'savage thought' operating any and all effort toward mental incorporation of the other. However, Milner concludes by agreeing with Lévi-Strauss' intellectualist stance as it pertains to translations across orders: 'Such conscious and logical models and structures may only appear to be necessary to us because we are not practitioners of Nuer or of Samoan culture, and consequently our emotions and . . . our intuition and its aesthetic media, are not involved. . . . But for us who stand outside the culture . . ., intellectual data will, as Bergson insisted, remain central and intuitional data peripheral' (Milner: 21–2).

all-pervasive order is through the experience of synesthesia, that tendency to intermingle different orders of sense impressions which is so prevalent in the experience of certain aesthetes. But apart from this flood of spontaneous feeling, synesthesia also refers to 'the deliberate trading on these couplings by artists— e.g. writing "white" with intent to suggest "pure" and so forth' (Lehmann: 211–12)—(an effort to give 'white' the power of *The Savage Mind*'s *'pensée'*?). This 'concocted' synesthesia—a process of realizing the correspondence of different orders—is analogous to the 'transformations' of Lévi-Strauss' natives who, like Baudelaire, utilize some unknowable (or uninteresting until systematized) nature as a source of units for syntheses. And we can again call on Balakian to stress how down to earth this process can be, even for Baudelaire, who establishes as doctrine the phenomenon of synesthesia in his 'Correspondances':

> Baudelaire reveals that the secret of attaining synesthesia is not through the inner eye and its contact with the divine, but rather in the connection of the mind (*l'esprit*) with the senses (*les sens*) by means of a natural stimulus, such as incense or amber (Balakian: 35).

This is strikingly and precisely what Lévi-Strauss demonstrates that preliterates achieve through mythic thinking. And any arguments over whether the process is divinely inspired or logically constructed are futile; for here the this-worldly and the otherworldly are quite one. Finally, where is the 'symbol' in all this 'Symbolism'? Johansen points it out expressly: 'The symbol is not a kind of perception, but the *expression* of a kind of perception, to wit that of synesthesia . . .' (Johansen: 73; my trans.).

While the clearest aspect of these matters is sensory correspondence, Lévi-Strauss emphasizes more radical analogizing in myth. Typically the classification which a myth embodies 'gives the group adopting it the means of "focusing" on all planes, from the most abstract to the most concrete, the most cultural to the most natural, without changing its intellectual instrument'

(L-S 1966a: 136). As in synesthesia, the manipulation of symbols enables a native 'to equate significant contrasts found on different planes: the geographical, meteorological, zoological, botanical, technical, economic, social, ritual, religious, and philosophical' (L-S 1966a: 93). Any symbol, then, exists simultaneously on several such analytically isolated 'planes': Baudelaire's 'cat' is just as much geographical (loins of sand), meteorological (magic star light), social (household resident), ritualistic (medium of resolution), religious (mystic infinity of eyes) and philosophical (juncture of thought and experience), as it is zoological. From a viewpoint apart from the poem the symbol is a unitary entity—a cat; if one situates himself within the poem, the symbol is a system which interrelates all those 'planes' just enumerated. Through a simple singular something a world of experience is attained. Once again a favorite authority on the Symbolists affords a description which is equally true of preliterate myth, as both seek to transform a world of experience into a world of thought-expression through

. . . the coupling of abstract and concrete characteristics whose relationship is not ascertained—all these devices being attempts to transcend direct meaning and to open up the vistas of conjecture, to raise the limited experience of man the poet and man the reader to a level of multiple possibilities (Balakian: 112).

In anthropology a particularly well documented type of taxonomy is afforded by the so-designated 'totemic type,' which is 'based on the postulate of a homology between two systems of differences, one of which occurs in nature and the other in culture' (L-S 1966a: 25) (the latter two categories are analytically distinguished). It is quite arbitrary whether the totem is seen primarily as a referent to some biological element which is then appended to a social group to form an analogy, or vice versa. Moreover, the totem is at once unitary and systemic, just as we have seen with Baudelaire's 'cat':

. . . in none of these cases can the animal, the 'totem' or its

species be grasped as a biological entity: through its double
character of organism—that is, of system—and of emanation
from a species—which is a term in a system—the animal
appears as a conceptual tool with multiple possibilities for
detotalizing or retotalizing any domain, synchronic or diachronic, concrete or abstract, natural or cultural (L-S 1966a:
148–9).

What results is 'a genuine system by means of a creature'; as
far as the example from our poem goes: by detotalizing, all
the disparate planes of existence are a cat; by retotalizing, a
cat is all the disparate planes of existence—depending on the
point of view.

Having thus discovered in totemic systems codes for the transposition of messages into other codes, Lévi-Strauss criticizes
past students of totems for trying 'to reify this form and to
tie it to a determinate content when in fact what it provides
is a method of assimilating any kind of content' (L-S 1966a:
135). Much the same criticism could be leveled at attempts
to understand poems like Mallarmé's 'Un Coup de dés'; rather
than trying as a final aim to determine precisely whose hand
is gesturing, where, etc., all the possible referents should be
enumerated and related to each other and to all the other events
and forms. We can, it seems to me, adopt a 'primitive' approach
to any poem, and to Mallarmé's poems especially, by considering its various 'levels' as 'stages or moments in a continuous
transition' (L-S 1966a: 138). And certainly this same poet's
ambitious goals for a total work, his dreamed of *Œuvre,* could
only have been achieved in the form of some set of transformable structures which could encompass all experience: *l'Œuvre*
as 'a method of assimilating any kind of content'! How else
might he have gone about creating a work so difficult to describe:

What? It's difficult to say; a book, . . . in many volumes, a
book which would be a book both architectural and pre-
meditated, and not a collection of chance inspirations however marvelous they might be . . . I will go farther, I will say:

the book, persuaded that . . . there is but one . . . the Orphic explication of the Earth, which is the sole duty of the poet and the literary game *par excellence* . . . (Mallarmé's letter of November, 1885, cited in Charvet: 67; my trans.).

(Perhaps Mallarmé attained his dream after all, since such an ultimate set of structures would logically be represented by silence—which is to say, total sound; only in undifferentiation are all categories perfectly transformable into all others.) Finally, the preliterates described by Lévi-Strauss are no more 'sentimental about vegetation' (or fauna) than was Baudelaire, who asserted that he could 'never believe that the *souls of the gods live in plants* . . .' (cited in Hyslop: 22). Geertz summarizes the preliterates' similar sophistication:

When [the informant] says that the members of his clan are descended from bear but those of his neighbors from eagle he is not giving forth with a bit of illiterate biology. He is saying, in a concrete metaphorical way, that the relationship between his clan and his neighbor's is analogous to the perceived relationship between species (Geertz: 29).

Preliterates smack of the poet insofar as they utilize the same sort of 'verbal classifications to impose order upon the human society as they use to impose order on the natural environment' (Leach 1965a: 25). Or, more precisely, the poet smacks of the preliterate in a relatively a-mythical world.

Just as Lévi-Strauss has criticized past students of totemism, his own studies of this particular variety of classification and more generally of myth have been challenged. Nur Yalman, for example, observes:

Regarding the 'oppositions', it is difficult to know whether they are merely heuristic devices to order the symbolism or whether they are categories of the native mind which evoke the myths by their interplay (Yalman 1967: 77).

This observation is accurate; it is difficult to know whether the oppositions are 'categories of the native mind' apart from

the fact that the opposition can be *demonstrated* to be stated—
usually quite unconsciously—in various 'texts' on various levels
which are reputed to have been produced by some 'native mind.'
In the absence of a privileged channel to that locus of authori-
tative veracity (i.e. someone's honest and straightforward
'mind') the difficulty detected by Yalman is in fact an impossi-
bility. Moreover, structuralism is itself a concerted effort to surmount this epistemological obstacle of inability to distinguish
'heuristic devices' of analysis from any 'true categories' generating texts (see L-S 1961b: ch. 6). It does this in part by utilizing the logically simplest heuristic device—namely, binary
opposition—as it seeks out systematization without worrying
whether its own process of *discovery* repeats any process of
formation which yielded the systems in the first place.[3] Then
Yalman goes on to ask, 'But what does this analysis show about
the thinking processes of the tribes in question? What indeed
is the relationship between the relatively formal myths and the
rest of the mental activity of the tribes?' (1967: 86). And at
least a partial answer is clear. Structural analyses of societies'
'texts' are no more primarily concerned with consciously produced systematic statements than was the article on 'Les Chats.'
Of course, any conscious systems ('native models') are just as
interesting as unconscious ones, at least as manifestations of
logical processes. But since the structuralist himself is in the
best position to detect structures—thanks to his cross-cultural
and sometimes temporal perspective, which points up differences that effect distinctive features—then his analyses can reveal
the 'realest' basis underlying, for example, myth. And if any-
thing can be said to 'evoke the myths,' this basis does. Finally,
we must remember that the basis of the structures is preeminently
'unconscious,' if, recalling our discussion of *langue*, we take
'unconscious' to refer to 'the mind's threshold of self-conscious
social awareness' wherein men define themselves by differen-

---

[3] Leach, then, is somewhat unjust here: 'Because he takes his cue from
Jakobson-style linguistic theory and the mechanics of digital computers,
Lévi-Strauss tends to imply . . . that the whole structure of primitive
thought is binary' (Leach 1967b: 8). As Lévi-Strauss suggests (e.g. L-S
1966b: 74n), binary opposition is principally an analytic device.

tiating themselves from other men and from features selected from their experience (see Boon 1971: 1003).

A related point is that one structural analysis can indeed be better than another, and such an analysis can be demonstated to be wrong. For example, I think Lévi-Strauss erred in the article (L-S 1963b: 136) where he claims that Malinowski's Omarakana village is dually ordered by the following: sacred/ profane, raw/cooked, celibacy/marriage, male/female, central/ peripheral. I would counter that the male/female dichotomy is inaccurate and that the data shows this; for the center is not where bachelors 'lived' but where they slept and experienced their period of pre-marriage intercourse with different partners. I would replace the male/female with free-sex/regulated sex. Doing so, the argument would run, opens up many more aspects of Malinowski's Trobriand data—especially myth and ideology and the notion of Tuma—to a more thorough and economic analysis. With proper documentation, then, the very possibility of any such argument refutes Burridge's conclusion (1967) that Lévi-Strauss' formulae are self-explanatory. The formulae are simply never final; there is always more to consider, more to be said. The formulae are indeed subject to testing, but not, as some would like, to absolutely conclusive tests.

Lastly, as for the 'rest of the mental activity of the tribes' inquired after by Yalman, we must recall Lévi-Strauss' very general designation of 'myth' already cited (on p. 33). For 'myth' is most generally any manifestation (chanted, spoken, acted, designed) of preliterate systematic 'thinking' which is accessible to an outside observer, i.e. which is *translatable*, which can be sensibly communicated to him out of the 'texts' by which he is confronted. And *pensée sauvage* is the effort towards that translation. Thus, 'myths' in the history of anthropology are just those involved and seemingly very systematic accounts gathered from preliterates which have also seemed most sensory—no doubt due to their concern with aspects of how the people in question relate themselves to their surroundings. And 'myth' is more translatable than, say, 'poetry'—which would be distinguished by some sort of formal criteria—because myth is *defined* as that which is intelligibly communicable.

It is for these reasons that Lévi-Strauss can be so nonchalant in *Mythologiques* about what sort of texts he means by 'myth.' For 'myth' is an operational concept, based on the reality of inter-translatability, and not the *designatum* of a particular form or sort of content.[4] Bickering over what is a myth and what is not is just as pedantically out of place—given the nature of the experience of data gathering in ethnography, or any data gathering for that matter—as it is to quarrel over how to spell correctly 'Nambikuara' when the name does not even exist among the various peoples it has been adduced by scholars to designate (see L-S 1946b).

Another sort of criticism of Lévi-Strauss centers on his discovery procedures. While it has been suggested that Lévi-Strauss fails to make these procedures clear, I would counter that he makes them so clear as to leave us incredulous before their simplicity. For nowhere has a method of analysis been more succinctly and straightforwardly outlined than in *Totemism* (L-S 1963a: 16–17). He looks at data from different cultures which bear on some analytic distinction, for example men/not-men. He detects two sets of oppositions in the two halves: for men there is an ordering by individual/group and for not-men by individual/species. He then sets up permutations: individual man/species-not-man, group-men/individual-not-men, etc. Finally he refers back to various data to see if these permutations occur, always hoping to be informed of additional oppositions.[5] Thus, we have a basis for comparing different types of 'totemism'

[4] Burridge fails to appreciate this fact when he summarizes: 'Lévi-Strauss' whole argument in "The Structural Study of Myth" rests on the direct translatability of myth, on the assumption that the language of myth is non-poetic, that a myth may be translated without any concern for the resonances of words on either hand' (Burridge: 111). For some further words on the 'mythic function' see my 'Lévi-Strauss and Narrative' (Boon 1970).

[5] See Mendelson (1967) for a still fuller summary of this method. Lévi-Strauss' analytic strategy is perhaps most readily apparent in 'The Bear and the Barber' (L-S 1963d). Note especially how this general comparative sketch of 'totemistic' as opposed to 'caste' modes of ordering societies begins with the most concrete of details from particular groups (p. 1). See also Lévi-Strauss' casual summary of his method printed from a broadcast by Michel Tréguer published in (Backès-Clément 177–9).

based on differences which should be operative in other areas of cultural life. Yalman (1967: 80) has noted that this same method continues in *Mythologiques*, but with a vastly increased comparative range and a greater number of levels (than just analytic 'social' as opposed to 'natural') examined to detect structures.[6]

I think the difficulty lies not in any duplicity on Lévi-Strauss' part as to how he proceeds in his studies, but rather to many readers' persistent expectation that he will eventually label some level of experience—such as 'social organization' or 'ideas'—primary or causal, which, as we have seen, he certainly never does. Or perhaps even more confusion arises from a failure to understand the direction in which Lévi-Strauss' thinking moves, or rather where it begins. Leach has recently exposed this problem most explicitly:

What will doubtless puzzle the novice . . . is how on earth Lévi-Strauss comes upon his basic oppositions in the first place. How could it ever occur to anyone that an opposition between roast pork and boiled cabbage might reflect a fundamental characteristic of human thinking, or that honey and tobacco (of all things) might come to have a significance as fundamental as that which opposes rain and drought? The answer, I think, is that Lévi-Strauss starts at the other end. He first asks himself: how is it and why is it that men, who are a part of Nature, manage to see themselves as 'other than' Nature even though, in order to subsist, they must constantly maintain 'relations with' Nature? He then observes, simply as a fact of archaeology rather than of ethnography, that ever since the most remote antiquity men have employed fire to transform their food from a natural raw state to an artificial cooked state. Why is this? Men do not *have* to cook their food, they do so for symbolic reasons . . . (Leach: 1967b: 8; repeated in 1970: 91–2).

[6] For an overwhelmingly schematic outline of Lévi-Strauss' discovery procedures in *Mythologiques* (more specifically in 100 pages of *The Raw and the Cooked*), see (Richard 1967).

Thus, in what one could call a very Symbolist-like fashion, Lévi-Strauss 'starts at the other end' from some overriding binary distinction that appears to pervade the data on a first perusal. He can then trace the distinction, as its sides break down into further distinctions, along multiple levels of texts. And as Leach appreciates, Lévi-Strauss does not just pull especially outlandish oppositions out of his hat. Rather he thinks in this way: If I were a native living in this particular ethno-botanical area, relatively isolated, and I wanted to differentiate myself from (or identify myself with) my surroundings or my neighbors, how would I do it, given the elements at my disposal? Furthermore, unlike most anthropologists he does not write up the results of the inquiry alone. Rather, especially in *Mythologiques*, he writes up the activity of the inquiry as such. As should later become clearer, critics who complain that Lévi-Strauss' works leave his discovery procedures vague fail to realize that it is an idealized retrospect of those very procedures that they are reading.

As for the problem of verification of his analyses, critics are right in saying that Lévi-Strauss' results are unverifiable, if they mean to say that there is no 'absolute domain'—social organization, material goods, etc.—any corroborating variables of which can be taken to prove authoritatively the validity of the findings in myth. But the findings can be relatively better verified the more they can be demonstrated to be expressed independently and at best *socially* across cultures. For Lévi-Strauss' structuralism employs the same *circulus methodicus* enjoyed by Panofsky in *Meaning in the Visual Arts,* a work which Lévi-Strauss has commended as authentically structural (see L-S 1965a: 127).

. . . the individual observation assumes the character of a 'fact' only when it can be related to other, analogous observations in such a way that the whole series 'makes sense.' This 'sense' is, therefore, fully capable of being applied, as a control, to the interpretation of a new individual observation within the same range of phenomena. If, however, this new individual observation definitely refuses to be interpreted

according to the 'sense' of the series . . . the 'sense' of the
series will have to be reformulated to include the new individual observation (Panofsky: 35n).

With myth we just have to keep trying, and liking it, somewhat in the manner of literary criticism.

Totemic systems are no more than particularly well-known
examples of man's general penchant to structure systems in
which 'there is a constant passage in both directions between
ideas and images, grammar and lexicon' (L-S 1966a: 154).
Whereas 'totemism' is on the one hand a fully structured
domain, it can itself serve as a 'unit' in the structures of the
society as a whole. For example, consider still another summary
by Leach of Lévi-Strauss' ideas:

> Thus Indian caste systems consist of endogamous groups
> which are distinguished by cultural criteria (occupations),
> whereas Australian aboriginal societies consist of exogamous
> groups which are distinguished by natural criteria (totems),
> yet considered as total systems, that is as structured arrange-
> ments of categories, these entirely different patterns of cul-
> ture are strictly comparable (Leach 1967b: 6).

The mind is a mediator—or is evidenced by the mediation—between analytically isolated nature and culture, drawing from
both realms to generate species:

> As medial classifier . . . the species level can widen its net
> upwards, that is, in the direction of elements, categories, and
> numbers, or contract downwards, in the direction of proper
> names (L-S 1966a: 149).

And that mediation which moreover bridges the analytic domains of the 'social' and the 'natural' has typically, and mis-
leadingly, been labeled 'totem*ism*.' Perhaps the slogan which
best clarifies Lévi-Strauss' concepts of thought is provided by a
chapter in *The Savage Mind*, 'The Individual as Species.' Just
as was true with 'cat,' even an ultimately particular and

K

individualizing proper name connects to systems which channel one back into diversified experience, as the mind continually passes 'from empirical diversity to conceptual simplicity and then from conceptual simplicity to meaningful synthesis' (L-S 1966a: 131). A striking example of this individual/species theme is afforded by linguistically 'aware' Symbolist works in which the word itself contains a species:

> The writer chooses a minute part among all the possibilities contained in the word (phonetic qualities, etymological tradition, semantic value) which he then enlarges in terms of that which he proposes to do. The word is at once an end in itself and the most marvellous point of departure (Uitti 1967: 361; my trans.).

Lévi-Strauss denies that he is viewing social life as a mere conceptual game lodged in the mind. Rather, he is suggesting that there exists a mediating conceptual scheme through which matter and form are realized as structures; the most elaborated realization of the scheme is a hypothetical superstructure:

> . . . the dialectic of superstructures, like that of language, consists in setting up *constitutive units* (which, for this purpose, have to be defined unequivocally, that is by contrasting them in pairs) so as to be able by means of them to elaborate a system which plays the part of a synthesizing operator between ideas and facts, thereby turning the latter into *signs* (L-S 1966a: 131).

Many Symbolists have a similar philosophy of expression, and they construct (reflect) that philosophy in their poems. They scrutinize language and come up with a super-structured poetry, a poetry of 'superstructures.' Or even in the absence of such complex structuring, they indeed create 'synthesizing operators':

> . . . il sonne une cloche de feu rose dans les nuages (Rimbaud: 230).

Symbolist works, native myth, and studies of both are all characterized by the same logical end point. They are 'totalizing
thoughts, which exhaust reality by means of a finite number of
given classes,' (L-S 1966a: 172) thanks to the phenomenon of
transformation or of contrived synesthesia. This totalistic
quality has paradoxical effects on the analytic categories of
method, doctrine, and—most severely—self.

Lévi-Strauss conceives of 'species' as an operator allowing one
to pass 'from the unity of a multiplicity to the diversity of a
unity' (1966a: 136). The species as operator is a methodological tool for classifying, but it can only be this insofar as it
reflects the way things are thought to *be*. In the concept of
species we find constituted 'the most direct manifestation [man]
can perceive of the ultimate discontinuity of reality. It is the
sensible expression of an objective coding' (L-S 1966a: 137).
That this merger of the categories of method and doctrine in
structuralist studies is a reflection of the latter's subject matter
is pointed out by Peter Caws:

> Language, myth, and so on represent the way in which man
> has been able to grasp the real [method], and for him they
> constitute the real [doctrine]; they are not structures *of* some
> ineffable reality which lies behind them and from which they
> are separable. To say that the world is intelligible means
> that it presents itself to the mind of the primitive as a message,
> to which his language and behavior are an appropriate re-
> sponse—but not as a message *from elsewhere*, simply as a
> message, as it were, in its own right (Caws: 81).

Again, you see, we are witnessing the death of dualism, and all
in the name of communication. This assertion of the primacy of
the messages in language and myth—with the accompanying
refutation of a source, an 'elsewhere' as pertinent—parallels
notions we have seen in Symbolists regarding the status of their
poetry, their doctrinal method of knowing (being) the world:

> Poetry is the expression, by human language brought back
> to its essential rhythm, of the mysterious sense of existence:

it bestows authenticity on our stay . . . (Mallarmé cited in Hartley 1965: xxiii; my trans.).

In our roles of Symbolists or structuralists, we can but study 'the shadows which are outlined in the depths of the cave, without forgetting that only the attention we lend them bestows upon them a semblance of reality' (L-S 1962a: 155; my trans.). 'The thesis of Claude Lévi-Strauss is in effect that the universe wherein live primitives is, as is ours, a universe of messages' (Cuisenier: 548; my trans.).

The circularity of this argument has vast implications for the concept of self. According to Peter Caws current structuralists are of the opinion that modern man's plight arises from his 'invention of the self *as an object of study*, from the belief that man has a special kind of being . . .' (Caws: 82). Their solution to the plight is achieved through a breakdown of the unity of 'self' in a fashion reminiscent of the tendency in Symbolists' works to make of the subject an 'organizational abstraction' (Lehmann: 67). Again, in his concise article on the French structuralist 'movement,' Caws deems the preoccupation with language doubling back on itself its hallmark:

> Whereas the civilized mind thinks itself capable of taking an objective stance and judging the adequacy of language or symbol (the signifier) to their meanings (the signified), the view of mind which emerges from ethnology and psychoanalysis suggests that the two realms are autonomous and that mind *is* precisely this adequacy, so that objectivity is impossible (Caws: 85).

It is recalled that Mallarmé yearned to achieve *l'Œuvre* 'in order that the universe regain in this (my)self its identity' (Mallarmé cited in Gibson: 85; my trans.). 'The ego that Mallarmé deals with is an *objective* ego (as is that of Rimbaud, Gide, Proust and, to some extent, Baudelaire) to be regarded dispassionately, impersonally even, not as interesting in itself but as a locale in which experiences take place' (Guthrie and Diller: 523). But it is not merely some amorphous, mystic,

vaguely narcissistic locale; it is a tensely structured, yet im-
minently transforming ego-world, such as that composed in
'Un Coup de dés.' And while Symbolist works are often extraordinarily hermetic, they are infinitely less so than would be
the alternative which they seldom lost sight of: the non-com-
municability of silence, that true mark of ultimate Narcissus.
The very fact that a Symbolist embodied himself in a text is
a call to *exchange*, which fact alone requires partners.

Thus, Symbolist poetry appears to afford prefigurations of
Lévi-Strauss' structural view of 'man, externalized by man'
(L-S 1966a: 220). In their poems the slogan of 'individual
as species' is exemplified in that particular guise wherein the
individual in question is the self. Ultimately, as realized by
Lévi-Strauss, the anthropologist's works fall into that same
guise. We have been suggesting analogies among Symbolist
poems and native myths, but Lévi-Strauss has somewhat sen-
sationally admitted that his own intelligence is neolithic (L-S
1961b: 56). It cannot be determined in his studies of natives
whether their thought takes shape under the operation of his,
or his under the operation of theirs (see L-S 1964a: 21). Since
his structural analyses seek to be as classificatory as the native
myths, Lévi-Strauss concludes in *Le Cru et le cuit*: 'Thus is
this book about myths, in its fashion, a myth' (1964a: 14; my
trans.).[7] Yet, if Lévi-Strauss is, in fact, constructing 'the myth
of mythology,' then, according to his own definition, he is
using a structure to create a set (object+event), i.e. a story.
But what is his 'story?' It seems that it could only be the
analyses themselves. If this is so, then might not the 'reciprocal
translatability' among different myths (demonstrated throughout *Mythologiques*) be based on correspondences just as arbitrary
as ' "A"-black' or 'redbird-sun'? One must, I think, answer

---

[7] If, as Lévi-Strauss asserts, language is a first order code, myth a second
order code, and *The Raw and the Cooked* 'a third order code destined
to assure the reciprocal translatability of several myths' (L-S 1964a: 20; my
trans.), then the Symbolists' philosophy of poetry would likewise be a
third order code, interrelating their second order poems which are inter-
transformable classes of language, and this study should be a fourth
order code, attempting the translation between third order structuralism
and Symbolism.

in the affirmative, since for transformations to be effected a system of equivalences has to be erected; and in the case of 'the myth of mythology' it is Lévi-Strauss who consciously erects them. Yet, the correspondences derived by Lévi-Strauss can be checked and cross-checked against a wealth of empirical data, in order to assess their generality and applicability. This does not make the correspondences any less 'arbitrary' (in Saussure's *a priori* sense), but rather shows the same sort of *a priori* arbitrariness to be universal. Then we can proceed to trace out the *a posteriori* set of restrictions in a given area. Lévi-Strauss is no material-oriented idealist; he is empirical and analytic, and he uses empirico-analytic methods to demonstrate that men in general are material-oriented idealists, if that can be taken to mean Symbolist-like sensory-constructionists!

In no way, then, should we despair in a bog of *dédoublement*. For in still another way any charge of this sort of arbitrariness would not disparage what Lévi-Strauss seeks to accomplish. For, always insisting that contents can only be known empirically (and then only as it is structured by the observer), he hopes to illuminate universal logical *processes*. It is not *what* his myths (analyses) say, it is *how* they derive what they say that counts most. Completely different stories can be generated by the same structures; and if the most general and widespread structures claimed to be more *absolute*, we would be right back with Baudelaire's transcendental tendencies. Lévi-Strauss seems to me to be offering less a way of *re*-constituting someone else's myth, than he is offering processes through which one can in *other*'s terms create one's own: instant poet. This much, at least, can be assumed for the moment: he relates a structuralist macro-myth to a 'demythologicalized world' of potentially native thinkers. If he is accused of circularity in so doing (circularity is an 'accusation' only if one assumes logic's 'natural' way to be linear), he can counter that he is circular only insofar as human thought must be, given that it is characterized by finite logical processes realizable through language. Admit the circularity and make a myth. The sensory units out of which to construct it are there for the taking in ethnographic accounts.

We need only be tolerant and comparative, all the while remembering:

> Tolerance is not a contemplative attitude, dispensing indulgence to what has been or what is still in being. It is a dynamic attitude, consisting in the anticipation, understanding and promotion of what is struggling into being. We can see the diversity of human cultures behind us, around us, and before us. The only demand that we can justly make (entailing *corresponding* duties for every individual) is that all the forms this diversity may take may be so many contributions to the fullness of all the others (L-S 1952: 49; my emphasis).

Lévi-Strauss has entitled his most recent series of studies '*Mythologiques*,' and therein, predictably, lies a fruitful ambiguity. For while the works are ostensibly a dramatically empirical investigation of relationships among portions of South and North American mythology, it seems that an accompanying aim is to demonstrate (indeed, advocate) mythic logics, *mythologiques*. Thus, through a method we achieve a doctrine in which we incorporate experience into the myth of ourselves. No less than Mallarmé, Lévi-Strauss constructs an ethic, as must anyone who constructs a logical universe:

> "The golden age which blind superstition situated behind or ahead of us is *in us*.' Human brotherhood acquires a palpable significance when we find our image of it confirmed in the poorest of tribes, and when that tribe offers us an experience which, when joined with many hundreds of others, has a lesson to teach us (L-S 1961b: 392).

And one need only add that every ethic is an aesthetic. The anthropologist can demonstrate what the poet senses,

> for, knowing as we do that for thousands of years past mankind has done nothing but repeat itself, we shall attain that noble cast of thought which, transcending all that has been

done and redone, assigns as the starting-point of our reflections that indefinable grandeur which is the mark of true
beginnings (L-S 1961b: 392).

After all, even though they do not *progress* any*where* beyond
themselves, there is nothing degrading about productions of
full circles of symphonic form.

V

Critical Ramifications

He was at the same time all the artists he had studied and all the books
he had read, and yet, in spite of this talent for mimicry, he remained
profoundly original (Baudelaire in Hyslop: 33).

G. C. Dans tout ce que vous dites il me semble qu'on voit percer les
    idées de Rousseau.
C. L-S. Pourquoi pas? (Charbonnier: 41).

Viewing Lévi-Strauss in terms of past literary works in no
way detracts from his achievement. For what have we been
discussing in this study, if not Baudelaire's category of constructive *imagination*:

[The imagination] is analysis; it is synthesis. . . . It is the
imagination which has taught man the moral meaning [*sens*]
of color, of contour, of sound and odor. It has created, at the
beginning of the world, analogy and metaphor. It decomposes
all creation, and, with the materials amassed and disposed
according to rules whose origin can only be found in the
utmost depths of the soul, it creates a new world; it produces the sensation of the new (Baudelaire 1951: 765 my
trans.).

Originality itself is a product of synthesis. Nor does comparing
Lévi-Strauss' empirical analyses with the creative works of
various aesthetes necessarily imply that the former is less 'scientific' (or the latter less aesthetic), although there has been a
tendency among Lévi-Strauss' critics to assume the two sides
of a science/aesthetics opposition to be mutually exclusive, and

to leave it at that. For example, Yvan Simonis (1968), in his review of Lévi-Strauss' entire corpus of work, concludes that his structuralism is a logic of aesthetic perception, that it cannot be a science but only a sort of artistic metaphor. However, it seems to me that this sort of conclusion begs one of the central questions repeatedly posed by Lévi-Strauss, among others: in what sort of terms can comparative social 'science' be scientific? Many students of culture would argue that 'natural science' models or 'laboratory, predicting science' models have failed, when applied to certain varieties of general human productions. In light of the failure, can we expect to achieve a 'science' other than a sort of applied comparative-artistic(?)-metaphor, extensively checked against cross-cultural documentation? And is not this actually the kind of operation many of the purer sciences themselves embody, if we allow for the additional coding device of some sort of calculus?—which, in fact, is just what Lévi-Strauss is trying to discover: a preliminary calculus, that is, of aesthetic (intersensory) perception and conceptualization. The status of Lévi-Strauss' 'science' is, of course, a central issue of debate. In Zimmerman's opinion, after he notes his efforts to delineate invariant structures: '. . . if what Lévi-Strauss does is science, then what the primitive does is not science but rather a phase in the development of science' (Zimmerman: 58). But, as I hope the present chapter will indicate, the issue is not quite so clear cut. Let us note for now that it is unwarranted simply to assume that an aesthetic is non-scientific. This is especially true in Lévi-Strauss' case, since his comparativist science is concerned with communication theory rather than any laboratory science theory, thus seeking to demonstrate pattern, complementarity and limits, rather than controlled predictability of observable fact.[1]

Lévi-Strauss himself frequently discusses the works of earlier classifiers, whether scientific, aesthetic or, otherwise—Rousseau, Marx, Weiner, Rabelais, etc.—and suggests how parts of their

[1] Lévi-Strauss outlines his ideas on the limits of comparative social science at length in (L-S 1964b). For a very different view from my own on the kind of theory Lévi-Strauss is or should be concerned with, see (Shankman 1969).

systems can be transformed into parts of his own. Above all, for our purposes the intimate affinities between Symbolist and structuralist understandings of human experience afford a fertile field for cross-disciplinary analogies. Thus this chapter seeks to demonstrate the logico-aesthetic implications of corresponding points of view.

Tristes Tropiques ('one of the great books of our century'— Sontag: 6), is a Symbolist narrative of a Symbolist's quest to disclose an ideal, primal realm of experience, 'to pursue "the primitive" to its furthest point' (L-S 1961b: 326). In the same way that Mallarmé and his followers sought the unattainable state of a perfected, universal *Rêve* (dream), Lévi-Strauss set out to find that primitive condition, as sensed in himself, more completely objectified in a people. He found his primitives, but at the same time found their state just as incommunicable as the Symbolist *Rêve*: 'They were as close to me as an image seen in a looking glass: I could touch, but not understand them' (L-S 1961b: 326).

L'Azur! l'Azur! l'Azur! l'Azur! (Mallarmé 1965: 28).

Later in the work the author includes systematic results of this incapacity to understand, in the form of structural orderings of that which he perceived. But, like Symbolist poems, these orderings are nowhere near 'the thing itself.' For the thing itself—these societies—cannot be grasped in and of itself, but can only be known indirectly across the fact of a relationship that is established between whatever that thing is and an observer. Well then, however, on second thought, if there is a 'society-thing' that *is*, it must itself be epistemologically grounded in some such observer-relation situation—hence the locus of Lévi-Straussian 'structures,' his re-discovery of subjectivity in the social sciences and the breakdown of observer/observed dualism, even in empirical investigations. Unable, then, to *know* the primal perfection, Lévi-Strauss determines to describe how he is unable to know it, and the result is *Tristes Tropiques*, an anti-ethnography.

It is in perfect irony that Lévi-Strauss obliges himself to

write something that will no doubt be received as that which he most loathes: objective accounts of 'travel.' Why offer accounts of what is almost all boredom and petty frustration? To overcome the dilemma involved in producing what will nevertheless be construed as a factual tale of adventure, Lévi-Strauss adopts a decidedly Symbolist approach by offering not reportage but remembrance. Thanks to the fifteen year interlude between the act of his necessarily fragmented fieldwork and the account of it, he can rest assured that:

> Forgetfulness has done its work among my recollections, but it has not merely worn them thin, not merely buried them. It has made of these fragments a construction in depth that offers firmer ground beneath the feet and a clearer outline for the eye. One order has been substituted for another. . . . Unrelated events, rooted in the most disparate of regions and periods, suddenly come into contact with one another and take shape as a crusader castle which owes its architecture not to my private history but to some altogether wiser designer (L-S 1961b: 45).

Yet Lévi-Strauss is fully aware that his readers—each of whom looms as a sort of ethnologist in his own right before the body of data that is *Tristes Tropiques*—will misconstrue the work as being an objective 'story'; just as so many professional ethnographers had misconstrued other data creatively ordered through hindsight by the natives themselves. And Lévi-Strauss warns us of this impending error by means of his hastily scribbled play interjected towards the end of the book, 'The Apotheosis of Augustus':

> Cinna had returned home loaded with marvels. Every hostess in Rome had put him at the top of her list. Only he knew, meanwhile, that the celebrity he had paid for so dearly was based on a lie. The experiences with which he was credited were a myth; the journey a deception; but all seemed true enough to those who had seen only its shadow.
> Camille has eyes only for her explorer, who tries in vain

to make her see how false are his stories. 'I did my best to explain the emptiness and futility of all that had happened, but no sooner were these transformed as 'a traveller's tale' than she was dazzled and all adream (L-S 1961b: 378–9).

To use this analogy is not to say that *Tristes Tropiques* contains false information. Rather it is an acknowledgement of two facts. In the first place the anthropologist's 'field' provides no absolute source of privileged insight into the nature of Man. No matter what the tribe or how long the duration of the ethnographer's stay, the fieldwork situation never amounts to any more than a man trying to communicate with men; and the degree of expertise a fieldworker has in a certain area can never surmount the fundamental imperfection characteristic of this situation. As Lévi-Strauss recognizes: '. . . did not my mistake, and that of my profession, lie in the belief that men are not always men?' (1961b: 326), i.e. that they are objects. Then too, he generalizes elsewhere:

> Without a doubt, the attempt will remain largely illusory: we shall never know if the other, into whom we cannot, after all, dissolve, fashions from the elements of his social existence a synthesis exactly superimposable on that which we have worked out. But it is not necessary to go so far; all we need—and for this, inner understanding suffices—is that the synthesis however approximate, arises from human experience. We must be sure of this, since we study men; and as we are ourselves men, we have that possibility. The way in which Mauss poses and resolves the problem in his *Essay on the Gift* exhibits, in the intersection of his subjectivities, the nearest order of truth to which the sciences of man can aspire when they confront this object integrally (L-S 1967c: 14).

Just as Mallarmé insisted concerning the description (evocation) of objects or events with words, Lévi-Strauss asserts (as noted by Pouillon):

> Authentic comprehension does not abolish the distance

between subject and object; it allows for the distance to be traversed, but does not surpress it . . .' (Pouillon 1956: 152; my trans.).

For an object is not an inert and nameable thing any more than a 'family' is (see L-S 1956). A family is an analytic cut across a system of relationships in process, as are societies—as is gradually recognized through the adventures of *Tristes Tropiques*.

The second fact acknowledged in 'The Apotheosis of Augustus' is that fieldwork itself takes on significance only through the faculty of creative and imaginative ordering—albeit true to the data—which might be based on intuitive inklings apart from supposedly pure and more essential experience in the field (whence fieldwork's character of 'myth'). Indeed, the reader is is almost constrained to read 'The Apotheosis of Augustus' allegorically, Cinna representing Lévi-Strauss' fieldworking half, which had sought to win Nature and might now 'rejoin society and continue to deny it,' and the ivory-towered Augustus being the anthropologist-intellectualist half which amalgamates Nature and Society, thus making himself a god among men. Which half wins? *Tristes Tropiques* leaves it at a stalemate and Lévi-Strauss himself confesses: 'I'm not really quite sure how it all ended' (1961b: 380). In fact, there is simply no way for one to rid one's observations of subjective whimsy—nor indeed are there any grounds for insisting that one do so, when we recognize that *any* analysis is not of some 'thing in itself,' but only of some assumed 'thing' in relation to a subject. Witness in this connection how Lévi-Strauss is infected with that perceptual-distortion tendency singled out by Proust as 'Place-Names: The Name' (Proust 1956a: 550), wherein the associations built up after the sounds in an area's name severely direct perception of the so-designated area 'itself':

I imagined Brazil as a tangled mass of palm-leaves, with glimpses of strange architecture in the middle distance, and an all-permeating smell of burning perfume. This latter olfactory detail I owe, I think, to an unconscious awareness of the assonance between the words '*Brésil*' (Brazil) and '*grésiller*' (sizzle). No amount of later experience, in any case, can prevent me from still thinking of Brazil in terms of burning scent (L-S 1961b: 49–50).[2]

Nevertheless, such an intuitive response might be of some value in a study of Brazil. The response at least starts one thinking; it at least puts 'order in some ideas, there where there had been none' (Mauss: 372). There is no logical reason for disparaging such intuition, since any eventual 'model' or explanation is always to be checked back against different data on different levels to determine its value. But regardless of the source of inspiration behind the 'genius' of any analysis— whether that source issues from the mouths of natives or the ruminations of self—the results are bound to be mistaken by many students of society for an attempt to represent some substantive 'thing.' While what in fact is offered is the structure of the communicated confrontation between two sets of terms, the one set being generally glossed as the 'self' of the ethnographer, the other set being the elements of those 'societies' which the ethnographer himself can isolate. Finally, we must be careful not to equate this structuralist position with one of total relativity. The position would be hopelessly relativistic only if all 'selves' were considered unique. But since a self likewise is only known in a state of relationship (i.e. as communicated), then, at some point exceeding individuality 'selves' are determined. Therefore what anthropologists have to work with is not an endless array of unique individuals garnering impressions of exotic societies, but a limited number of *ways* that communication is affected between a finite number of different cultural systems and a finite number of different self-systems.

Thus in *Tristes Tropiques* Lévi-Strauss recounts the confrontation of a Symbolist *esprit* with various ethnographic situations (callings to translate) the world over, and how it

[2] Barthes has noted (1967: 157) the parallel between Proust's use of proper names to launch his reminiscence and the observations Lévi-Strauss makes on such procedures in *pensée sauvage*.

got there. As is generally true of Symbolist narrative, the objects described 'exist only in relation to the particular mind of the artist and his persona' (Freedman: 142). But in Lévi-Strauss' case it is not exactly the artist and his persona, rather the anthropologist and his natives. Yet the precariousness of 'objective' existence remains: 'As for the creations of the human mind [*esprit*], they are meaningful only in relation to that mind and will fall into nothingness [*se confondront au désordre*] as soon as it ceases to exist' (L-S 1961b: 397). In truth, Lévi-Strauss' narrative is a far cry from a linear travelogue (of the sort exemplified by those slide shows which inspired him to begin his quest). We are presented instead the temporally and spatially collapsed world of recollection. When he writes of 'Le Retour', it is not a question of a particular voyage home, but rather of all his multiple voyages home, be they from South America, Asia, or anywhere. Furthermore, the traveler reflects:

. . . Instead of opening for me a new universe, my adventurous life restored for me the old. . . .
Was travel then but this? An exploration of the wilderness of my memory rather than of that which was surrounding me? (L-S 1955a: 406, 408; my trans.).

This suggests that Lévi-Strauss' 'Return' is not so much from voyages or particular peoples but rather from adventures in his memory—and to what?—to the self of creative intellectualizing in which memorable events are reviewed and classified. i.e., created as narrative. After all, the book begins with 'la fin des voyages'. (Unfortunately, the English translation misses the significance of Part I by translating its title 'Destinations' rather than 'The End of Travels.' Moreover, the English version deletes the clearly non-South American chapters, apparently to make *Tristes Tropiques* appear more like an ethnography in the tradition of space isolates and objective reportage.)

Equally applicable to *Tristes Tropiques* in this respect is Karl D. Uitti's description of Gourmont's Symbolist work *Sixtine*, which 'just like traditional novels possesses a chronological beginning, development, and end; but this sort of temporal progression is but anecdotic' (Uitti 1967: 351; my trans.). Likewise relevant is that 'ideological structure of *Sixtine*, that psychologico-aesthetic idealism' (p. 349)—with the restriction that, unlike a novelist, an ethnographer does not fabricate events or objects. Moreover, perhaps what has been termed the 'solitude à trois' point of view typical of Symbolist novels also occurs in this structuralist novel, with one alteration. We find the interpretations of author (Lévi-Strauss in his retrospection) and hero (Lévi-Strauss on the road); but instead of the reader who comes into play in Symbolist narrative, there is a new third party—the natives and their own views of their systems. (Of course, as Leach has appreciated in his [1965c] review of *The Raw and the Cooked*, the creative participation of the reader, qua *bricoleur*, can also have a place in experiencing Lévi-Strauss' works—this resulting, I suppose, in a 'solitude à quatre'.) The crucial fact to note is that none of these points of view is given the upper hand: take any 'thing,' for example a village lay-out, and the ethnologist has a model of it (a systematic representation built up out of features selected from it); the ethnographer had a model; the natives may have one or more models. And it is only across all these models that the 'thing' can to some extent be 'known' in terms of the *structure* relating their differences.

Thus it is that Lévi-Strauss elevates ethnological sensitivity to the level of the modern novel as it was at an early stage embodied in Symbolist narrative. For, in criticizing 'history' as well as standard 'monograph' approaches to human groups, Lévi-Strauss is saying of 'societies' what modern writers maintain in regards to their characters: '. . . they too (more or less consciously) are guided by the consideration that it is a hopeless venture to try to be really complete within the total exterior continuum and yet to make what is essential stand out' (Auerbach: 485). And the same consideration guides (unconsciously) the natives he studies. Moreover, Lévi-Strauss' approach can be placed alongside that of Erich Auerbach's 'modern writers', in particular Virginia Woolf and Marcel Proust, in these terms as well:

L

These are the forms of order and interpretation which the modern writers here under discussion attempt to grasp in the random moment—not one order and one interpretation, but many, which may either be those of different persons or of the same person at different times; so that overlapping, complementing, and contradiction yield something that we might call a synthesized cosmic view or at least *a challenge to the reader's will to interpretive synthesis* (Auerbach: 485; my emphasis).

But whereas Proust, or even more so Virginia Woolf, might often just juxtapose multiple views of the same object or event and leave the rest to us, Lévi-Strauss almost always proceeds to set up a formalized pattern which interrelates the sets of differences among those multiple views. Thus, rather than leaving us suspended in indirect statements, he grounds us in the abstracted residue of those statements, i.e., in their 'structure'. And this structure lies behind the 'thing,' insofar as the latter's multiple manifestations will allow. Delineating such structures is Lévi-Strauss' comparativist's task; it makes of his open-ended critical operations a science, the results of which can be checked back against further data.

It is, then, in *Tristes Tropiques* that Lévi-Strauss most clearly demonstrates his own personal basis of Symbolist sensitivity. This book alone would justify our placing him at the end of a thematic line of aesthetic synthesizers traced in a book by E. Fiser, who, arguing mainly from analogy, delineates critical affinities among the works of Wagner, Baudelaire, Mallarmé, and Proust, all of whom strived to create in terms of a view best clarified by Bergson, by which 'an ideal perception would thus contain in a single present object the totality of the sensible universe, and in a single remembrance the totality of the past. Ordinary perception is a *diminution* of this ideal perception' (Fiser: 16; my trans.). The problem becomes one of synthesizing ordinary, diminished impressions in a way that will re-approach that ideal impression, fully accessible only through intuition. Lévi-Strauss suggests that pre-literate classificatory procedures are a response to this same problem—once we realize

that Bergson's ideal totality can only be assumed at the level
of the communicating and self-differentiating group. In *Tristes
Tropiques* the anthropologist effects a synthesis of his diminished
impressions of natives synthesizing their diminished impressions
in a manner which, as we shall later appreciate, recalls Proust:

> Impressions such as those which I was endeavouring to analyse
> and define could not fail to vanish away at the contact of a
> material enjoyment that was unable to bring them into
> existence. The only way to get more joy out of them [*de les
> goûter davantage*] was to try to know them more completely
> at the spot where they were to be found, namely, within my-
> self, and to clarify them to their lowest depths (Proust 1956d:
> 203).

Viewing *Tristes Tropiques* in the above light lends credence
to Geertz's observation that 'all ethnography is part philosophy
and a good deal of the rest confession' (Geertz: 25)—an observation which points our way directly to Jean-Jacques Rousseau.
In addition to discussing the confessor-philosopher in several
works, Lévi-Strauss has written an article on his own affinities
with Rousseau and has alluded to a possible book on the subject.[3] Thus anyone interested in the full range of outlooks
shared by these two students of cultural 'texts' should consult
the article and hope earnestly for the book. The theorists coincide most obviously in terms of the contents of their concerns:
'such fields as literature, poetry, philosophy, history, ethics,
political science, education, linguistics, music, and botany—to
mention only a few' (L-S 1962c: 10). But more importantly
it is a particular attitude—a certain *critical* attitude—toward
whatever phenomena are in question, that is first manifested by

[3] Rousseau is especially apotheosized in *Tristes Tropiques* (L-S 1961b:
389ff.) and *Totemism* (L-S 1963a: 99–103); his *Emile* helps orchestrate
Mythologiques III (1968). The article 'Rousseau, Father of Anthropology'
appears in abridged form in UNESCO (L-S 1962c). Lévi-Strauss mentions
a future book on Rousseau in (Gramont 1968). The article on Rousseau is
very useful, since it takes up again certain ideas of applying anthropology
to ourselves—a sort of *anthropologie morale*—earlier outlined in *Race and
History* (L-S 1952).

Rousseau. For he discerned that human differences should be appreciated and studied in their own right. But the danger was that the self of the student would stifle those differences in the act of studying them. As a result that self would never be able to appreciate or study itself, since it itself could be truly known only in terms of its own differences from others. And, as we have just mentioned, these differences seem unable to survive the efforts to study them. Or, as Lévi-Strauss coins the message of Rousseau:

> . . . man must first come to know himself as 'another' before he can hope to think in terms of himself (L-S 1962c: 13).

Rousseau's solution to this dilemma is the establishment of a critical capacity relatively independent of the will or opinions of his first-personness. It is through this ingenious application of his own notoriously schizoid nature that Rousseau can achieve strikingly modern accomplishments in an age most generally characterized by Voltaire's all too ironic smile, which tends to eradicate the other by coyly and neatly assimilating it to its own terms.[4] Observe, for example, Rousseau's groundwork for an ethnomusicology, when he notes how the *esprit* of a particular nationality determines its sensory-based acceptance of particular *accens*, with the formidable conclusion that:

> Il faut à l'Italien des airs italiens, au Turc, il faudroit des airs turcs (Rousseau 1864, vol. III: 516).[5]

Likewise, through such self repression he strives by means of botany to assimilate himself to nature's terms, thereby challenging the strict man/nature dichotomy prevalent in his time.

[4] See, for example, Voltaire's handling of the Quakers in his *Lettres philosophiques* (1964: 19–40). Never once removing tongue from check, he thinks only of using this curious group to advance his own libertine attitude. He makes them a foil for himself, without ever stopping to wonder what *they* are. Thus, while Rousseau is the father of anthropology, Voltaire is, at least in part, the father of *Time Magazine*.

[5] 'In Italy they need Italian airs; in Turkey, they should have Turkish airs' (my trans.).

It is, then, thanks to these inter-illuminating dialectics between self and other—as facilitated by the cultivation of a critical, yet open-minded, distance—that Rousseau paves the way for ethnography and ethnology. All of this is not even to mention the stylistic (perhaps I should say syntactic) affinities between Rousseau and Lévi-Strauss, which reflect a particular mode of delight through paradox. Witness, for example, Rousseau's sparklingly concise statement of the nature of his ideal 'social contract':

> In short, each giving himself to all, gives himself to nobody; and as there is not one associate over whom we do not acquire the same rights which we concede to him over ourselves, we gain the equivalent of all that we lose, and more power to preserve what we have (Rousseau 1967: 18).

For both theorists such is the stuff of 'society.' Moreover, it is pleasing to express the fact: we need only recall Lévi-Strauss' discussion of exchange (see p. 80). It is on this sort of issue that continental rationalists dwell, in order to indicate the breakdown of 'common sense,' that brain-child of empiricists.

Lévi-Strauss pays Rousseau's *Confessions* the supreme compliment when he states that its treatment of Mme de Warens at last brings to Western literature the opposition of mother/mistress thoroughly developed in South American myths. Following through on this, which is yet another primitive/sophisticate analogy, he reflects:

> It is accounts of this kind . . . which can convey to us, in a brief and vivid illumination, the feeling charged with an irresistible evidence that these primitives, whose inventions and beliefs we manipulate with an offhandedness that would only suit clumsy productions, can prove themselves capable of an aesthetic subtlety, of an intellectual refinement, and of a moral sensibility which ought to inspire in us as much scruple as piety (L-S 1966b: 156; my trans.).

'Pourquoi pas?' It is not surprising that Rousseau is the source of a striking opposition; for, as the poetic old paranoid reviews his lifetime, he inevitably describes himself and all around him in terms of dualities, one term of which expressly contradicts the other. I have extracted from his *Confessions* just a few examples of this tendency and will present them to you at this time: effeminate nature/indomitable; woe/sensuality; sickness/ health; to tremble/to laugh; calm/passion; sordid avarice/ scorn of money; sublimity/baseness; fictitious/real; misanthro-pic/too affectionate; saint/bandit; diabolical/angelic; Achilles-hero/Thersites-good-for-nothing; lively passion/slow ideas; no-thing to say/frenzy to wish to talk (Rousseau 1965: 31, 36, 55, 64, 67, 70, 72, 75, 75, 107, 140, 148, 181, 185). Rousseau proves his individual uniqueness by first embracing both sides of the opposition with which he (often half at the suggestion of others) describes himself and then proceeding to resolve its inherent contradiction by incorporating the function of Time. For example, while his acquaintances label him a misanthrope, he senses himself to be too filled with love; the paradoxical conclusion is that both are accurate—misanthrope today, humanist tomorrow. The only means of deriving constancy from this confusion is to wait and look back through time in order to structure the flux that is the reality of himself: isolate the oppositions and intellectualize them into their resolution (sickness/health resolved in masochism; fiction/real resolved in imagination remembered). Build yourself a myth; build your-self, a myth.

Thus one comes to realize something rather striking con-cerning that critical capacity which Rousseau learned to dis-tinguish from any fundamental first-personness: the former is just as essential for establishing the latter as vice versa. In other words the self itself is a vibrating dialectic between event and postponed constructionism. Rousseau's confessional—and even more so, his *Rousseau, juge de Jean-Jacques* (1884, vol. IV)— provides an early example of conceiving of the individual, not as an entity that can be represented by a single label, but as a species—mutable as the viewpoint or circumstances change: unit *and* system. He thereby foreshadows ideas of the self in Symbolist narrative as well as in the ethnological technique of *Tristes Tropiques*.

Yet, it is not just the self that is built up in this way, it is all experience. As Rousseau attests:

> I have studied men, and I consider myself a fair observer; however, I know not how to see anything of what I see; I see well only what I recollect, and I possess *esprit* only in my memories (Rousseau 1965: 184; my trans.).[6]

Through such *Tristes Tropiques*-like reflections one senses that experience realized is the result of a 'mythic' operation, in that it is the translation of the *other* (in this case the lived) into patterns of conception that themselves comprise the structure of the self translating. And across these patterns alone can the self, the 'je', be known, in light of that continual flux wherein:

> Everything changes around us. We ourselves change and no one can be assured that he will love tomorrow that which he loves today (Rousseau 1960: 119; my trans.).

But what are the materials out of which the 'conceived' is constructed? They are the residue of perceptions in the form of those intermingling sensory impressions that occasionally assert themselves, in instances such as this:

> Not only do I recall the times, the places, the persons, but also all surrounding objects, the temperature of the air, its odor, its color—a certain local impression which made itself felt there alone, and the memory of which transports me there again (Rousseau 1965: 195; my trans.).

We should note the relevance of Rousseau's impressions to a generalization by Balakian: 'When a unilateral externalization of the inner mood occurs, rather than an elevation, then we

[6] The original is much smoother: 'J'ai étudié les hommes, et je me crois assez bon observateur: cependant je ne sais rien voir de ce que je vois; je ne vois bien que ce que je me rappelle, et je n'ai de l'esprit que dans mes souvenirs.'

are indeed at the origins of Symbolism' (Balakian: 37). The elements—particles of some hypothetical, totalized sensory input —out of which Rousseau's conceptual orders are built are the same that underlie Baudelaire's 'Correspondances' doctrine; the same that enable Lévi-Strauss to delve back into his field experiences; and the same that are patterned into the 'concrete logic' embodied in preliterate mythic texts. They are the stockpile of *terms* through which experience is made meaningful, i.e. ordered in other terms, and thus in terms of which experience is made.

Thus Rousseau employed the same creative strategy that is the subject of this study. Moreover, as Lévi-Strauss has emphasized, Rousseau applied his strategy to the same issues that loom large in cross-cultural analysis: '. . . the triple passage (which is really one) from animality to humanity, from nature to culture, and from affectivity to intellectuality . . .' (L-S 1963a: 101). Ironically these very issues form the basis for Rousseau's peculiarly down to earth humanism, for he comes to define the natural condition of man as 'compassion' or 'identification with another':

> It is because man originally felt himself identical to all those like him (among which, as Rousseau explicitly says, we must include animals) that he came to acquire the capacity to distinguish *himself* as he distinguishes *them*, i.e., to use the diversity of species as conceptual support for social differentiation (L-S 1963a: 101).

Yet for our purposes Rousseau does reveal one important limitation. For he seems to have constructed the all-inclusive, retrospective myth just once and linearly. Because of this solitary step by step ordering of a life-time's 'odds and ends,' Rousseau lacks either that diachronic complexity or a cross-cultural one that results only when there exist multiple versions of the same myth across space or time. It is perhaps only with Proust that this full implication of such multiplicity—in his case due to time passing—is captured. For Proust's narrator has experienced a series of interpenetrating orderings each time his 'involuntary memory' was triggered. This enables him to move back and forth between different conceptualized versions of what constituted any particular event. He can conceive of the event as the narrator remembering it, as the narrator thinking of it while living it, as the narrator remembering remembering it during an instance of 'involuntary memory' (etc.?). Rousseau lacks this structural depth through multiple 'texts' on himself experiencing; yet he prefigures it.

But at present, let us advance our cross-disciplinary analogies by making of Mallarmé an ideal native-anthropologist, for Proust will be conclusive. It has been said that Mallarmé's poem 'Le Tombeau de Charles Baudelaire' (see Mallarmé 1965: 91) reveals 'the poet's essential role of critic' and that it bears 'a terrifying weight of relationships with the past and the future, with Baudelaire, with all poets, and with man in general' (Fowlie 1962: 65). When Mallarmé refers in that work to 'the buried temple,' I like to think he is being coyly literal. For, we recall that in Baudelaire's view, 'Nature is a temple.' Thus, what is it that is buried in Mallarmé's 'The Tomb of Charles Baudelaire?' Quite obviously, it is Baudelaire himself; yet in the first line it is a temple, or in Baudelaire's terms Nature. Therefore, the person of the poet is his own temple, i.e. his own 'forest of symbols.' And a poet-temple under the earth becomes a tomb, Nature itself, composed *of* Baudelaire—'Le Tombeau de Charles Baudelaire.' All of this is just my way of suggesting that Mallarmé considered the contents of systems to be quite arbitrary: they are buried with (as) their creators; they are universals (content-wise) only in the creator's constructs.

Therefore, the fact that Mallarmé's own systems of analogies are most strikingly arbitrary should in no way reduce their significance. As Calvin Brown observes:

Mallarmé's mind operated by means of analogies to an extraordinary degree, and it has long been recognized that one of the difficulties of correctly interpreting his 'hermetic' poems is simply the problem of determining the usually unstated analogies on which the poems are based (C. Brown: 67).

It is open to discussion whether Mallarmé would have expected or even conceived of a 'correct' interpretation of his poems; after all, in his own words 'every thought sets forth a toss of dice,' and not one of them ever abolishes chance (see Mallarmé 1965: 207–33). Nevertheless, certain varieties of analogy seem to predominate in his works, as is indicated in the following description:

> There is the accumulation of images related imaginatively to each other as well as syntactically to the theme of the poem (in *Brise marine* the whiteness of paper suggests the milk of the young wife feeding her child; in *Don du Poëme* the woman's voice that recalls a viol does so not merely because it is musical, but because that instrument . . . is a symbol of birth through its very shape). Here the imagery becomes multivalent by its own nature and also because of its place in the poem. Later the individual image was to be profoundly eroded by its integration into the poem (Hartley: xxix).

How absolutely primitive! Extend this already ample spectrum of analogy principles to Mallarmé's numerological play (such as the 'sevens' in 'Un Coup de dés') and to equivalences set up between certain letters of the alphabet and gender (e.g. feminine 'v'), and the resulting world is exactly parallel to the ones Lévi-Strauss describes, in which:

> A logical structure—initially a simple opposition—thus fans out in two directions: one abstract, in the form of a numerology, and the other concrete, first of elements and then of species. On each level semantic short-circuits permit direct connections with the level furthest away (L-S 1966a: 146).

Indeed, as has been observed by Cohn, 'Mallarmé . . . operates out from such simple oppositions, which finally "reduce" to cosmic ones' (Cohn: 4). Mallarmé's 'white paper logic' conjures up some of those marvelous preliterate systems of multiple logical axes with characteristics like the following:

Relations may be established, in effect, on either the sensible level (the bodily markings of the bee and the pythons) or on the intelligible level (the function of construction common to the bee and the carpenter): the same animal, the bee, functions, as it were, at different levels of abstraction in two cultures. Again, the connection can be close or distant, synchronic or diachronic (the relation between squirrels and cedars for instance on the one hand, and that between pottery and elephants' footprints on the other), static (mush and goat) or dynamic (fire kills animals, rain 'kills' fire; the flowering of a plant indicates that it is time to return to the village), etc. (L-S 1966a: 63).

This manner of significance constructing becomes paramount in both the subject matter and the analytic method in Lévi-Strauss' *Mythologiques*. For the message conveyed by the preliterate mythic *esprit* parallels that of Mallarmé in regard to literature:

 ... things exist, we do not have to create them; we have only to take hold of their relationships; and it is the threads of these relationships which form lines of poetry and orchestras ... (Mallarmé 1945: 871; my trans.).

Moreover, just as Hartley observes for Mallarmé's imagery, Lévi-Strauss discovers in New World Indian texts certain imagery which 'becomes multivalent by its own nature.' This is not at all to espouse a theory of universal 'archetypes'; it is rather to assert that not only are some things 'good to think' (L-S 1963a: 89), but certain things may be better to think (for certain purposes). Certain things may be obviously more fruitful sources of diacriticals for maintaining semantic universes. Take frogs. Frogs are manifestly *naturally* very 'good to think.' They are seasonal (temporally discontinuous); they are vocal; they are notoriously bipolar in that they bridge the water/land opposition and undergo observable metamorphosis; they are colorful; they lay eggs in a semen-like substance; they unabashedly climb onto each other's backs during copulation; they have peculiar motility habits and appear twice their size when fully extended; who could ask for anything more?[7] Thus, through frogs one can encode many other aspects of nature, such as seasonal ones, colorful ones, back-adhering ones, and so forth. Frogs present a wealth of potential distinctive features for sets of contrasts. It is no wonder, then, that frogs are frequently encountered in New World mythology; they are so naturally multivalent.[8] But they are not encountered *qua* 'frogs' as content, but rather *qua* their potential as keys to systems of signification. And whether the frogs' repeated appearances across space is indicative of diffusion or of independent invention is a moot question. For, from a structural point of view they would have *persisted* throughout diffusion for the same reason that they might have been independently *invented*: the reason being their capacity to act as operators in the establishment and maintenance of meaning.

Finally, many myths are found which lack specific references to frogs, but which do reveal certain of those froggish aspects which we have enumerated. For example, there are tales concerning back-adhering characters. Now, in the context of the semantic field so far outlined, we could designate such tales 'frog-myths,' simply because they center on a relationship we have seen fit to place under the rubric 'frogs.' For we should not be thinking of a frog as a 'critter'; rather it is the label for that assortment of potentially 'markable' features listed above— which taken together generate the structure of some ideally multivalent 'frog,' but no individual frog, rather an intellectual-species-frog. Thus, some story dealing with back-adhering relations—which are a portion of the structure that is a frog— would be a 'frog-myth.' And in trying to discern what sort of significations this back-adhering relationship might tie in to, it would not be foolish to check back through other instances

---

[7] See Lévi-Strauss' treatment of 'frogs' in (L-S 1966b: pt. II) and (L-S 1968: 57ff.).

[8] And imagine the present author's delight upon discovering in Kidder's 'Two Peruvian Frogs' the following: 'In view of the importance of felines, probably jaguars, pumas, or smaller wild cats in Mochica art, composite frog-cats would not be surprising' (Kidder 1968: 9).

of different frog-myths for clues; since any frog-myth might
at least possibly embody a back-adhering relationship which—
thanks to the concatenation of significations bundled around
the observable, natural *frog*—could specifically indicate something else. Then we could check back into the first text in
question to see if the clue from some other frog-myth is useful
in the former's terms.[9]

What one must guard against is making this analytic procedure sound wilder than it in fact is, as some critics have done
by citing bits and pieces of *Mythologiques* without explicating
the total semantic universe in whose terms they are composed.
Take, for example, a summary passage from *L'Origine des
manières de table*:

> A comparison extending over the two Americas has enabled
> us to consolidate certain myths which appeared to arise
> from two distinct groups; those which have as heroine a
> burr-woman, and those wherein this role recurs in a frog-
> woman. In effect, the two groups of myths transmit the
> same message which every time concerns a clinging woman,
> although she can be such in the literal sense or in the
> figurative sense.
> . . . the man with the long penis and the burr-woman
> have symmetrical values: he is able to attain a lover at a
> distance, she can be a spouse only in adhering to the body of
> her husband.
> In the final analysis, certain myths, which appear hetero-
> geneous by their content and distinct geographic origins, all
> show themselves to be reducible to a unique message which
> they are limited to transforming on two axes—the one stylis-
> tic, the other lexicological. Certain ones of the myths express

[9] See also Lévi-Strauss' (1970) review of Wasson's opus on Soma. Lévi-
Strauss appreciates the various modes in which different cultures have
encoded the hallucinatory mushroom; but he is careful to point out
that the natural item is not a simple determinant, but rather a bundle of
distinctive features, certain ones of which can be selected by different
cultures. This holds true even for the hallucinatory effects that the mushroom might yield.

themselves literally, the others figuratively. And the vocabulary that they utilize refers to three separate orders: the real, the symbolic, the imaginary (L-S 1968: 68; my trans.).

Considerable debate has arisen over the sorts of analytic procedures involved in the above. In this example Lévi-Strauss treats a selection of myths about a sexually rampant man with an errant penis; he opposes this to myths about a truncated spouse who cannot leave her husband's back (whether stated figuratively or directly). The man with the long penis and the back-adhering woman take on significance when placed in opposition to each other: one suggests a situation where the group is expanding outward and achieving inter-group relationship; the other suggests the inverse. Lévi-Strauss notes this and also looks for some single 'text' that would state more directly such opposition by inversion, to justify further this interpretation of the 'message.'

What matters from now on is how fully other 'texts' can be brought to bear on the opposition, how fully this 'message' can serve to interrelate elements in other myths. What does not matter is how Lévi-Strauss came by the *idea* for this opposition or whether only Lévi-Strauss—with all his eccentricities—could have come up with such a thing. Call it genius, witchcraft, intimate familiarity with a wealth of data, mystic access to truth, crafty manipulation of obscure texts, etc., if you wish. But answer to the analysis—after having clearly ascertained its frame of reference, which is to analyze New World myth in terms of all of New World myth, gathering keys from where you will—with a better analysis. Or else argue specifically against the worth of such an analysis, which is of course an altogether different issue. Above all, do not take such a passage out of context!

Moreover, any text that is found which states the opposite of a posited signification does not refute the signification but supports the assumption that the terms in question are encoded by sets of contrasts to yield meaning. Thus, Leach is wrong to criticize *Mythologiques* as follows:

... the whole system seems to have developed into a self-fulfilling prophecy which is incapable of test because, by definition, it cannot be disproved. For example, a footnote to *Mythologiques III* reports on ... a Choco myth which uses wild honey as a metaphor for human sperm. Since the 'philosophy of honey' which Lévi-Strauss has painfully extracted from the piled up detail of *Mythologiques II* is 'inspired by the analogy between this natural product and menstrual blood' one might have expected that Lévi-Strauss would be somewhat disconcerted ... (Leach 1970: 117).

Leach subsequently reveals his surprise over the fact that Lévi-Strauss, rather than despairing over this contradiction, welcomes the new data as a supplementary dimension. Leach then concludes: 'But if "supplementary dimensions" can be added to meet every contrary case then the main theory can never be put to a critical test at all' (p. 117). What Leach fails here to appreciate is this: the very inversion of the honey-menstrual blood signification into a honey-sperm signification proves that 'honey' is a device for encoding 'sex,' especially if some other text can be found that states menstrual blood as the inverse of sperm. Leach seems still to be concerned with contents rather than with differential relationships between contents. Furthermore, we have already seen how structural theory can indeed be put to a critical test of sorts (on p. 127).

The above discussion suggests in part the kind of method Lévi-Strauss employs in examining a vast array of mythic texts from all over South and North America. In so doing part of what he is saying is, I think, this: even in the absence of diffusion theories, it would be equally justifiable to approach these diverse documents as manifestations of a semantic universe as it is to approach something like 'Western literature' or 'the Trobriand islanders' or 'the poems of Mallarmé.' Mallarmé might have written a whole array of completely unrelated individual poems; but empirically (and according to himself) there seem to be various consistencies in his orderings of significance across the works. Lévi-Strauss maintains that empirically the same thing is true of New World myth. And he examines the consistencies—the hidden bases of which are sometimes highly debatable—in order to trace the structure of the 'imagination' (in Baudelaire's sense) of New World preliterates, as far as their 'texts' allow. Of course, we must bear in mind our loose usage of 'text' and Lévi-Strauss' interest in any sort of manifestation of mental activity on the part of the populations studied. 'Myth' as translatable encodings of significance can be stated through house plans, grooming or cooking customs, astrological schemes, etc., just as well as verbally or graphically. Moreover, we must also bear in mind that these 'texts' for social discourse are not acknowledged consciously by the peoples whose meanings they delimit. As Pouillon here puts it:

> The indigenous one—and who is not indigenous?—does not understand the myth that charms him, not because of intellectual incapacity, but because of position; it is also because of position that the ethnologist, because he knows other myths elsewhere, can understand it (Pouillon 1966: 104; my trans.).

But thus far I have avoided the most controversial issue in *Mythologiques*: the deterministic nature that is attributed to the structures finally identified from preliterate texts. For, once Lévi-Strauss has delineated many of these structures, which state the principles for transforming one system of interrelated units into another such system bearing a related message, but with distinctive differences, he makes the famous assertion:

> And if the question arises as to what ultimate signified is referred back to by these significations which signify themselves one to another—but concerning which it is indeed necessary that, in the final analysis and all together, they be related to something—the sole response suggested by this book is that the myths signify *l'esprit*, which elaborates them by means of the world, of which it itself is part (L-S 1964a: 346; my trans.).

Or, as Pouillon has paraphrased it, myths provide an image of the world 'because they make manifest the "natural" functioning of a constrained and unconscious thinking which is itself part of the world' (1966: 105; my trans.). But what exactly is part of the world? None other than those system-rendering *processes* which lie close to the surface of preliterate texts (as we see them) and which are the stuff of the analytic method used to translate them among each other and into our own logical terms in *Mythologiques*. The *esprit humain* which is part of the world, is simply that which is attested in the following process:

> Rather let us say that by the term *pensée sauvage* I am designating the system of postulates and axioms required in order to found a code, enabling one to translate with the least poor rendering possible 'the other' into 'the our' and reciprocally. . . . In the main, '*la pensée sauvage*' is in my intention none other than the locus of encounter, the effect of an effort of comprehension, of *me* putting myself in *their* place, of *them* put by me in *my* place (L-S 1963c: 634; my trans.).

This, if we discount for a moment Lévi-Strauss' empirical dimension, leads us round again to Mallarmé. For, Mallarmé too, in spite of (really by means of) all his wildly impressionistic, idiosyncratic correspondence building, was striving towards an absolute. Marcel Raymond appreciates this fact:

> Let us remember besides that this poet, individualistic and impressionistic as he was in so many respects, wished . . . to compose a book which was The Book, a poetry which was Poetry, as if the structure of our *esprit* were marked on the seal of the entire universe and 'poetic instinct ought to conduct us blindly to truth' (Raymond: 35; my trans.).

But where in the sorts of works Mallarmé produced or yearned to produce lies the potential for this completeness and truth? First, we find that aspect of his poems which prefigured modern attempts at '*simultanéisme ou synchronisation*' (Orliac: 238), whereby the syllables and sounds of any given phrase can be

M

read in multiple ways and cross-referenced to many features of the work's written-spoken words—which through their graphic peculiarities afford potential for pictorial and gestural systems as well as verbal ones. More importantly, the multiple meanings of the verses themselves can only be discerned through such cross-referencing and detailed attention to context, since, as has already been mentioned, Mallarmé's efforts toward meaning parallel those of the preliterate texts analyzed by Lévi-Strauss.

But there is another source of truth potential in Mallarmé's works, which, while complementary to their characteristic *synchronisation*, is independent of it. For, while Mallarmé strived to attain simultaneity, he sought as well to purge specificity. His entire career can be seen as an effort to extend to the limit his theory of indirect statement, summarized in the formula:

> To evoke, in a precise obscurity, the object hushed, by allusive, never direct, words, reducing themselves to uniform silence, tentative behavior near creating [*comporte tentative proche de créer*] (Mallarmé 1945: 400; my trans.).[10]

It is this aspect of his effort—so manifest in his constant reworking of poems, in order to avoid direct reference, in order to heighten the obscure possibilities of their connotation—which has polarized his readers into proclaiming cults or condemnation.[11]

Can anthropology elucidate esoterism? Through this juxtaposition of Mallarmé and *Mythologiques*, the effort will be made. Debates over the increasing obscurity that Mallarmé sought to instil in his verses often center on whether or not the changes resulted in a 'better' poem. Regardless of this question, it is certain that one result of the changes was to make of the poem a far more challenging and difficult object to be confronted by the reader. In fact, if I might become a bit parochial,

[10] Évoquer, dans une ombre exprès, l'objet tu, par des mots allusifs, jamais directs, se réduisant à du silence égal, comporte tentative proche de créer' (Mallarmé 1945: 400).
[11] To follow this kind of reworking of a poem, see (Mondor 1948).

I would claim that what Mallarmé eventually constructs is not at all unlike what the ethnographer is 'naturally' cross-culturally confronted with. His later poems present the reader with something almost thoroughly *other* (i.e. in terms that are not his customary ones), yet something which affords inklings of systematization, of potential communicability. Furthermore, in his efforts to comprehend what Orliac calls 'la réalité unique du moi-créateur' (Orliac 233), Mallarmé tends increasingly to induce his readers to conjure up their own *moi-créateur,* their own capacities to effect translations from another system of significations into their own. As he rewrites vagueness into his poems to increase the initial obscurity of the fundamental situation of creative void which they depict, it is as if he seeks to oblige himself to be approached cross-culturally, insofar as remaining in French will permit. By thus making of him*self* another order (another culture?) he forces us into the *process* of an aesthetic-intellectual effort toward interpretation. Yet, he must not go too far but must leave enough surface attraction and initial charm so that the fuller effort *will* be made. (For poetry readers are not so patient as anthropologists.) I would guess that what mattered to Mallarmé was the process of the effort to analyze into understanding a text that verged on the incommunicable—with Truth lying in the fact that it could eventually be transformed into ever fuller significance. And I would further surmise that it was in this heroic effort-towards-discerning-significations (his from the texts of experience, his readers' from the text of him)—in this 'comporte tentative proche de créer'—that Mallarmé sensed his *Grand Œuvre* to lie in waiting.

This potential for universal Truth comes from ever so gradually attaining an understanding of multivalent texts, always in accompaniment with the vague suspicion that there may really be nothing sensible there to understand. Thus, the very process of reading Mallarmé echoes his favorite poetic device, a variation on Baudelairian correspondences, here pinpointed by Cohn:

> All of his favorite symbols, flower, window, feather, siren, bird, star, hair, and so on, are at a crossroads of cognate

polarities—up-down, static-kinetic, light-dark, male-female, cold-hot—that emanate from a parent pair, Being and Nothingness ... (Cohn: 4).

Baudelaire keyed his correspondences to a traditional metaphysics. Mallarmé's more extended, dispersed and elliptical correspondences key only to themselves, and they are rendered worthy by the sense of void they deny. Lévi-Strauss searches the same sort of 'cognate polarities' among preliterates to ferret out both these and other varieties of correspondences across cultures. But only with the more imaginative texts of *Mythologiques* can he concentrate fully on those particularly Mallarmé-like correspondences (or more precisely on the structures constraining them) that loom as man's first line of defence against spiritual darkness in the realm of the imagination.

Thus we have Mallarmé centrifugally translating himself into other orders and Lévi-Strauss centripetally translating other orders into himself. That Mallarmé's direction is centrifugal makes him idealistic, individualistic, and, some would say, solipsistic (but I still insist on the fact that one writes himself to be read). That Lévi-Strauss' direction is centripetal makes him empirical, collectivistic, and humanistic. This leads us to still another definition of 'culture(s)', as it befits any study in anthropology to spawn. At this stage of our inquiry cultures (as 'texts') can be regarded as a maze of subtle 'Mallarmés' that somehow got inter-individually contracted in analytically imposed space-time isolates; and anthropology is their literary criticism. While this definition would place emphasis on the semantic issues involved in confronting both Mallarmé's poems and other cultures, no claim is made that such issues exhaust the reality of that which is 'a poem' or 'a culture.' There are, as can be sensed, ineffable poetic qualities in Mallarmé's work and a host of complex sociological, psychological, transcendental, etc., factors in cultural life. But insofar as any relationship between ourselves and another set of poems or cultures can be *articulated*, the basic issue is one of structuring transformations across different systems of signification. And this issue appears to me as the motivating force behind both Lévi-Strauss' *Mythologiques* and aspects of the poetic language of Mallarmé.[12]

Through Mallarmé our discussion modulates into music. Amid the array of musings over relationships between Symbolist poem and symphony, Calvin Brown discusses the view of Mallarmé's works as 'a contrapuntal effort':

> Cohn's language implies that he considers the counterpoint a metaphor rather than a fact, but that such a metaphor can explain something of the effect. . . . Suzanne Bernard sees Mallarmé as making a definite attempt at an actual linguistic counterpoint. 'Mallarmé truly wants to incite us to a *simultaneous* reading of the different motifs, well differentiated by the typography' (C. Brown: 76–7; my trans. of Bernard).

Mallarmé represents the culmination of the Symbolists' tendency to use musical metaphors and to seek methods of incorporating the genius of experiencing a musical score into lines of verse. Two major currents of the trend are most clearly revealed in the works of Verlaine. Obviously that poet could concern himself with images of instrumentation and the musical qualities of sounds, (en)chanting the well-known lamentation:

> Les sanglots longs
> Des violons
> De l'automne
> Blessent mon coeur
> D'une langueur
> Monotone   (Verlaine: 56).

[12] Before leaving Mallarmé I should note my gratification on reading a recent confirming opinion by Octavio Paz on the ideas in this section. Paz has this to say: 'His [Lévi-Strauss'] effort reminds me, on another level, of Mallarmé's: "Un Coup de dés" and *Le Cru et de cuit* are both devices for meaning. This is not a fortuitous coincidence. . . . Mallarmé proceeds from poetic (primitive) thought toward logic, and Lévi-Strauss from logical thought to the primitive. At the same point in time that logical reason annexes the symbols of poetry, critical reason annexes the logic of the senses' (Paz: 46–7). Paz also mentions that when he reads Lévi-Strauss he feels a little as if it were Proust (p. 5).

On the other, more controversial, side Verlaine could attempt to adapt certain forms and techniques of music to poetry, such as the traditional sonata form. Given our concern with contrived constructionism, this latter interest in musical composition, which was likewise revealed in the quotation about Mallarmé's counterpoint, is the more critical. For, 'it must not be thought that by music the Symbolists mean pleasing, harmonious sound. Music is essentially a matter of order, proportion, relation, and architectural construction. It is the art that is nearest to mathematics' (Guthrie and Diller: 451–2). Or, as Mallarmé phrased it: 'On the other hand, Music is calculation: it offers the intelligence an immense domain of pure combinations—another subject of envy for the poet' (cited in Gibson: 185; my trans.). And beyond this architectonic aspect of music is a greater situational one that Mallarmé suggests when he considers concert attendances to be modern society's 'sign or substitution for ritual. . . . Music is the last human cult, the final vestige of celebration and mystery' (Fowlie 1962: 239–40).

Similar ranges of musical interest characterize Lévi-Strauss. His thoroughly Proustian sensitivity in this field is displayed during the travels of *Tristes Tropiques*:

> For weeks on end, on that plateau of the western Mato Grosso, I was obsessed not by my surroundings, which I should never see again, but by a hackneyed tune that my memory deformed still further: the third of Chopin's Etudes, op. 10, which seemed to me—and I well knew how bitter was the irony of it—to summarize all that I had left behind me (L-S 1961b: 375).[13]

This interest in music might first seem to bear only a superficial relation to Lévi-Strauss' studies, resulting in little more

[13] The original French has a less nostalgic, more Proustian, flavor: '. . . j'avais été obsédé, non point par ce qui m'environnait et que je ne reverrais jamais, mais par une mélodie rebattue que mon souvenir appauvrissait encore: celle de l'étude numéro 3, *opus* 10, de Chopin, en quoi il me semblait, par une dérision à l'amertume de laquelle j'étais aussi sensible, que tout ce que j'avais laissé derrière moi se résumait' (L-S 1955: 407).

than some playful elements such as the orchestral organization of *Le Cru et le cuit*, with its dedication 'à la Musique' through the lyrics: 'Mother of memory and wet-nurse of dream, it is you whom we take pleasure today to invoke 'neath this roof' (L-S 1964a: dedication; my trans.).[14] But we have already learned to take heed during these playful moments. Both here and in the Chopin opus of *Tristes Tropiques* Lévi-Strauss associates music with a particular (and, we must assume, a logical) state of mind. One apparent reason for his valuing music is summarized by Leach:

> Lévi-Strauss seems to claim that we respond to the patterned structures of myth in much the same way as we respond to the repetitions of counterpoint and to the combinations of harmony. On this analogy the details of particular mythical stories are like the melody of a particular musical phrase, and melody is a relatively trivial element in the communication that is achieved when we listen to music (Leach 1967a: ix).

Now, in *Le Cru et le cuit* Lévi-Strauss does allude to questions concerning the way a preliterate in fact experiences a myth being told. He suggests that somehow the *structure* of mythic conceptual imagery underlies a basic sensory response to the myth, in much the same way as musical pattern somehow directs the nostalgic emotions it arouses. Yet, in the overture to *Mythologiques'* opening number, this matter is left as inexplicit as the following aphorism suggests: 'Le mythe et l'œuvre musicale apparaissent ainsi comme des chefs d'orchestre dont les auditeurs sont les silencieux exécutants' (L-S 1964a: 25).[15]

This leaves us with the problem of justifying the construction of *Mythologiques I*. For, borrowing metaphors from musical

[14] As George Steiner has already observed in regards to the Overture and organization of *Le Cru et le cuit*: 'The conceit is not new: one finds it in Baudelaire's theory of "correspondences" (to which Lévi-Strauss implicitly refers), in Mallarmé . . .' (Steiner: 249).

[15] Aproximately: 'Both the myth and the musical work thus appear as orchestra leaders whose listeners are their silent players' (my trans.).

composition, the myths related in *Le Cru et le cuit*, rather than being linearly ordered, are dispersed around a single, often repeated basic mythic opposition (raw/cooked), which through the myths' terms is stated, developed, transposed, reiterated, expanded—i.e. elaborated in various ways we might deem 'musical.' And the process is totally engrossing, even though the number of units for contrast is very finite, indeed.

This organization is not to be taken as a simple indication of the way a preliterate responds to any of the myths as isolated and recorded in the book. For the indigenous inhabitant cannot be aware of the cross-cultural semantic ramifications of the units in his myths. What the book's organization does have to do with is *our* response to the book itself. Given our cross-cultural perspective and ethnological distance, we (readers of *Mythologiques*) are in a position to experience a series of inter-relatable mythic texts from different cultures in a way which parallels—but on a more conscious level—the way a preliterate must come to experience his own culture's entire corpus of myth in context: by having our sensory reflections loosely ordered and subtly related to other sensory orders. For the preliterate his myths' loosely connected orders vaguely relate—perhaps only after inversion, transposition, or the like—to each other and to the other aspects of his culture (kinship rules, house plans, etc.). This enables his entire cultural experience to be held together by what I like to call AN INKLING OF DÉJÀ VU· Analogously, for readers of *Mythologiques* the loose orders in one mythic variant vaguely relate to those in another, until Lévi-Strauss (in his role of ethnomythicologist) suggests one of the ways in which the relationship can be specified. Thus, we readers attain something the native does not have: knowledge of cross-cultural structural operations that constrain conceptual orderings of sensory experience. But we do this in a way which echoes the way that experience-conceived is attained in the first place. Moreover, Lévi-Strauss starts writing *Mythologiques* like a Wagnerian music drama, in order to induce a variety of semi-sensory, semi-intellectual retrospective experience. But he feels obliged to apologize for failing to achieve this goal, even before we start:

When I consider this crude and confused text, I come to doubt that its audience will derive from it the impression of listening to a musical work, as its design and chapter titles would have one believe. . . . Here and there . . . music is absent (L-S 1964a: 40; my trans.).

Having already prefigured Proust and with the above in mind, we can better appreciate Lévi-Strauss' acknowledgement of the service he has always rendered 'at the altars of the "god Richard Wagner"' (L-S 1964a: 23; my trans.).[16] It is here that his musical interests most notably coincide with those of the Symbolists, for whom 'Wagner was the great apostle of "transposition" (embodying the qualities and modalities of one art in the practice of another). He was at once poet, dramatist, musician, and critic' (Guthrie and Diller: 453). Of course, one obvious source of interest Wagner provided the Symbolists with was his intense concern with corresponding visual, literary, and musical messages. Baudelaire called Wagner's dramatic art 'the *coincidence* of several arts, as art *par excellence*, the most synthetic and the most perfect' (Baudelaire 1951: 1041; my trans.). And Wyzéwa announced: 'With [Wagner], Art is no longer in painting, nor in literature, nor in music, but in the strict union of these genres and in the total life which is born thereof' (cited in Lehmann: 201; my trans.). While Bayreuth's complete life of inter-corresponding media for the re-creation of national legends would seem to prefigure Lévi-Strauss' ideas of the totality of myth, this point is easier to sense than it is to establish. For Lévi-Strauss' 'totality' is mentalistic, bearing more on the mind-boggling, simultaneous complexities within the operatic score itself than on the sensory flood throughout the site of its performance. Indeed, he seldom concerns himself with actual ritual situations characterized by multiple media (situations that would be more analogous to operatic spectacles).

[16] Blackès-Clément (1970: 61) has explained Lévi-Strauss' interest in Wagner by some affinity he has for plot lines and themes based on incest. This explanation appears to me far too contents-oriented and not a very 'structural' way of looking at things, since Lévi-Strauss studies incest only insofar as it is a necessary principle for the establishment of systematic kinship practices.

He concentrates instead on discerning logical patterns in whose terms portions of such performances can be *compared*.

I would argue that the anthropologist's principal attraction to Wagner stems from a more intellectual interest in his works, likewise shared by the Symbolists, as indicated by Duthie:

> It is Wagner who was the great revelation in music for Baudelaire, Mallarmé, and the symbolist generation. It is not the simple melodies of former times, it is Wagnerian polyphonies that attracted them and that they dreamed of reproducing through their efforts of written orchestration (cited in Lehmann: 194n; my trans.).

Having once singled out Wagner's particular achievement as the resurrection of polyphony (back to Bach), multiple threads of this study come thundering together. With polyphony serving as key, Wyzéwa provides the keyhole:

> Wyzéwa . . . invents a dialectic for the emergence of polyphony, corresponding to a shift in social emphasis: 'For simple uncultivated souls, melody, song; for many the more perfect melody of opera; for certain ones the complex languages of counterpoint, the nuances of accent and timbre' (cited in Lehmann: 203n; my trans.).

And the door crashes open, cosmo-logically, à la Richard Wagner. (Throughout the following discussion, I hope the reader will bear in mind these words of Proust: '. . . the objective precision of a writer's judgements on an art other than his own are without importance. What matters, what sets him dreaming, is the fact of his admiration, even when it may be given to what is unworthy' [*Chroniques*, p. 218, cited in Strauss: 56].)

The concepts of polyphony and homophony remain a source of fruitful debate in music theory. For the purposes of an eventual music-mythic analogy, let us view the concepts in a way that stresses the potential acoustical and temporal dimensions of experience that can be differentially activated and arranged in 'music.' We note that music is relatively more polyphonic as a greater number of equally important lines (voices) of counterpoint are placed in harmony. Conversely, music is more homophonic (melodious) as a single voice's line of counterpoint takes precedence: you can whistle it. Homophony is defined in terms of a horizontal dimension—the syntagmatic association of note after note—and is thus analogous to what results from the metonymic function in language (see chapter III). Absolute homophony would be, I suppose, a single sustained note with no period of vibration; therefore, silence. Now, polyphony can be defined in terms of a vertical dimension (the harmonic one, which is predominant) *and* a horizontal dimension: a chord is more polyphonic than a single note (harmonically = vertically); and a move from a loud eighth note to a soft triplet is doubly more polyphonic than a move from a loud eighth note to another loud eighth note (contrapuntally=horizontally, due to the two added dimensions of a contrast in volume and a contrast in rhythm). An absolute, vertical = harmonic polyphonic arrangement would be, if you will again permit me, an instant of total sound—i.e. silence. Thus, in the abstract sense in which we are employing the concepts, all music has both homophonic and polyphonic aspects: homophonic insofar as the music is moved as a unit through time; polyphonic insofar as the music displays more contrastive features distributed over time and what we might call 'sound-space.' Normally, in the broad Western music tradition Bach is seen as the crowning point in a long line of polyphonic church music; as Leonard Bernstein lauds:

> Bach fuses the vertical and the horizontal in so marvelous a way that you can never say of any piece of his, 'This is only counterpoint,' or 'This is only harmony.' He fashions a kind of sublime crossword puzzle in which the notes of the across 'words' and the down 'words' are interdependent, where everything checks and all the answers are right (Bernstein: 238).

Then Haydn and Mozart led into the tuneful, more homophonic romantic period—until Wagner, who not only re-instated poly*phony*, but cross-referenced visual and verbal texts as well.[17]

Rich analogies can be drawn with Lévi-Strauss, advocate of the polyphonic mind. He views the multiple logical axes of myths (metonymy + metaphor) primarily as polyphonic-type arrangements (horizontal + vertical). This is to say that there are multiple lines of conceptual counterpoint running simultaneously, with no single line predominating (no story-line 'melody'), just as we have found in Mallarmé's poems and in 'les Chats.' Any mythic arrangement has a metaphoric dimension (vertical-harmonic 'pool' of choices from the culture's total repertoire of verbal images, one of which is selected at a time in a myth); this metaphoric dimension pertains to something like a *langue* level of that culture's perception and conceptualization. Any mythic arrangement also has a metonymical dimension (multiple, horizontal-contrapuntal strings of related images). It is these multiple strings of images which can be clarified most readily by cross-cultural analysis (see especially L-S 1963b: ch. XI). And pursuing such analysis gradually maps the total *langue*-like repertoire of images that are selectively activated in the metonymic dimension. Finally, there is in any myth-as-performed what we might call an intra-metaphoric dimension which sets up multivalent correspondences across verbal images in these strings ('voices'), just as the selecting of these images had set up multivalent correspondences within the repertoire

[17] There is no intention here of denigrating the significance of symphonic form as 'the dynamic treatment of tonality,' as 'a reaction against the tonal passivity of earlier music. The important thing to remember about it is that the revolt was vital and constructive, positive—it threw away nothing, not even counterpoint' (Simpson: 14). The only trouble with a symphony is its danger of being mistreated by inattentive listeners, who come to take portions of the work's melodic motifs for the work itself, thereby impoverishing it. More polyphonic music is less at risk on this score.

Also, the reader who would like to pursue the ideas in our necessarily brief allusions to music theory is referred to Langer (1953: Ch. 7–8). What I have placed under the rubric of music's homophonic aspect she discusses in light of Bergson's insights into musical duration; and the varieties of contrastive features most readily detected in polyphony she treats as the 'musical matrix'.

of perception and conceptualization. An ideal, totally sensitive preliterate would be subsidiarily aware of these latter vertical intra-metaphoric relationships in experiencing a mythic text being performed—somewhat as the connoisseur of Western music can be aware of the several voices comprising a passage of harmony. The anthropologist—in addition to his comparativist task of mapping *langue* level semantic repertoires as coded into interwoven strings of images—might, I suppose, attempt also to achieve the very same sensitivity to a text being performed that that ideal native would have. However in *Mythologiques* Lévi-Strauss does not attempt this. It is basic to his approach that the outsider might be able to appreciate *how* an indigenous one experiences his myth, but he cannot match that experience. Yet, we can perhaps achieve a feeble echo of intra-metaphoric ('harmonic') sensitivity, through the orderly comparison of contrasts among related mythic variants across cultures. This possibility will receive more attention as we proceed.

Most obviously opposed to the 'semantic polyphony' we have been discussing is the homophonic tendency in technical ('rational') thought, where a single linear thread of 'because A, then B' comes to predominate, much to the dismay of William Blake and probably most of the writers in this study: 'May God us keep From Single vision & Newton's sleep!' (Blake: 420). For few of them would agree with Ruwet, when he asserts:

> Simply, language excludes polyphony; in the domain of language one can never come upon simultaneously different traits *belonging to a like dimension* (to a like parameter), as one can in music (Ruwet: 577; my trans.).

Baudelaire and Mallarmé, at least, tried to arrive at a demonstration of the contrary.

It appears that Lévi-Strauss considers industrial society a homophonic world of metonymical, technical pursuits. But he realizes that there is no such thing as absolute homophony: there must be some harmony-rendering modulations even in a single line of the same note; and it is this bedrock of language-based, polyphonic (mythical) logic that he wants to unearth. The West's fall from myth must have begun sometime in the latter Middle Ages when, as goal-oriented linearity arose, simultaneous inter-dimensionality was forced to retreat to the protected zone of ecclesiastical music. The low point came during the eighteenth century, which saw the rise of reasonable, linear prose—interestingly enough, at the very time that even polyphonic music was on the wane. The literary exception to this generalization is, of course, Rousseau. For overly-alphabetized man it is easier to keep in mind a romantic symphony than it is a Bach toccata; he can say, 'Certainly I know Beethoven's Fifth,' and proceed to whistle four notes to verify the fact. Likewise, he can *handle* a story *line* better than he can multiple levels of thought in myths or Symbolist poems. As another champion of simultaneity has put it:

> . . . there is nothing subliminal in non-literate cultures. The reason we find myths difficult to grasp is just this fact, that they do not exclude any facet of experience as literate cultures do. All the levels of meaning are simultaneous (McLuhan: 72).

The sort of logical restriction typical of moderns is essential for 'progress.' But symphony conductors, certain poets, ideal preliterates, and Lévi-Strauss are different. They do not need abbreviated handles—tunes or synopses—to keep such complex arrangements 'in mind.' (It should be noted that Beethoven can be just as polyphonically aware as Bach, even in emphasizing a melodious theme; it is his listeners who might tend to reduce their perception of his music to its more homophonic aspect.) These polyphonically-minded people can keep track of the multiple strains of myths, poems, or musical scores, all simultaneously.

But what is the point in this admittedly over-played surmisal concerning individual minds attending to actual performances, which is outside the *social, langue* focus of this study? The point is that one has no need of summary handles unless what is summarized is seen 'progressively' as a means to something else. But neither myths, Symbolist poems, nor a Bach toccata are 'going' anywhere; they *are* the where: worlds of interrelating, sense-bound units, which can totally occupy, in fact totally consume our logical powers. Finally, the fact that Lévi-Strauss finds such productions in the most diverse areas—myth, race-horse names, music, medieval transubstantiation (in *Du Miel aux cendres*, L-S 1966b) and so forth—should remind us once more of that fundamental message in his quest for polyphony. Remember, from what we have seen in *Tristes Tropiques*, it would not really be a matter of going 'back to Bach,' but rather of going 'in to Bach.' Music is there to remind us that experience is a synchronized symphony of contrastive sensory features—all ours for the playing.

Music is also there to reveal the limitations involved in trying to logically encode sensory-based texts which are not our own. Cross-cultural 'textual' criticism is to myth, ritual, and so forth what musical analysis is to complete compositions performed. An analyzer's powers are restricted to the following: the demonstration of the various processes of opposition, inversion, homology, etc., which technically (and theoretically) 'generate' the whole of European symphonies (once given a store of units with which to work), as well as the whole of human phonemics (whose units are limited by the presumed *nature* of human vocal apparatus), as well as, according to Lévi-Strauss, the whole of man's semantic universes as established and maintained through metonymy and metaphor. We cannot 'know' or 'experience' another's myth cross-culturally any better than we can another's music. For myth and music are keyed to a culture's panoply of interrelated sensory systems from experience; this very fact enables the mythic and musical forms regularly to suggest multivalent associations for anyone who has grown up in their terms. (As Proust said somewhere, 'Music synthesizes the essential experiences of the interior life' [my trans.].) Thus, thanks to the lifetime of sense relationships orchestrated by mythic and musical forms, a native inhabitant—like Proust's artist—can experience the 'form as an emotion' (see Moss: 102). Outside observers on the other hand—like

Proust's connoisseur Swann—can do little more than experience emotions another's forms set free. Of course, there are degrees to all of this. And we can trust that the more myth or music we succeed in interrelating analytically, the more we ourselves will have built up a store of retrospective associations that will eventually facilitate our experiencing another's form as an emotion, but not, of course, just like his (let us say indigenous) emotion. This, at least, is the hope behind *Mythologiques*.

Music, then, provides the most ready examples of those 'significant forms' (Langer: 202) behind experience, which are more difficult to perceive through words. Or, in the ruminations of Proust:

> And, just as certain creatures are the last surviving testimony to a form of life which nature has discarded, I asked myself if music were not the unique example of what might have been—if there had not come the invention of language, the formation of words, the analysis of ideas—the means of communication between one spirit and another. It is like a possibility which has ended in nothing [*qui n'a pas eu de suites*]; humanity has developed along other lines, those of spoken and written language (Proust 1956c: 349).

Indeed, Claude Lévi-Strauss has Marcel Proust in mind. This is the Proust in whose prose 'symbolism bloomed' (Fiser 11; my trans.), the Proust who 'revolutionizes the novel in bringing to it poetry' and who 'takes up poetry in the revolution it had just experienced—that of Baudelairian correspondence' (Picon: 175; my trans.). Unfortunately, if the discussion of the preceding literary correspondences has seemed cursory, imagine our present plight. Nevertheless, the affinities are there, and we must at least begin to appreciate them.

In *Structural Anthropology* Lévi-Strauss literally concludes that 'any myth represents a quest for the remembrance of things past' ('tout mythe est une recherche du temps perdu' [L-S 1958: 225]). From this allusion to Proust's work he goes on to note that 'in industrial civilization there is no longer any room for mythical time, except within man himself' (L-S

1963b: 204). In another passage the anthropologist offers the following discussion of the problem of the unconscious:

> We might say, therefore, that the preconscious is the indi-
> vidual lexicon where each of us accumulates the vocabulary
> of his personal history, but that this vocabulary *becomes*
> *significant, for us and for others,* only to the extent that the
> unconscious structures it according to its laws and thus trans-
> forms it into language (L-S 1963b: 203; my emphasis).

It might be profitable carefully to relate Lévi-Strauss' usages of 'preconscious' and 'unconscious' to Proust's varieties of memory which, while often designated simply as 'voluntary memory' and 'involuntary memory,' are more accurately classi-fied by Moss as conscious memory, unconscious memory, and involuntary memory (see Moss: 94). Although the effort to interrelate these concepts will be confusing, it is worth the try; and part of the point lies in the confusion itself. Our principal concern is that opposition between lived/conceived (*parole/ langue*, events/structure, etc.) previously alluded to (on p. 91.

The 'unconscious memory'—by which Moss means the past connection of events which has been, in Freudian language, painfully repressed—is easily handled, because it is of least importance in Proust's work. Likewise, Lévi-Strauss is not con-cerned with Freudian depths, and they are not what he means by 'unconscious.' Now, with 'preconscious' Lévi-Strauss is re-ferring to the continuous input of sensory data out of which experience must be ordered. (This sensory data is itself built up from 'matter' unknowable as such: '. . . one will bow before the fact that matter is the instrument, not the object of signi-fication' [L-S 1964a: 346–7; my trans.].) Through 'conscious memory' Proust can recall only scattered and impoverished portions of such input which have been tidily ordered according to Habit. Yet richer stores of the preconscious remain in reserve; and they become accessible through the 'involuntary memory,' which occasionally yields overwhelming recall when triggered by a new instance of a formerly experienced, multivalent sen-

N

sation. Of course, the fuller order of events to which Proust thereby accedes has been a part of himself all this time. In fact, the order of events is apart from time, because events come to be seen as something they were not seen as when they occurred. Furthermore, we—Proust's readers—never gain direct access to his narrator's involuntary memory, since he must employ his conscious memory to recall the instances of involuntary memory he writes about. (Of course, the various memories need not remain so distinct as this discussion implies). For it is only in his writing that the *parole* of all varieties of memory attains the level of communicable *langue*.[18] But where have we left Lévi-Strauss? The point eventually to be made is that Lévi-Strauss' 'unconscious' involves a bit of Proust's 'involuntary memory,' but with the additional thesis that to an extent such memory exists socially (inter-individually). And the representation of that memory is what we call 'myth.'

Actually, Proust's involuntary memory is not just a way of remembering more of what we have seen: 'Involuntary memory induces perception and is not a repetition but a revelation' (Moss: 94). What is more:

The true power of involuntary memory lies not in *what* we remember but in the process of memory itself (Moss: 96).

This memory is a faculty, often never discovered, whereby an individual can know not so much how things happened, but what things *are*, in terms of their relations to other things. Through his work Proust teaches that everyone can be his own Symbolist poet. The proof that such capacity is inherent in each of us lies in the *déjà vus* and the shudders of sensory induced (especially musically induced) recollection-plus that all persons have experienced but few have articulated. Moreover, in the end Proust is a full-fledged determinist, because everything has been there all along—the structure of his involuntary memory, whereby water lilies are Aunt Leonies and all levels and sensory modes interrelate in totalized harmony—prefiguring his per-

[18] For an application of the concepts *langue* and *parole* to Proust's work, see (Uitti 1963).

ception and post-figuring his recall. 'Just as Proust argues that all creation is re-creation, so all cognition is recognition' (Macksey: 107). Moreover, each individual artist has his own particular harmonious synthesis to offer in discovering that structure of himself—his vision—in ever greater detail as he goes on seeking connections.

But what does one man's 'réminiscence créatrice' (Picon: 125) have to do with the empirical facts of myth? I suppose I am merely arguing that a notion such as 'societal involuntary memory' would be a useful tool for appreciating Lévi-Strauss' concept of myth. For myth is neither a record of what happened, nor an aspiration about what ought to have happened, nor a license for what is happening. Myth is seen as an articulation of happenings in terms of various codes; and this articulation itself affords elucidation (revelation?) in the process of being formulated. Above all Lévi-Strauss' myth is neither *fact*ual nor univocal, both of which qualities bear on Proust's arch-enemy habit, at least in one of its aspects:

Habit is a half-remembered metaphor in which one term has lost its original relevance to the other.

Why is memory a metaphor? Memory connects two things through some object or sensation by sensing a correspondence between them. How does it differ from habit? Habit disconnects the past stimulus from the present response. Memory seeks the connection (Moss: 92–3).

Lévi-Strauss condemns the discipline of History in the same terms we see here applied to habit. On the other hand myth is seen as incorporating history (i.e. time passing), but always *in terms of a present response*, as it refuses to be alienated from any feature of existence deemed significant. We remember, however, that 'conscious memory' is habitual and supposes it knows *the* connection. Thus, it is more precisely 'involuntary memory' that 'seeks the connection.' For Proust, then, involuntary memory is the phenomenon of access to his own metaphorical systems, to the set of connections throughout his sensory input that constitute his essential being. Similarly, Lévi-Strauss' category of 'unconscious' is only the locus of the structuring whereby individual sensory inputs (preconsciouses) are communicably interrelated (i.e. where they become 'significant, for us and for others'). One might say that empirically 'involuntary memories' are partially shared, at least if images and metaphors can indeed be communicated (as we hope they can). Thus, myth now looms as any concise representation of multiple sensory-based systems which themselves relate to a backlog of experiential input, some of it consciously remembered, much of it involuntarily remembered (at least potentially) only on certain instances.

Furthermore, we can perhaps see from this point of view why myth should be typically emotion ridden. Contrary to some critics, I think that Lévi-Strauss, rather than ignoring the emotive aspects of classificatory behavior, has through his extended analogy with music de-mystified them and indicated a way of 'explaining' those aspects. For, if Proust's narrator can hang volumes of creative reminiscence on a single musical phrase; or if on the social level that same Atlanta high school class (see p. 101) might be reduced to simultaneous tears by a few bars of *that song*, which is little more than several rhythmic repetitions and melodic transpositions, but which relates to certain sorts of events and certain kinds of times; then imagine how more complete what we scorn as a momentary lapse into sentimentality could be for a face-to-face community, the semantic universes of whose members display extensive overlap, and who, again, have nowhere *progressively* to go! For such a group its corpus of myth—merely through the down to earth function of simultaneously corresponding disparate portions of experience transposed across different sensory orders—could provide a cohesive force that would leave our mass media, with their sundry devices, wanting.

A more readily documentable allusion by Lévi-Strauss to Proust comes in the chapter of *The Savage Mind* entitled 'Time Regained' ('Le Temps retrouvé'). Having thus signalled the culmination of Proust's opus, Lévi-Strauss discusses how over time a native classification 'tends to be dismantled like a palace swept away upon the flood':

The problem [totemism] has never ceased presenting to theorists is that of the relation between structure and event. And the great lesson of totemism is that the form of the structure can sometimes survive when the structure itself succumbs to events (L-S 1966a: 232).

This usage of 'the form of the structure' and 'the structure itself' could lead to confusion, especially in the context of the present study, which has tried to maintain a clear view of the concept 'structure' as a delineated relationship between sets of differences (the latter being themselves distinctive features of systems from different orders). To recall from chapter II: a sexually specific housecat (as systematically posed in Baudelaire's poetic language) is related to an androgynous, star-studded sphinx through the structure of inversion and exteriorization. But, if we likewise recall the discussion of meaning from Saussure *et al.* (chapter III), we remember that by shifting our point of view enough, everything becomes 'structure': e.g. a 'cat' itself is a particular relationship between the sets of differences which generate our categories of 'animals,' of 'female-types,' etc. Thus, to clarify the above quotation concerning totemism, we can imagine the following situation: a set of differences which generates a category in the natural order (e.g. the category of 'animals') is related to one in the social order (e.g. 'clan system'); this *structure* is stated in the *form* of particular clans having rights on particular areas associated with particular animals. The 'structure itself' (the relationship) would succumb to events if, for example, one of the clans died off; yet the 'form of the structure' (the statement of the 'structure itself') might survive and be employed for new significations. This simplified example should suggest why some critics have complained of the difficulties in keeping track of Lévi-Strauss' concept of structure, difficulties which are exacerbated by translation problems. Yet, I think the concept is easily kept in focus. We need only remember that the point of view is shifting and try to bear in mind what the phonetic model teaches about ordering a domain out of combinations of contrasts in binary opposition. But, whereas the phonetic model supposedly has a bound set of possible vocal features to work with, the conceptual universes studied by Lévi-Strauss are vastly more complex, with multiple analytically imposed levels (imaginary, historical, social, ritual, real . . .) in many varieties of elements employed by different cultures (sounds, colors, directions, shapes, gestures . . .).

In this state of mind one can appreciate why such surviving 'forms of structures' are crucial to achieving 'Time regained.' For insofar as they are indices on the social level of distant, intrinsic codes of order, these forms of structures can serve a function similar to that of Proust's involuntary memory on the individual level. The forms yield insight into structure itself. And structure depicts the codes for corresponding orders of experience, which are the most fundamental basis of what a culture *is*, or, to put the matter more comparatively, of what a culture can *communicate*. Moreover, just as Proust sees the worth of each individual artist to be his representation of his own particular constellation of metaphors, so Lévi-Strauss sees 'cultures' as certain permutations on a theoretically finite number of interrelatable systems across orders; and:

> *The anthropologist is the astronomer of the social sciences*: His task is to discover a meaning for configurations which, owing to their size and remoteness, are very different from those within the observer's immediate purview (L-S 1963b: 378).

Through a consideration of affinities between Proust's and Lévi-Strauss' views of Time and the status of experience transcending Time, we have arrived at the notion of cultural *temps perdu*s (essential systems of connections out of which a group's perception and conceptual contents derive) which the anthropological-outsider is in a privileged position to discern. Proust achieves a similar privileged position on his own perception and conceptual contents by coming to see Time for what it is:

> This destroyer of all external objects of desire becomes, in turn, a creative force: it allows recollection. Value resides

only in past experience possessed and translated in the present. The artist's two means to achieve this vital simultaneity are memory and metaphor. Both require for Proust, as for Coleridge, 'the reconcilement of opposite or discordant qualities: of sameness with difference' (Macksey: 119).

The *recognition* of sameness with difference here accorded through Time is the same recognition attained through distance in *Tristes Tropiques*. From this vantage point additional similarities appear in how Proust and Lévi-Strauss conceive of themselves and the role of their work in the context of their experience. In the first place there is a mutual negative note, as struck again by Moss in regards to Proust:

Proust is the most honest of novelists because he shows us not only how little we know about other people but how impossible it is to know them. It is a suspicion we have always had but hate to see confirmed (Moss: 38).

As has already been suggested, the incapacity acknowledged by Proust to directly *know* the assortment of 'texts'—mutable over time—which compose personages we encounter, was the same incapacity—only now exaggerated—which Lévi-Strauss appreciates in anthropology's particular version of a self in confrontation with the 'other'. Moreover, as was partially evident from *Tristes Tropiques,* what Lévi-Strauss determines to do in spite of 'how impossible it is to know them' is reminiscent of Proust. For, both come to deny any substantial being to the *self* as well as to *others*. Unable to know either of these supposed entities, they turn to the creative synthesis of elements which are sensed to constitute communication between the entities. While the 'person' Swann is different each time that Proust's narrator confronts him or hears tell of him, the narrator can still structure the sets of differences among the various manifestations of the person, to know, as it were, 'Swann.' Analogously, Lévi-Strauss can know 'a myth'; and both Proust and Lévi-Strauss can know themselves.

As always in such a procedure there is the problem of knowing just what it is that one is *really* getting to know. For example:

> No one can deny that antinomy there is in Proust's philosophy between Platonic idealism and its negation; a tendency to attribute supreme importance now to the idea and to the artist as 'déchiffreur' of a spiritual reality, now to the senses, to the object itself as a path leading to the spiritual (Mein: 111).

But the fact to note is that the senses (i.e. sensory data) enter into Proust's scheme only insofar as they go to constitute parts of an idea. The worth of a sensory impression is judged by precisely how much else it can be intellectually, retrospectively related to, as Proust goes about detecting correspondences between artistic and experiential 'texts' (e.g., most simply, a portrait and a face remembered). Or to put the matter another way, an idea enters into Proust's scheme only insofar as it relates to multiple, cross-temporal or inter-order, sensory impressions. A systematic musical pattern does not exist in the abstract, but only in conjunction with a host of visual, olfactory, other auditory, tactile, and gustatory associations which—as we learn through time—can themselves be just as systematic and causally evoked by the musical pattern alone. Here then in Proust we find that very same refusal to differentiate sharply between real, 'on the ground' sensory input and mental orderings *of* it that characterizes Lévi-Strauss' preliterate *pensée sauvage* and his own studies of this—all of which results in the difficulty encountered when critics attempt to label them either materialist or idealist. 'Here again one will bow before the fact that matter is the instrument, not the object of signification. In order that it yield to this role, it is first necessary to impoverish it: retaining from it only a small number of elements suitable for expressing contrasts and for forming pairs of oppositions' (L-S 1964a: 346–7; my trans.). Here also we find the 'need to organize his experience in terms of paired opposites':

> This habit of mind is at the very heart of his almost sacerdotal

attention to metaphor, to synaesthesia, to puns, to stylistic devices such as syllepsis and oxymoron—all pivots on which to engage opposition. . . . Out of opposites, however, is generated the dynamism toward a dialectic (Macksey: 107).

The subject here described is Proust.

Above and beyond this lie the most striking affinities between Proust and Lévi-Strauss, which bear on their ambitions to do critical justice to various bodies of 'texts'—Proust to a selection of sensory systems which constitute portions of Western art and literature, Lévi-Strauss to a selection of preliterate expressive classificatory procedures—in their search for meaning. In conjunction with this shared ambition is found a common effort to make of extensive critical analysis in prose an exercise after the fashion of what Brooks notes in Donne, whereby: 'The poem is an instance of the doctrine which it asserts; it is both the assertion and the realization of the assertion' (Brooks: 17). What results is on the one hand a novel and on the other hand an anthropology which, especially during the former's more analytic moments and the latter's more florid, reveal distinctly similar visions (of how to gain significance through interminable critical procedure).

Lévi-Strauss offers a four volume *Mythologiques* with no subject, no beginning, and no end. His method, in part patterned after musical structures, consists of threading through the data of New World myth, sometimes performing closely controlled comparisons of neighboring mythic corpuses, at other times swinging widely between distant versions to detect clues for possible significations of given elements. In so doing he traces a methodological rose-window with repeating loops of inquiry swerving back through the same item of empirical data from different angles—from different vantage points afforded by comparing mythic variants with similar themes (e.g. seasonal periodicity, the origin of agriculture). Through this re-ordering of elements in mythic texts, and only after following up every lead as to any possible significations that an exhaustive familiarity with the whole of New World data (plus anything else that comes to mind) can suggest, Lévi-Strauss achieves a 'myth of mythology.' The myth is in no way finished, in fact, could not conceivably be finished: '. . . mythic thought never executes a completed course: there always remains for it something to accomplish' (L-S 1964a: 14; my trans.). But occasionally this methodological spiral is temporally arrested, as bits of the store of 'odds and ends' comprising the original field of inquiry fall into place, acquire demonstrable signification, as do the particles of a kaleidoscope at stages of its rotation. In this way a 'possum' can eventually be seen to be equivalent in New World imagery to 'rot,' or one sort of 'fire' can be shown to be codified as the inverse of one sort of 'water'—the reason being, for example, that fire can be shown to be equivalent to something which is itself equivalent to the specifically stated inverse of water in another mythic variant (see L-S 1964a: 230). Thus, a shift occurs from one set of terms to another to justify a particular opposition; and tangible empirical problems—such as how a possum functions in various people's mythologies—are solved.

As far as we have gone, Proust performs a similar task with his own experience. Proust's mind's eye is likewise kaleidoscopically oriented (rather, in his imagery, like a magic lantern, but projecting back in on himself rather than out onto other cultures). His narrator effects similar spiraling loops back through memorable 'odds and ends' as time passes, searching different angles or new perspectives, in order to distinguish new significations in retrospect for the ostensibly same elements of experience. There is no set subject (the work is not simply an autobiography or the history of an epoch), no beginning or end: *À la Recherche du temps perdu*, though conclusive, is, like *Mythologiques*, '*interminable*' (L-S 1964a: 14). And Proust likewise achieves *en route* satisfactory solutions to particular empirical problems: For example, why emotion x occurs under stimulation y can be 'explained'—through analogy—by detecting the equivalence of y and a prior stimulation z with its own welter of contextual associations which are themselves now the cause behind the intensity of x. Thus, stimulation z (in Proust's most famous example, a tea cake), once it has happened, can never again be just z, but only z plus the potentially recallable perception of its context—to which stimulation y (= stimulation z again

later) yields access through its equivalence to the z that was—
whence x! And if Proust works it right, x can signal the acti-
vation of involuntary memory, i.e. recall through all the contextual associations of all the y's that have been since z.

But such schematization of the particular problems solved is
far from the whole of what Proust is about. For, essentially,
Proust's work is both world *and* procedure; or an instance of
the doctrine which it asserts; or: '. . . Proust, especially, omits
nothing in his effort to fuse conception and execution . . .'
(Mein: 119). In 'Time regained' Proust concludes: 'Thanks to
art [of which his novel is an example], instead of seeing only
one world, our own, we see it under multiple forms . . .' (Proust
1956d: 225). And in reference to his readers he later discloses:

> For, as I have already shewn, they would not be my readers
> but readers of themselves, my book serving merely as a sort
> of magnifying glass, such as the optician of Combray used
> to offer to a customer, so that through my book I would
> give them the means of reading in their own selves (Proust
> 1956d: 384).[19]

It is by now a commonplace in Proustiana to observe that he
not only professed *that* time can be transcended through creative
reminiscence, but demonstrated time regained while describing
the fact, as he finally obliges the reader to regain the very time
that has elapsed during his own reading of the demonstration
that time is to be regained. At the novel's end we are induced
into recall of the novel's beginning, as set in still fuller relief by
our having experienced the whole of the novel. Time is regained,
but not nostalgically—rather creatively, absolutely. Proust,
then, concludes his opus with a monumental, 'See, I told you so.'
Reading Proust is doing what he is convincing you is done.

I would deem the tactics in Lévi-Strauss' *Mythologiques*
essentially parallel. The world of South American and North
American myth is interesting in its own right, but how much

[19] 'For the Eye altering alters all' (Blake: 84). (For the I altering
alters all. For the I altaring altars all—all Proust requires is some haw-
thorn blossom or Aunt Léonie's medicine table.)

more so if the fashion in which that world is described is itself
a demonstration of the processes by which that world is constructed: Take a few sets of contrasts; accrue to them ever
fuller ranges of experience, always bringing the totality to bear
on the present stage of the spiraling procedure. Ever since considering the title of *La Pensée sauvage* (see ch. I), we have
noticed this tendency in Lévi-Strauss to do what he is demonstrating. In *Mythologiques*, Proust-like, he induces us to do
likewise from text to text to text. He thus brings to anthropological analysis the contrived complexities Proust brought to the
novel—and all to help show that the kind of re-ordering and
transposing of sensory units from one experiential 'text' to another is itself sufficient to generate rich worlds of signification, as
we ourselves amass step by step a universe of meaning through
retrospect. Reading Lévi-Strauss is doing what he is convincing
you is done. And the procedure is a legitimate one, as long as
we realize that there is no claim made to *re*-trace the actual
development of meaning throughout New World myth. The
history of the creation of *Mythologiques* lies largely in the dark;
and the causes governing *change* cannot be proved by structural methods. Change, in fact, is not embraced as a basic problem, since it is encompassed in the first assumptions of
structuralism: namely, that men classify their experience and
that they actively differentiate themselves in groups from other
groups. These assumptions have *change* built in, since contem-
plative self-differentiation, rather than inertia, is the norm; and
any 'cause' of change (at least of conceptual change), such as
war, plenty, earthquake, invasion, etc., appears rather as an
'excuse.' The terms in which men conceptualize do not *have*
to change; but they *do* change, whether or not there happens to
be a 'cause' adduced as such through hindsight. Thus, a group
with a myth which sets up a correspondence between animal
actors and events concerning the invention of agriculture might
set itself off from another group by changing the animal to
human actors—but complementary changes would eventually
be expected to occur throughout the group's orderly conception
of experience, so as to keep their various systems (mythological,
sociological, zoological, etc.) in tune with each other. Finally,

we must note again: what any mythic element means depends on the particular body of 'texts' in whose terms it is to be deemed significant. Lévi-Strauss is not finally concerned with what one tribe's myth means in terms of the social experience of the members of that tribe, but rather with what any New World myth means in terms of as much as we can know of New World myth—myth itself being a more or less independent category of mutable sense-bound correspondences, which are, however, *limited* (directed, skewed) by the very first set of correspondences established, and therefore no longer random.[20] With this large scale meaning as his goal, Lévi-Strauss' mythological approach to *mythologiques* (his contrived realization of his own assertion) is no sleight of hand, but an additional form of evidence.[21]

Still in addition to this lies the affinity between Proust and Lévi-Strauss concerning their efforts to demonstrate an answer to the critical question *par excellence*: given a store of 'texts' (poems, essays, paintings, myths, rituals, house plans, church plans, symphonies, opera, cooking customs, and so forth), what are we, in light of our potentially comparative viewpoint, to *do* with them? Proust's work is about this problem. He sets out to undermine various standard justifications for being interested in sensory-bound, systematic orderings of experience (call it

[20] This is to say that once instigated, the systems of correspondences are no longer completely *arbitrary* in the Saussurian sense (see p. 69ff). For once any correspondence has been established, there is some*thing* set to take into account henceforth.

[21] Lévi-Strauss is very sensitive to this problem of the extent of the 'textual framework' that bounds a given analysis. It is no doubt this sensitivity which provoked his well-known assertion, alluded to in note 12 of ch. III: 'Therefore, not only Sophocles, but Freud himself, should be included among the recorded versions of the Oedipus myth on a par with earlier or seemingly more "authentic" versions' (L-S 1963b: 217). This is to say that he is not treating the Oedipus-myth-in-relation-to-the-experience-of-classical-Greeks. Rather, he is treating more generally various efforts to come to terms with several sets of contradictions, such as 'how *one* can be born from *two*.' Sophocles provides a version that can be interpreted as such an effort; so does Freud. Of course, as noted by Lévi-Strauss the Oedipus example is a bad one, since its terms have been literarily developed, thereby removing it somewhat from that ultimate mythic level of non-self-consciously aware classification and differentiation.

'art'). On the one hand Sainte-Beuve's notion that a great 'work' reflects a great 'man' is false; on the other hand the connoisseurship of *snobbisme* leads us up a painfully restricted alley, as demonstrated by Swann. So on, step by step, Proust eliminates all bases for considering 'texts' other than the critical process of synthesizing and interrelating the texts themselves, which is, after all, one fashion of creating them: experience is metaphor. (For it is to be recalled: '. . . Marcel Proust intends by metaphor "the encounter-sensation-remembrance-by-analogy" which is in reality the dynamic or literary symbol' [Fiser: 169; my trans.].) And the grandest human achievements turn out to be—cathedral-like, according to Proust's principal image—products of such synthesis and correspondence among multiple orders across time. Indeed, human life—through perception and retrospective conceptualization—is itself such an achievement.

On Lévi-Strauss' side *Mythologiques* would seem to be more than anything else an attempt to demonstrate what is left to be done, once all of the false assumptions as to why one should be interested in preliterate classifications are eliminated. Ironically: through advances in scholarly-scientific thinking, he argues against antiquarian interests; evolutionary assumptions; Boasian reality-mirroring and Malinowskian society-licensing (since myths can state conditions which contradict what is 'really found,' or have little bearing on it); Jungian universal archetypes; materialist interpretations; and social anthropology's assertion of the primacy of social organization; as well as the Hegelian thesis of direct interrelationship among various orders of society. There remain incredibly rich codes from experience which—although they bear on natural elements, human relationships, historical events, rules and norms, etc. (and although all these things, if pertinent, should be taken into account to understand the codes)—do not relate *directly* to anything other than those logical functions by which they are generated. Thus, in considering myth Lévi-Strauss proceeds in scientific and scholarly fashion to dispense with demonstrably unjustifiable assumptions; and he ends up with myth—plus cross-cultural checks, in order that *a* meaning can be refined more and more

toward *the* meaning. And the grandest human achievements turn out to be—*bricoleur*-like, according to Lévi-Strauss' principal image—products of such synthesis and correspondence among multiple orders across time. Indeed, human life. . . .[22]
How perfectly what Samuel Beckett says of Proust applies to Lévi-Strauss' ideas on myth:

> The Proustian world is expressed metaphorically by the artisan because it is apprehended metaphorically by the artist: the indirect and comparative expression of indirect and comparative perception (Beckett: 67–8).

Myth is the *indirect* and comparative expression of indirect and comparative perception (of experience). The 'myth of mythology' (*Mythologiques*) is the indirect and *comparative* expression of indirect and comparative perception (of myths). Therefore, Lévi-Strauss can conclude his introduction to the processes of mythic thinking as follows:

> We have had to wait until the middle of this century for the crossing of long separated paths: that which arrives at the physical world by the detour of communication, and that which as we have recently come to know, arrives at the world of communication by the detour of the physical. The entire process of human knowledge thus assumes the character of a closed system. And we therefore remain faithful to the inspiration of the savage mind when we recognize that the scientific spirit in its most modern form will, by an encounter it alone could have foreseen, have contributed to legitimize the principles of savage thought and to re-establish it in its rightful place (L-S 1966a: 269).

In an interesting aside Lévi-Strauss divides his corpus of writings into two principal stages: the first is best exemplified by *Les Structures élémentaires de la parenté* (1949) and the

[22] It is suitable to note here Leach's reflection: '. . . . an appreciation of existentialist philosophy may be necessary to understand Lévi-Strauss' position . . .' (Leach 1968: 344).

second commences with *Le Cru et le cuit* (1964a); in between comes *La Pensée sauvage* (prefaced by *Le Totémisme aujourd'-hui*), which is characterized as a sort of pause for reflection (see L-S 1964a: 17). Lévi-Strauss apparently intends by this division something which can perhaps be clarified by comparing earlier Symbolists with Proust; it is all just a matter of Time, i.e. of an increased complexity because of the number of 'texts' to be interrelated. In the nineteenth century Symbolist novel there is a concept of self which is less complex, which allows for no changing through time. For example, as regards the hero Entragues in Gourmont's *Sixtine*, 'the reader . . . has the impression of coming face to face with an enormous (and fascinating) cross-word puzzle and of having but to fill in the empty squares. Entragues has no *history*' (Uitti 1961: 63–4). This point calls to mind a complaint by Baudelaire:

> More than once I have tried . . . to confine myself within a system in order to preach freely. But a system is a kind of damnation which forces us into a perpetual recantation; it is always necessary to invent another, and the exertion required, is a cruel punishment. And my system was always beautiful, vast, spacious, convenient, neat, and above all complete. At least, it seemed so to me. . . . [but] No matter how much I changed or broadened the criterion, it always fell short of expressing universal man and never caught up with the multiform and multicolored beauty that moves in the infinite spirals of life (Baudelaire in Hyslop: 12–13).

Mein suggests one recourse taken by Baudelaire:

> It was Baudelaire who, to the intense wonderment of Thibaudet, combined 'une intelligence critique' and the spirit of poetry. Baudelaire, like Proust, was subject to an indecision about form, then turned his hesitancy to rich effect in the intermingling of techniques of 'les Correspondances' (Mein: 118).

But the rich effects are not rich enough, and Baudelaire can only fully overcome his dilemma by positing the existence of a transcendental realm. Proust, on the other hand, settles into the 'damnation' of a system, but he expands its potential through an incorporation of the dimension of Time: all of the separate systems of correspondences he perceives and constructs can themselves be interrelated transversely, diachronically, thanks to creative reminiscence. But Proust's diachronic dimension is not *history* as *lived*; it is *process* as *conceived*. As Picon remarks: 'Proust encounters instances of poetry where the poet encounters them: in the horizontal time of coexistence. But while poetry as a form is founded on their abstraction, Proust chooses to evoke them concretely, to leave them in their context' (Picon: 166, my trans.). Then he can critically interrelate the instances of poetry through comparison.

In a parallel way Lévi-Strauss enters into that alluded-to second stage of his effort with an emphasis on the transformations across systems (including transformations both within one culture among different orders, and within one order among different cultures, and both), since any other emphasis would likewise fall 'short of expressing universal man.' His first stage (L-S 1949a) reveals how one particular order (that of kinship) can be differentially organized according to socio-logically basic marriage rules which can be compared across cultures. Then, after the modulating breath of *The Savage Mind*, he expands to encompass the interrelationships among systems in as many orders as he can, by means of the insights of myth.[23]

[23] There is a notable parallel between Lévi-Strauss' efforts to stave off final criticisms of *Mythologiques* before completion of its multi-volumed full-circle, and Proust's difficulties on the same count. Richard Macksey brings together sources that summarize Proust's concern: '. . . Proust wrote in his first letter to Jacques Rivière with an enthusiasm born of anxiety: "At last I have found a reader who has hit upon [qui devine] the fact that my book is a dogmatic work and a construction! . . . In this first volume you have seen the pleasure afforded me by the *madeleine* dipped in tea: I say that I cease to feel mortal etc., and that I do not understand why. I will not explain until the end of the third [i.e., last] volume. The whole is so *constructed*." To Benjamin Crémieux, who was later to defend him as the master of the "composition en rosace," . . . Proust wrote: "Thank you for comparing my book to a city. . . . People fail only too often to realize that my books form a construction, but drawn

o

From this lower key affinity it will perhaps be less abrupt to arrive at a conclusion, since there is no end to the analogies to be drawn between Proust and Lévi-Strauss. With indiscriminate relish Proust manipulates the 'odds and ends' of past critical, literary, musical, and visual productions and of elements in his daily experience, while he specializes in Western synthetic arts; Lévi-Strauss does likewise, while he specializes in preliterate 'texts.' In the sense in which we have come to understand the term, Proust puts the 'myth' in literature, Lévi-Strauss puts the myth in anthropology. Both build myths and offer their results in 'Le Temps retrouvé'—Time regained being in truth the *structure* which relates the systems of correspondences comprising experience as conceived. Proust describes in a novel the structure—the timeless—of himself. Lévi-Strauss moves toward describing the structure of the data that has come under the purview of ethnographers. In a Proustian fashion Lévi-Strauss denies that *histoire* can be grounded in anything other than 'a spurious intelligibility attaching to a temporary internality.' From there he proceeds, almost stoically, to assert:

> I am not however suggesting that man can or should sever himself from this internality. It is not in his power to do so and wisdom consists for him in seeing himself live it, while at the same time knowing (but in a different register) that what he lives so completely and intensely is a myth—which will appear as such to men of a future century, and perhaps to himself a few years hence, and will no longer appear at all to men of a future millenium (L-S 1966a: 255).

It is this very human dilemma that is confronted—on the individual level—in the art of Marcel Proust.

But let a sound already heard or an odor caught in bygone years be sensed anew, simultaneously in the present and the

to a compass so vast that the structure—a rigorous structure to which I have subordinated everything—takes rather a long time to discern. There will be no denying it when the last page of *Le Temps retrouvé* (written before the rest of the book) closes precisely on the first page of *Swann*" ' (Macksey: 104–5).

past, real without being of the present moment, ideal but not abstract, and immediately the permanent essence of things, usually concealed, is set free and our true self, which had long seemed dead but was not dead in other ways, awakes, takes on fresh life as it receives the celestial nourishment brought to it. A single minute released from the chronological order of time has re-created in us the human being similarly released, in order that he may sense that minute. . . . situated outside the scope of time, what could he fear from the future? (Proust 1956d: 198).

Beyond the shadow of a doubt, retrospection is in order. What are the unifying features of this series of critical ramifications extending from novelistic Lévi-Strauss to anthropological Proust?

One theme that has run through this chapter is the use of *distance* as an analytic and poetic device—distance being that removal from the event itself, which facilitates determining the significance of the event. Rousseau has been hailed as 'the first critic of alienation, the first unmasker of culture' (Becker: 32). He recognized that to analyze behavior, one must stand abstracted from it, whether it is the behavior of others or of oneself. Even in daily experience, Rousseau confesses how he had to wait until *after* any personal confrontation to think of what he should have said. For, only in the distance of retrospect can the significant features of the whole event (along with the most appropriate response to them) be discerned. That is why he writes. Proust too makes of temporal removal an operational principle for disclosing the meanings and interrelationships of the everyday; and he at last translates this *time* into his work's final metaphor of spatial elevation on a pair of stilts—from which vantage point he attains his vision of unity. What Proust does for the experience of personalities, Lévi-Strauss envisions comparative human science doing for grouped man, by adding cross-cultural space to history's time:

It was necessary to await anthropologists in order to discover that social phenomena obey structural arrangements.

The reason is simple: it is that structures appear only through observation practiced from outside. Inversely, this observation can never grasp processes, which are not analytic objects, but the particular fashion in which a temporality is lived by a subject. This is to say, on the one hand, that process exists only for a subject engaged in his own historical becoming, or more exactly in that of the group to which he belongs; and, on the other hand, that in a given group, processes are numerous enough—and sufficiently different from each other—for there to exist sub-groups of identification: for an aristocrat and for a *sans-culotte*, the Revolution of 1789 is not the same process. And there exists a 'meta-process' integrating these irreducible experiences only for historically posterior thinking ... (L-S 1962d: 44–5; my trans.).

Ideally anthropology employs both sorts of distance—spatial (cross-cultural) and temporal. History's procedural drawback is that historians generally study their own societies, thus lacking comparative perspective. Anthropology's circumstantial drawback is that preliterate groups lack historical records. But ideally anthropology should utilize both varieties of distance in discerning the structure of cultural experience, just as Proust's narrative technique does so by establishing the point of view of a narrator who is both outside and later than the changing self of the novel's hero. As Richard Macksey observes:

> The point of view from which the action is seen is curiously divided between the Marcel of past time who acts and grows old through the course of the narrative, and the Marcel who recollects him from the distant vantage and is at last joined by him to pass, with the final footfall, into time regained. The situation is not unlike that of 'Rousseau juge de Jean-Jacques'. . . .
> Thus the action can be likened to an odyssey or pilgrimage where the traveler in time has forgotten the location of the homeland or the significance of the shrine (Macksey: 108).

The traveler of *Tristes Tropiques* adopts a similar technique but incorporates into the procedure the rescue of *other* cultural forms; for, the self cannot be rescued from time unless articulated into distinct relief by the *other*. Lévi-Strauss chooses man and tries to rescue the other, too.

Related to this theme of analytic distance, the present chapter has, in fact, traced the history of the increasing denial of what might be called *substance* (as contrasted to *structure*). Simply and schematically, Rousseau showed how there was no substance to the self which must be reconstructed *ex post facto*. Then, Mein observes:

> Baudelaire and Proust, with their conception of personality as a series of successive states, are prone to analyse ways of escaping the fate of even appearing to have a single, official identity (Mein: 124).

Then too, Mallarmé evokes the lack of substantive contact between ourselves and the ordinary objects comprising the experience of our surroundings. In fact, the hazy web of astoundingly could-be relationship which makes up his 'Afternoon of a Faun' is a pristine embodiment of Lévi-Strauss' savage thought which 'does not distinguish the moment of observation and that of interpretation' (L-S 1966a: 223). At last, Proust literally demonstrates that just as there is no self nor substantive *milieu*, there are likewise no substantive *others*, no archetypical incarnations of certain, fixed personalities along life's path. His finale likewise demonstrates what to do about this problem, as he induces us to realize that the very stuff of inter-personal experience must be reconstituted through time.

Yet a literary finale is not the only kind. And Lévi-Strauss goes on from that moment in *Tristes Tropiques* (see p. 141) to argue that there are likewise no substantive others in other milieus, even though many observers had assumed the contrary, thinking that men could be approached as objects. Yet, even in the absence of simple, whole man-objects, we must proceed by translating any texts *they* provide into structures which can then be related to the structure of the text that is ourself (cf. Rousseau), everything being just a matter of corresponding sets of relationships from semantic universes that have come into confrontation. Moreover, Lévi-Strauss argues that this conceptualization in terms of bundles of relationships (rather than in terms of fixed labels for substantive objects) is precisely what is manifested in many of the modes of communication that anthropology studies. And no more than a Symbolist work could be understood by assigning specific designata to the terms composing it, can many varieties of anthropological data be approached as statements about substantive things. Louis Dumont discusses this issue in terms of 'traditional mentality' versus 'modern mentality.' On the one hand there is the modern way, whereby:

> . . . a system is conceived of as formed of objects, all of which have their own being [*être*] and act on each other by reason of this being and through a law of determined interaction; for example, physical bodies all have their own mass and act on each other in a measure determined by this mass and their relative position. This manner of thinking, which separates individual being and relation, is principally modern. It can no doubt be found elsewhere, but it is modern in its full development and its exclusion of the following (Dumont 1967: 60–61; my trans.).

The following is, then, traditional:

> Or indeed to the contrary, an abstraction can be made of the 'elements' in themselves, of which the system seems to be composed, and they can be considered as merely resulting from the network of relations of which the system would thus be constituted. A phoneme has only the characteristics which oppose it to other phonemes; it is not some thing but only the other from the others, thanks to which it signifies some thing. We will talk of structure exclusively in this case: when the interdependence of the elements of a system is so tight that they disappear without residue as soon as the inventory of the relations among them is made—in sum a system of relations and no longer a system of elements. The passage from one

mentality or from one *esprit* to the other, from the world of structure to the world of substance, is no doubt the major problem for the comparison of societies (Dumont 1967: 61; my trans.).

Elsewhere Dumont argues for the logical priority of traditional mentality, i.e. structure: '. . . *structure or complementarity is necessarily and historically prior to substance and individuality,* and in that sense complexity is prior to, and more explanatory than, simplicity' (Dumont 1966: 238). Clearly then, structure as contrasted to substance parallels 'wild thinking' (*pensée sauvage*) as contrasted with technological (I would add therapeutic) thinking. Moreover, according to Lévi-Strauss, if the human sciences want to be comparative, the only way to approach an unbiased comparison of different systems is by structural methods. Thus, 'traditional mentality,' i.e. the world of structure, i.e. *pensée sauvage* wins out in the final analysis. And the circle is complete.

A final thrust of retrospection should highlight this chapter's relevance to that general tendency in communication theory to disregard problems concerning the source of phenomenal data. In the first place the self is *known* only insofar as it communicates to itself. Gilbert Ryle emphasized this point from ordinary language philosophy in his famous treatise against Cartesian dualism's doctrine that some ghostly 'mind' must be assumed to lie behind mental activity as manifested through acts of the bodily machine. During the course of his argument that any data indicative of 'mind' should be accepted without worrying about where it comes from, Ryle states the following:

The way in which a person discovers his own long-term motives is the same as the way in which he discovers those of others. The quantity and quality of the information accessible to him differs in the two inquiries, but its items are in general of the same sort (Ryle: 90).

The point is that there is no privileged source of information about the self or about where it is going. As Rousseau,

Baudelaire, and Proust wrote, all there is is an input of data, better seen through hindsight, which makes it appear as if one had been moving towards something. For, even if one were to assume that there exists some noumenal self-mind, it would not enter (communicably) into communication:

> Speaking to others (or to myself), I do not speak *of* my thoughts; I *speak them*, and what is between them—my after-thoughts and under-thoughts (Merleau-Ponty 1964a: 19).

Or, with more specific reference to society:

> Communication between individuals or groups is not, in effect, a consequence of life in society, it is this life itself, on the condition, of course, that it is not limited solely to oral or written communication (Pouillon: 1956: 158, my trans.).

This variety of reflection is generally summarized in communication theory through the assertion that, while *messages* can be assumed to be conveyed from a sender to a receiver, really all we have to go on are the messages themselves. For the sender and receiver can only be known across their messages, which is likewise true of oneself, at least in the view of Symbolists and structuralists. Yet the disintegration of 'self' or 'person' or 'substantive object' is no cause for alarm, since there still remain, existentially, worlds of translatable (interrelatable) messages— messages which, remembering music and myth, are *both* formally regulated *and* sensory-bound. And even if the source of the messages lies beyond us, even if progress through time toward truth from message to message cannot be demonstrated, it is still to be assumed that we can achieve greater understanding of the messages by inter-translating them more and more.

This view has been with us from the start of this study. It lies behind the loose usage of 'text' according to which our experiences of 'self,' of 'anthropological and poetic writings,' and of 'other cultures' are all epistemologically par. All these things are more or less 'texts'—sensory-bound systematic messages—that are there for the assimilation. This same view of experience was seen in Baudelaire's 'Correspondances,' one line of which also shows the key to expressing the view in French. The line is this: 'Les parfums, les couleurs et les sons se répondent.' And the key is the French reflexive. This particular verb form affords a ready means of suggesting interrelationship without having to specify either of the following: first, the locus of the relationship need not be determined; second, the reflexive form does not automatically imply the existence of some agent behind the state described analogous to the 'by whom or what' expected of the English passive often used to translate the reflexive. Thus, a condition of intertwined existence can be simply and satisfyingly stated as unelliptically there. Contrasted with this subtle reflexive is the necessarily cumbersome English translation of the above line: 'Perfumes, sounds, and colors answer each to each' (Scarfe's Baudelaire: 37).

Nor are the consequences of the reflexive mode of organization restricted to poetry. In fact, I would say that such readily stated, ungroundable existentially given, reciprocal *being* is a cornerstone of French *sociologie*. Take, for example, the following evidence from Durkheim's discussion of the role of a clan's mythic ancestor as a means of expressing 'the collective unity' characteristic of the clan:

> Masse homogène et compacte où il n'existe pas, pour ainsi dire, de parties différenciées, où chacun vit comme tous, ressemble à tous, un tel groupe *se représente à lui-même* cette faible individuation, dont il a confusément conscience, en imaginant que ses membres sont des incarnations à peine différentes d'un seul et même principe, des aspects divers d'une même réalité, une même âme en plusieurs corps (Durkheim 1896: 52; my emphasis).

Sagarin's translation skirts the difficulty by imposing a transitive, thus diminishing any sense of cognition:

> A homogeneous and compact mass where there exists, so to speak, no differentiated parts, where each one lives like all and each resembles all—this is the clan. Such a group *sees*

its own image in terms of a feeble individuation, of which it has a vague consciousness, by imagining that its members are incarnations, hardly at all different, from one and the same principle; they are various aspects of the same reality, a single soul in several bodies' (Sagarin's Durkheim: 88; my emphasis).

Durkheim's whole point is right there in the untranslatable reflexive. He is talking about a phenomenon which—like 'exchange' or the 'social'—most basically involves *two* and cannot be reduced to anything individual (such as one acting on another). And this whole notion simply comes out more easily, thanks to the French reflexive—e.g.:

> . . . la musique se vit en moi, je m'écoute à travers elle (L-S 1964a: 25).

Regardless of how pervasive such thinking has been throughout French *sociologie*, it is central in Lévi-Strauss. As we have already detected, as far as he can know, men and mankind are a composition of messages—manifestations of communicative thought. He expresses the limits of his knowledge by means of the reflexive, especially when asserting that he seeks to show 'how myths think themselves in men.' While this particular assertion by Lévi-Strauss has aroused considerable controversy, there have been similar statements by other modern students of perception and conceptualization. For example, in *Sense and Non-Sense* Merleau-Ponty describes the creative process of Cézanne:

> The picture took on fullness and density; it grew in structure and balance; it came to maturity all at once. 'The landscape thinks itself in me,' he said, 'and I am its consciousness' (Merleau-Ponty 1964c: 17).

This is Cézanne's way of stating he himself exists in the forms his brush applies; they are evidence of him. He might exist through other forms as well—e.g. words he utters about his work. But at the moment of creating the painting Cézanne's being is a function of the landscape; and his vision derives from a perceptual grammar which cannot be solely his. This is very important to Merleau-Ponty, because he sees such painting as a representation of creative perception (the only kind) which in its simplest form still contains all those differential additives from which the whole of experience is built. In Merleau-Ponty's phenomenological view nothing is perceived without all sorts of supra-sensory qualities—such as back-sidedness—being attributed to it. Thus, perception can claim primacy since it contains from the start all those mental complexities characteristic of the highest philosophies. For Merleau-Ponty perception itself is message (rather than something sensed by another thing), and a painting is a picture of message, of interrelationship irrespective of the sender or receiver. This is true both of the painting being painted and of the painting being seen:

> I would be at great pains to say *where* is the painting I am looking at. For I do not look at it as I do at a thing; I do not fix it in its place. My gaze wanders in it as in the halos of Being. It is more accurate to say that I see according to it, or with it, than that I *see it* (Merleau-Ponty 1964b: 164).

And concerning Cézanne's art he maintains that it is neither imitation, nor tasteful or instinctual construction; rather:

> IT IS A PROCESS OF EXPRESSING (Merleau-Ponty 1964c: 17; my capitals).

We can be satisfied with painting as ungrounded message, as a picture of a process of expressing, regardless of *by* whom or *of* what, because of the following notion:

> Ultimately the painting relates to nothing at all among experienced things unless it is first of all 'autofigurative.' It is a spectacle of something only by being a 'spectacle of nothing,' by breaking the 'skin of things' to show how the things become things, how the world becomes world (Merleau-Ponty 1964b: 181).

How like Lévi-Strauss. For that is exactly what human social experience is: a process of expressing. And myth is a picture of that process (showing how intersensory order *becomes* inter-sensory order), and must be understod as such. Elsewhere Merleau-Ponty offers this clarification:

> Expressive operations take place between thinking language and speaking thought; not, as we thoughtlessly say, between thought and language. It is not because they are parallel that we speak; it is because we speak that they are parallel.
> The weakness of every 'parallelism' is that it provides itself with correspondences between the two orders and conceals the operations which produced these correspondences by encroachment to begin with (Merleau-Ponty 1964a: 18).

In this anti-parallelism view, then, what matter are the processes interrelating analytically isolated orders of expression. The different orders cannot be distinguished and labeled as substantial things (since, remembering Saussure, there is no*thing* to label until at least two orders are in *fact* interrelated). And in the absence of substance there can be no directional determinism between orders. Thus, unlike material-oriented Marxists, idea-oriented Hegelians, or transcendental Baudelaire, Lévi-Strauss leaves us with message—in texts—alone. Experience, including change, stands as a concert of interpenetrating, cross-referring orders, all of which can be rewritten somewhat differently in the others' terms. Change is a variation, to or fro, on a set of principles, which are themselves the structure that summarizes the relationship of the differences in a series of similar events. In other words and in reverse: if we take an object or event, it is known by means of a sensory-based *system*; take a similar object or event, likewise known, and detect its differences from the first. Then, state the relationship between the two sets of differences, and you have the *structure* of a series which might represent, for example, an earlier and a later view of the same 'object,' or *our* and *their* view of the same 'event,' and so forth. All of this is highlighted in anthropology because the *our* and *their*, and sometimes the earlier and later, are intrinsic to the nature of the inquiry. But two points must be borne in mind: first, that there can be no perception without differentiation among a series (i.e. without the stuff of *structure*); second, the differences between members of a series of systematic perceptions (i.e. the elements of the members' *structure*) are at first selected *arbitrarily* (whether by natives during perception or by anthropologists during comparative conceptualization).

In this light we can see the answer to a rhetorical question recently posed in irony by Korn:

> How can it be that 'structure' is 'the very content' but at the same time 'is not related to empirical reality'? How can it be that it is 'the very content' and it is also 'rather a method'? (Korn: 6; my trans. of Korn's quotations from Lévi-Strauss' French).

This assortment of features attributed to 'structure' appears outlandish only if one fails to note how much Lévi-Strauss' work is involved with theories concerning the grounds of perception and communication, as well as our limitations in arriving at an understanding of these processes. While a structure is built up from differences selected from empirical reality, it need in no way directly relate to whatever that 'reality' might be, even if the reality could be directly *known*. For to order empirical reality is to transcend it or at least to *deny it as a feasible category*. Moreover, structure can indeed be 'the very content' and also 'rather a method,' because (à la Proust and Merleau-Ponty on Cézanne) content is really relationship mistakenly substantized; and relationship is only communicably experienced as systematic process (one might say, methodically). Proust offers a similar vision of 'reality':

> An hour is not merely an hour. It is a vase filled with perfumes, sounds, plans and climates. What we call reality is a certain relationship between these sensations and the memories which surround us at the same time (a relationship that is destroyed by a bare cinematographic presentation, which gets further away from the truth the more closely it claims to adhere to it) the only true relationship, which

the writer must recapture so that he may forever link together in his phrase its two distinct elements. One may list
in an interminable description the objects that figured in the
place described, but truth will begin only when the writer
takes two different objects, establishes their relationship—
analogous in the world of art to the sole relationship in the
world of science, the law of cause and effect—and encloses
them in the necessary rings of a beautiful style, or even when,
like life itself, comparing similar qualities in two sensations,
he makes their essential nature stand out clearly by joining
them in a metaphor, in order to remove them from the con-
tingencies of time, and links them together with the indes-
cribable bond of an alliance of words. From this point of view
regarding the true path of art, was not nature herself a beginning of art . . .? (Proust 1956d: 217–18).[24]

Lévi-Strauss thinks so, precisely. Furthermore, not only does
the anthropologist argue that it is pointless to seek as final aim
the reality behind the process of expression; he also denies the
utility of any hard and fast analytic differentiation of various
orders of expression, since any such order is always *becoming*
in a continual dialectic of inter-signification with all the other
orders, simultaneously. This, then, is the savage mind; and in
face of such mind about all one can do is delineate structures,
thereby effecting correspondences among sensory systems and
only (if ever) *finally* determining their logic.

[24] A few pages earlier Proust makes the same point, but with more of
an emphasis on schools of literature: 'An hour is a vase filled with perfumes, with sounds, with moments, with changing moods and climates.
Consequently, that literature which is satisfied to "describe objects," to
give merely a miserable listing of lines and surfaces, is the very one
which, while styling itself "realist," is the farthest removed from reality,
the one that impoverishes and saddens us the most, for it sharply cuts
off all communication of our present self with the past, the essence of
which was preserved in those objects, or with the future, in which they
stimulate us to enjoy the past anew. It is that essence which art worthy
of the name must express and, if it fails to do this, one can even then
draw a lesson from its failure (whereas one draws no lesson from even
the successes of realism) namely, that this essence is in part subjective
and cannot be communicated to others' (Proust 1956: 212–13).

VI

Interpretations and Conclusion

THROUGH LITERARY CORRESPONDENCES
TOWARD A CROSS-CULTURAL ESPRIT

Ainsi que nous analysions le mécanisme des correspondances ou celui de
la création, nous aboutissons à la même conclusion: dans les deux cas
il s'agit de *transposer*, soit une sensation en un autre domaine de sensations, soit une émotion en une oeuvre d'art (Fiser: 206–7).

But a theory of mind whose keynote is the symbolific function, whose
problem is the morphology of significance, is not obliged to draw that
bifurcating line between science and folly (Langer 1951: 246).

SURFACE INTERPRETATION

'Neologics' is one man's name for a portion of Lévi-Strauss'
game—namely, Theodore A. Cheney's in 'The Power of Irrelevant Thinking' (1968). Cheney's Neologics has to do with the
preverbal thought of our forefathers in which 'any particular
experience was stored as a memory of what it sounded like, what
it smelled like, how old it was, what season it happened, how
hairy it was, how soft, how hard, etc.' Derived from the sup-
position that man still cross-files on 'sensory barbs,' the doctrine
is as simple as it is total:

> Neological theory holds that there is an interrelatedness
> about the world which means that almost anything may
> turn out to be relevant to something else, if looked at in a
> different light (Cheney: 42–3).

As might be expected, this doctrine fathers a method. When

confronted with a traditionally logical impasse, Operational Neologics advocates judgment suspension, silence and soliloquy, distraction, and irrelevance: one 'uses peripheral reading, environmental scanning, analogies, metaphorical play and accidents in the hope that at least one will turn out to be relevant.' In thus espousing the science of uninhibited thinking, Neologics comes up with an ethical (aesthetic) programme which might well summarize that of most creators mentioned in this study:

SINCE IT TURNS OUT THAT PERHAPS NOTHING YOU DO IS IRRELEVANT, LIVE LIFE TO THE HILT—BUT FILE IT AWAY FOR LATER REFERENCE (Cheyney: 42–3; my caps.).

The relevance of the above ideas (which were discovered during a period of suspended judgment facilitated by distracting peripheral reading) to Lévi-Strauss is clear, in light of one lesson implicit in all his works: 'One understands the thought of savages neither by mere introspection nor by mere observation, but by attempting to think as they think and with their material' (Geertz: 30). And that Neological, preverbal, sensory-barb cross-filing is exactly the means of organizing that Lévi-Strauss finds in preliterate *bricoleurs*, that we have found in Mallarmé, and that was evidenced in 'Les Chats.' Moreover, Bernard Pingaud appreciates how Lévi-Strauss himself has been *bricoleur*ing since childhood but offers the following words of warning: 'Thus nothing would be more incorrect than to imagine the child-collector as simply a maniac over classification; if he classifies, it is so that he may the better feel, and feel *truly*.' And later: 'Nature put in order is not a different nature; it is the same, finally seen, finally felt, mastered in its profusion' (Pingaud: 2, 3; my trans.).

Not only is Lévi-Strauss stimulated by myth, poetry, and virtually all cultural productions to reason 'irrelevantly,' he induces us to do likewise: 'Faced with the challenge of a new point of view one is suddenly able to see the familiar in quite a different way and to understand something which was previously invisible' (Leach 1967a: xviii). Furthermore, this non-

Academic outlook—absolutely contrary to 'linear' *raison*—typifies the whole 'structuralist movement' centered in Paris; Peter Caws suggests its importance to various scholars:

> Why, Foucault asks, do we find Borges' imaginary Chinese classification so preposterous? Into what intellectual straitjacket has our own history forced us? And he concludes that our resistance to this kind of spontaneous absurdity, our demand for logical coherence even where it is unnecessary, is again a product of the invention of *man* as an embodiment of analytic reason (Caws: 86).

Perhaps France's ingrained Academic and encyclopedic traditions of *raison* and *bon sens* afford a solid foundation for negative reactions such as Symbolism and structuralism (but then stifle their '*fleuraison*'?). Be that as it may, this common interest in 'preposterous classifications' is partly responsible for the fact that many different sorts of current scholars in France have received the label 'structuralist'.

In addition to recognizing that his own methods are inspired by mythic logic, Lévi-Strauss praises previous thinkers who had similar inclinations. For example, Bergson and Rousseau seem to have penetrated 'the psychological foundations of exotic institutions . . . by a process of internalization, i.e., by trying on themselves modes of thought taken from elsewhere or simply imagined' (L-S 1963a: 103). Neologics! Thus, while certain periods or groups may tend more toward Symbolist-structuralist patterns of conceptualization, the latter are always potential: '. . . every human mind is a locus of virtual experience where what goes on in the minds of men, however remote they may be, can be investigated' (L-S 1963a: 103). Lévi-Strauss credits Bergson's insights into totemism to the fact that 'his own thought, unbeknownst to him, was in sympathy with that of totemic peoples' (the Sioux):

> What is it then that they have in common? It seems that the relationship results from one and the same desire to apprehend in a total fashion the two aspects of reality which the

P

philosopher terms *continuous* and *discontinuous*; from the refusal to choose between the two; and from the same effort to see them as complementary perspectives going on to the same truth (L-S 1963a: 98).

This same resolution between discontinuous and continuous relates to the Neological creed of 'filing it away for future reference.' The resolution is analogous to one between synchrony and diachrony that we have found characteristic of native myth and of both the forerunner and the culmination of our Symbolists—confessing Rousseau and Bergsonian Proust. The lived-to-the-hilt, continuous and unorganized present is filed away in the symbols of native myths, in the self-conscious repressions of Rousseau, and in the voluntary and involuntary memory of Proust. The future reference is made later when a myth is constructed, or when Rousseau and Proust set about recollecting their past, i.e., when new discontinuities are precipitated out of those prior discontinuities comprising the original perception of experience. The future reference to the already perceptually segmented stockpile of sensory input can be conscious or unconscious, but it is certainly Neological, bringing Proust in line with the Sioux.

Perhaps the most general characteristic of advocates of Neological codes is a devaluation of what Norman Brown designates 'Protestant literalism':

The return to symbolism would be the end of the Protestant era, the end of Protestant literalism.

Protestant literalism: the crux is the reduction of meaning to a single meaning—univocation.

Protestant literalism is modern scholarship.

Modern humanistic, literary, and historical scholarship . . . is the Renaissance counterpart of Reformation literalism (N. Brown: 191–4).

In his aphoristic *Love's Body*, Norman Brown pits against such literalism a host of thinkers including Freud, Blake, Durkheim's and Frazer's primitive groups, Mallarmé seen through Richard,

Nietzsche, McLuhan, Pascal, and Lévi-Strauss. The direct relationship between this anti-literalism and Symbolist criticism
is immediately obvious, when one remembers that it was Baudelaire who deemed the only valid commentary on a work of
art to be a poem: imaginative, although representative, constructs out of imaginative, although representative, constructs
out of. . . . Moreover, I would equate 'Protestant literalism'
with that very 'austérité du savant' which 'les Chats' seeks to
surmount as it bares crossed analogies; Lévi-Strauss bears an
analogous cross, in spirit, even if always limited by empirical
fact. The latter point brings us to the next level of this summary of various *non*-mutually-exclusive aspects of Lévi-Strauss'
work.

MIDDLE PATH OF INTERPRETATION

Some would say that what we have here are varieties of idealist
tendencies. And the present work might have been entitled
'Idealism as a Species,' as I now propose a system of transformations leading from one brand of idealism to another, in
order eventually to transform out of it. We have seen throughout both our -isms how the self is 'made manifest in "experience"'
and how character is constituted more by language than the
facts of experience (Uitti 1961: 47). From any idealist viewpoint this language-experience exists in and of the subject; for
scholars with structuralist tendencies 'the subject is an activity,
not a thing. . . . The subject produces itself by reflecting on itself,
but when it is engaged on some other object it has no being apart
from the activity of being so engaged' (Caws: 85). The ultimate denial of any possibility for a science of the subject stems
from the feeling that 'the subject cannot be the object of science
because it is its subject' (Caws: 85). Yet, once the self is
equated with processes of conceptualizing experience, there is
still an open range of idealist attitudes that can be assumed.
Both Symbolists and myth-makers ground 'reality'-as-conceived
in the structure of the transformations (correspondences) among
systems in orders arranged analogously. If the transformations
are regarded as *fixed* and permanently embedded in the person

of the creator (to which the world of experience is subordinated), what results is the narcissism such as that set forth in novelist Maurice Barrès' early work *Le Culte du Moi*. It is a somewhat different case when Lehmann speaks of the Symbolists' 'vulgar solipsism': 'At that level "idealism" meant simply the inalienable right to look on the world in whatever way one pleased; or to invent worlds on an equal with the "common sense world" ' (Lehmann: 40–44). From this vantage point any tendencies to consider, for example, Baudelaire's systems of correspondences fixed and 'natural' appear solipsistic. In the eyes of sympathizers Baudelaire would escape this charge through his assumption of a different realm which transcends the forest of symbols suggesting it. Both of these strains of idealism (narcissism and solipsism) would fall into Robert Champigny's first definition of Symbolism in which there is 'a symbolic usage of language in which the first signified is material and the second signified is spiritual' (Champigny: 128; my trans.). In Champigny's terms, Barrès' spiritual signified would be the psychological realm of himself and Baudelaire's would be a metaphysical realm; in both cases this spiritual signified is *ranked* above the material entity signified by the same language unit.

The binary opposition of the distinctive feature of these first two idealisms generates a second variety: idealisms of *non-fixed* systems of analogies. Mallarmé's arbitrarily, but consistently, constructed codes of symbols demonstrate this variety, as do the analogously structured native myths—whether consciously (analytically?) or not—from the analyzer's viewpoint. (Analogies are always fixed from a viewpoint within the poem-code or myth-code—i.e. from a non-comparative viewpoint). Champigny distinguishes this kind from the others by pointing out the absence of any hierarchical aspect:

Finally let us suppose that the relation between the signifieds be rendered symmetrical. One will thus have texts which are more or less clearly polysemic, wherein the themes will not each constitute an autonomous domain of meaning but will inform themselves one to the other in order to compose the global meaning. . . .

wherein the diverse themes outlined would inform themselves
one to the other (by correspondences, by resonances) (Champigny: 129–30; my trans.).

It is, of course, this 'modern' variety that has been a principal
concern in the present study.

If one then takes this rejection of an assumed hierarchy in
any particular set of transformable systems and applies it to
all systems—language especially—with equal enthusiasm, the
resulting brand of 'idealism' is what has been deemed, among
other things, the 'new humanism.' Take for example, Ernst
Cassirer:

> A 'humanistic philosophy of culture' is needed . . . to do
> justice to man and his freedom. The whole gamut of cultural
> phenomena bears witness to man's 'will to formations.' 'What
> man achieves is the objectification, the intuition of himself,
> in and through the theoretical, aesthetic, and ethical form
> which he gives to his existence. This is exhibited even in the
> very first promptings of human speech and it is unfolded and
> developed in rich and many-sided forms in poetry, in the
> fine arts, in religious consciousness, in philosophical concepts'
> (Hendel in Cassirer: 63).

Thus, if one remains skeptical over Lévi-Strauss' efforts to be
moving toward a demonstration of final structures of the human
esprit, he could still greet his work as this sort of humanism. Far
from brandishing a bland solipsism, Lévi-Strauss in light of
cross-cultural evidence determines to make of human productions Symbolist poems and of the producers poets, himself
not excluded. Like the Symbolists he admits his incapacity to
cope with 'crowds,' of the sort depicted in *Tristes Tropiques,*

> the agglomeration of individuals whose *raison* is to be ag-
> glomerated by millions, whatever the real conditions. Filth,
> disorder, promiscuity, caresses; ruins, shanties, mire, rubbish;
> humours, dung, urine, pus, secretions, sweat: . . . all that
> which we detest, . . . all these by-products of cohabitation . . .
> (L-S 1955: 133; my trans.).

Such bestial degradation, all too reminiscent of the state of humanity witnessed in the hold of his war-time ship of exile, leads Lévi-Strauss to seek out what elevates men onto the plane of culture. He proceeds to observe natives effecting their systems of aesthetic symmetry and asymmetry in spite of their material poverty and in spite of the desperate situation of an overpopulated and culturally intermingled world:

> Tu m'as donné ta boue et j'en ai fait de l'or (Baudelaire 1961: 220).[1]

Lévi-Strauss amasses evidence that what we are calling a Symbolist mode of encoding the *other* is universal in systems of meaning. And the general moral feeling that results is somewhat as follows: while we may never confront the other directly (substantively) in communicable terms, nevertheless, thanks to the human 'texts' that abound (which are, of course, always distorted by any subject collecting them), we at least have the fraternal comfort of knowing *they* are 'out there' translating; and we can too. Through his portrayal of this anthropological moral stance, through his taking possession 'of that untamed [*sauvage*] region of himself, unincorporated in his own culture, through which he communicates with other cultures' (Merleau-Ponty 1964a: 120), Lévi-Strauss has come to influence French intellectual life in general. For the suggestion that the stark relativity of cross-cultural experience eventually fulfills the individual by disaggregating his cultural self-centeredness complements a general thread of French moral thought. This notion of the individual as a potential locus of inter-communication in turn reflects a notion of life itself:

> Just as with discourse things, signs, and persons intertwine themselves in a single continuous fabric whose internal logic we unravel; so it is with life (Ortigues: 147; my trans.).

The striking feature of Lévi-Strauss' anthropology is that this Symbolist conception of existence does not justify withdrawing

[1] 'You gave me your mud, and I made of it gold' (my trans.).

from the world, but engaging in the world, the experience of which engendered the conception in the first place. And Lévi-Strauss comes to bear on his age:

> Faced with the two temptations of condemning things which are offensive to him emotionally or of denying differences which are beyond his intellectual grasp, modern man has launched out on countless lines of philosophical and sociological speculation in a vain attempt to achieve a compromise between these two contradictory poles, and to account for the diversity of cultures while seeking, at the same time, to eradicate what still shocks and offends him in that diversity (L-S 1952: 13).

It is against the above background that his structural approach to cultural phenomena has been accorded in France the rank of an '-ism.'

Yet what is now being summarized as a humanism—although negatively inspired, and most forcefully set forth in the invocation of Buddhism at the conclusion of *Tristes Tropiques*—has impressed other commentators as just the contrary. Kahn (1967), among others, considers structuralism to be an 'anti-humanism' which denies man's creative capacity. And Furet, in the wake of that confrontation between Lévi-Strauss and Sartre (see L-S 1966a, ch. 9), which aroused much of this sort of discussion, concludes as follows:

> Like Hegel and like Marx, Sartre as yet describes an advent (*avènement*), a history which realizes man; Lévi-Strauss reduces multiple man to his common mechanisms, dissolves him in universal determinism, displays him at the extreme as a natural object. His books, somewhat affectedly rigorous, are a commentary without hope on the nothingness of man (Furet: 9; my trans.).

However, this sort of criticism is misdirected. In the first place Lévi-Strauss' books would appear affectedly rigorous only if the reader assumed the author were merely trying to fabricate a view of human worth or lack thereof. But Lévi-Strauss does more. In fact, he primarily poses answers for empirical problems—such as 'why' (structurally) Australians classify their clans, as they *do*, or why New World Indians put canoes in the stars, as they *do*—which, then, appear to relate to more general aspects of human experience. Moreover, if Lévi-Strauss denies the intrinsic value of history, it is only in order to establish a firmer ground for humanism: to wit, human experience itself, which from its logical inception contains the principles whereby out of the nothingness of undifferentiation entire symphonies of interrelatable, sensory-based, self-fulfilling experience can be more or less communicated. There are limits, and if Lévi-Strauss is right, deterministic ones, but they are only demonstrable in the reasoned communication of the symphony, and not in our potential of feeling or living it. Furthermore, David Michael Levin has treated the Lévi-Strauss/Sartre issue as follows:

> The structural anthropologist, then, far from being detached from the life of man in any significant sense, *refuses* to understand existence in a purely formal manner, nor does he wish to construct a perfectly intelligible, perfectly ordered world with the arbitrary imagination of the poet; he is strongly committed, in fact, to the idea that the task that confronts the social scientist is, as Merleau-Ponty expressed it, 'to deepen our insertion in being.' Thus, contrary to what Sartre argues in his *Critique de la Raison Dialectique,* the anthropologist is not engaged in studying man the way entomologists study ants; but he must certainly have the faith, which Sartre apparently does not have, that history is not merely a 'rational disorder' (Levin: 73).

In sum, if I were looking about for a way to characterize the sort of humanism indirectly embodied in the works of Lévi-Strauss, I would borrow Michaud's description of Mallarmé's message:

> A metaphysics of nothingness and of absence, which is rather a refusal of metaphysics, wherein the *esprit* itself denies itself through affirming itself; an aesthetic which turns its back

on the real, but affirms essential relationships among things and obstinately seeks the infallible utterance which will re-produce the structure of them; rare poems, finally, feeble echoes of this sovereign utterance, detached fragments of the Work, but which each time reproduce its ordinance . . . (Michaud: 197; my trans.).

Mallarmé tries such affirmation himself; Lévi-Strauss tries it with the help of *others* first—different points of departure, but analogous points of view. And the points of view are directed toward the same locus of human experience-expressed in for-mulation—the locus here noted by Fiser on Proust:

This first confused impression opens the way towards the most obscure regions of the soul. Exploring this unknown depth [*ce fond inconnu*] is the goal of all symbolist art. And music is particularly designed to show us the richness, the variety of this part of our soul that we have taken for emptiness and nothingness (Fiser: 174; my trans.).

This *fond inconnu* becomes manifest in the effortful synthesis of disparate orders of experience, as when Mallarmé's Faun strives to piece together dream and reality. Symbolists generally leave the effort to the individual creator. Durkheim, reflecting on tribe-life, deemed the effortful synthesis the *social* and pro-claimed a new extra-individual 'level' for the ground of ex-perience, truly generating something out of what had been taken (analytically) 'for emptiness and nothing.' The *fond in-connu* surfaces during that moment of profound scintillation in which Lèvi-Strauss almost understands a Tupi-Kawahib; in which 'Ich liebe dich' makes *sense* to a two-week's student of German at his first performance of *Tristan*; in which a Faun nearly achieves perception through the sunlight of reawakening. It is the moment where one order encounters another and an effort toward translation is made. The *locus of this effort* is the subject of both Symbolism and structuralism. 'It is thus perfectly conceivable that ethnology represents a method of approach as eternal as humanity itself' (L-S in Gramont: 37).

DEEP STRUCTURAL INTERPRETATION

But we must take up the threads of our attempt to generate
'Idealism as a species.' For have we not moved out of reach
of the very category with its pre-requisite that two 'mega-
orders' be clearly delineable?

We had arrived at that modern variety of idealism which
entails two corresponding orders of significance (for example,
a so-called material order and a so-called conceptual one) with
no determinant direction specified. Yet curiously, when confronted with this modern variety, many observers sense an immediate need to impose a determinant direction. This is especially
true in the case of that peculiar combination of apparently
far-fetched analogies plus radical empiricism that distinguish
the orders interrelated in Lévi-Strauss' studies. Highlighting
the dilemma provoked by Lévi-Strauss, Robert Murphy ponders
in his article on 'Zen Marxism':

> Can one be positivist and a dialectician at one and the same
> time? This is a rather difficult feat, for positivism, the posi-
> tive definition of reality, is the philosophic obverse of dialects,
> or the negative definition of reality . . . (Murphy 1963: 18).

Yet Lévi-Strauss' refusal to categorize himself and his approach
in such terms is steadfast. Not only does he consider it futile
to try and specify whether the material determines the conceptual or vice versa, but he is remarkably cavalier in regards to
the question of whether native texts shape his analyses or his
analyses shape their texts. This latter attitude directly chal-
lenges the feasibility of maintaining one of anthropology's principal concerns: 'Is my analysis *my* idea of what the natives do
or their idea?' Furthermore, Lévi-Strauss' decided refusal to
assign any direction to communicated messages—for example,
whether material messages inform ideational ones or vice versa,
or whether his messages inform his natives' messages or vice
versa—is interpreted by many anthropologists as crafty solipsism
supported by distorted data. Furet summarizes several of these
controversial issues brought out by Lévi-Strauss' work:

. . . one never really knows if the logical structure brought to light by the analysis is of the same nature as the material, produced by the material, or if on the contrary the structure informs reality. In fact, the problem of knowing if he is himself materialist or Kantian . . . is of little interest to Lévi-Strauss, who appears to accept both hypotheses: that is to say that in any case he is but secondarily interested in his philosophical relationships with Marxism (Furet: 10; my trans.).

This reluctance to so characterize his work is topped off by Lévi-Strauss' assertion that he is finally concerned with some sort of *esprit*, which is itself likewise difficult to pin down as ideational, material, or just what.[2] But Lévi-Strauss will not co-operate with those who seek to apply such labels, because he is engaged in demonstrating the lack of suitability of the labels themselves. There is order, but not on the level of perceivable phenomena as generally conceived. Thus, the order must be on some other level, to which direct access (at least by rational means) is denied. One is limited to effecting interpolations onto the level of order from empirical data ('texts') which itself reveals order only indirectly. Lévi-Strauss' program, then, joins that very 'death of dualism' which we have persistently

[2] Leach's complaint is voiced in this fashion: 'Lévi-Strauss' *esprit* appears in sundry guises. In 1952, originally in English, he/it was a personalized "human mind" . . .; in the earlier chapters of *La Pensée sauvage* he is perhaps the *bricoleur* . . .; at the conclusion of *Le Cru et le cuit*, in more abstract and more serious [?] vein, *esprit* seems to be a kind of limiting characteristic of the human brain mechanism. . . . Elsewhere again *esprit* seems to correspond to that very mysterious something which is a mediator between "praxis et pratiques" and which is described as "le schème conceptuel par l'opération duquel une matière et une forme, dépourvues l'une et l'autre d'existence indépendante, s'accomplissent comme structures, c'est-à-dire comme êtres à la fois empiriques et intelligibles' ['the conceptual schema through whose operation a matter and a form, each of them deprived of an independent existence, are accomplished as structures, that is to say as existences at once empirical and intelligible' (my trans. of Leach's quotation from L-S 1962a: 173)]. Now although I am entranced by the images which such verbal felicity calls to mind, I have to confess that, when it comes to the crunch, I have no clear idea of what it is that Lévi-Strauss is really talking about. This is my deficiency not his . . . (Leach 1969: 25–6).

encountered along the course of this study. A final encounter is called for.

In *The Phenomenon of Life* Hans Jonas describes both the intellectual contradictions left by the rigid Cartesian distinction between 'mind' and 'matter' and also a means to resolve those contradictions. He summarizes the resolution in this way:

> It follows that in the postdualistic situation there are, on principle, not one but two possibilities of monism, represented by modern materialism and modern idealism respectively: they both presuppose the ontological polarization which dualism had generated, and either takes its stand in one of the two poles, to comprehend from this vantage point the whole of reality. They are thus in their origin, though certainly not in their intention, partial monisms. . . . There is no returning to this: dualism had not been an arbitrary invention, for the two-ness which it asserts is grounded in reality itself. A new, integral, i.e., philosophical monism cannot undo the polarity: it must absorb it into a higher unity of existence from which the opposites issue as faces of its being or phases of its becoming. It must take up the problem which originally gave rise to dualism (Jonas: 16–17).

Jonas argues that the problem can best be taken up by considering the situation of the human *body* in experience:

> Dualism, when its work was done, had left behind the 'extended' as the lifeless and unfeeling, and the body undeniably is a part of this extended: either, then, it is essentially the same as the extended in general—then its being alive is not understood; or it is *sui generis*—then the exception claimed for it is not to be understood and calls into question the whole rule, i.e., the materialist interpretation of substance as such along the pure properties of indifferent extension. The same goes, *mutatis mutandis*, for the other side, that of idealist consciousness. . . .
> . . . life and inwardness are really extended through [the body] ('to the tips of my fingers'), it really is 'I'—then it is, even

though phenomenally extended, not an *idea* of consciousness but the actual outward extent of its own inner spatiality which itself occupies space in the world: and therewith it calls into question the whole idealist interpretation of consciousness as opposed to the entire world of extension (Jonas: 18–19).

As we have seen, Lévi-Strauss' mythic thinking calls into question the same idealist interpretation. His refusal to accept any idealist/materialist dichotomy and his acknowledgement of the label 'Kantism without a transcendental subject' (which is no Kantism at all) suggests how near Lévi-Strauss is to the position of William James, as reassessed by John Wild in light of recent phenomenologists (especially Merleau-Ponty):

. . . James holds the seemingly paradoxical view that it is precisely the bodily self, as an object among others in experience, that also knows and finds meaning in the world. It is precisely the objective self that is directly felt to be the subject of experience. But in the Kantian scheme, there seems to be no place for any direct self-consciousness of this kind. The objective self never knows itself as a subject, and the transcendental subject never becomes a real object by inserting itself in the world. This is the most basic difference between the two theories. . . .

By bringing a multiplicity of data to be known *inside* the mind, Kant has confused the unitary act of knowing with the plurality of objects to be known, and has thus ignored the intentional structure of all objective knowledge (Wild: 108–9).

Mention of the 'bodily self' recalls to mind Merleau-Ponty and his concern, derived from Gestalt psychology, with the body as the locus of sight in experience (experience which includes sight of the body itself). Merleau-Ponty proclaims dualism's demise through the circuit constituting human vision in the act of seeing:

Vision encounters, as at the crossroads, all the aspects of Being. . . .
There is no break at all in this circuit; it is impossible to

say that nature ends here and that man or expression starts here. It is, therefore, mute Being which itself comes to show forth its own meaning. . . .

Suppose, then, that one answers that no thought ever detaches itself completely from a sustaining support; that the only privilege of speaking-thought is to have rendered its own support manageable; that the figurations of literature and philosophy are no more settled than those of painting and are no more capable of being accumulated into a stable treasure; that even science learns to recognize a zone of the 'fundamental,' peopled with dense, open, rent [*déchirés*] beings of which an exhaustive treatment is out of the question —like the cyberneticians' 'aesthetic information' or mathematical-physical 'groups of operations'; that, in the end, we are never in a position to take stock of everything objectively or to think of progress in itself; and that the whole of human history is, in a certain sense, stationary. *What*, says the understanding, like (Stendhal's) Lamiel, *is it only that*?

Is this the highest point of reason, to realize that the soil beneath our feet is shifting, to pompously name 'interrogation' what is only a persistent state of stupor, 'research' or 'quest' to call what is only trudging in a circle, 'Being' to call that which never fully *is*?

But this disappointment issues from that spurious fantasy which claims for itself a positivity capable of making up for its own emptiness. It is the regret of not being everything, and a rather groundless regret at that. For if we cannot establish a hierarchy of civilizations or speak of progress—neither in painting nor in anything else that matters—it is not because some fate holds us back; it is, rather, because the very first painting in some sense went to the farthest reach of the future. If no painting comes to be *the* painting, if no work is ever absolutely completed and done with, still each creation changes, alters, enlightens, deepens, confirms, exalts, recreates, or creates in advance all the others. If creations are not a possession, it is not only that, like all things, they pass away; it is also that they have almost all their life still before them (Merleau-Ponty 1964b: 188, 189–90).

While any judicious balance between quotation and exposition would have required me somehow to abbreviate the above, I could not see how to do it. How fitting that Lévi-Strauss dedicated *La Pensée sauvage* to the memory of Merleau-Ponty. And how fully *Mythologiques* comes to bear on this vision of the limitless creative potential that can be achieved simply through transformations across systems of sensory orders—the transformer himself (truly of the world) being such a transformation, through communication with his *social* order.

Indeed, Merleau-Ponty's own interest in anthropology 'From Mauss to Lévi-Strauss' testifies his appreciation of the fact that comparative studies (showing how men become socially-and thereby self-conscious) can be put with other processes of highlighted sensory perception (such as the process of painting) to reveal how 'things' become:

> There thus appears at the base of social systems a formal infrastructure (one is tempted to say an unconscious thought), an anticipation of the human mind [*l'esprit humain*], as if our science were already completed in events [*les choses*], and the human order of culture a second order of nature dominated by other invariants (Merleau-Ponty 1964a: 118–19).

Throughout these sorts of observations, in the absence of any determinant direction among analytic orders, a determinant structuring 'somewhere else,' beyond the individual, is posited. As Gaboriau notes:

> If we abandon unification by history, do we not risk falling back into pure diversity? Lévi-Strauss avoids this danger by seeking unity at a more radical level: that of the conditions for the possibility of any social organization (Gaboriau: 583–4; my trans.).

At times Lévi-Strauss is very explicit in maintaining that cultural productions can serve as a vehicle for expressing, sometimes quite straightforwardly, orderings to be found in nature: 'But the outstanding fact about style is that the human mind is working unconsciously along lines similar to nature's' (L-S in Tax: 62). Or consider the following suggestion:

> I think nothing would be more urgent in the field of cultural anthropology than to make a topological theory of string figures, because this would show that, according to the population which is being considered, certain sets of topological transformations were chosen while other sets were ignored, and it would be important to find out whether in kinship, mythology, or linguistics we are confronted with the same basic choices (L-S in Tax: 306).

Thus cat's cradles, for example, are a picture of mind, a picture of ordering a natural element uninteresting in its own right. While further levels of significance may be encoded in the string figure's terms—such as personages it represents or legends it recalls—basically the figure manifests the expressing of order, call it *esprit* if you will. The important fact is that sets of topological contrasts are selected, as are sets of phonological contrasts, as are sets of color contrasts, as are sets of rhythmic contrasts, and so on through all the distinctive features of perception. And the sets themselves are more or less interrelated, likewise by contrast and analogy. Thus Nature becomes communication, and a tautology is in order:

> If the passage from laws of nature to laws of information is legitimate, then the passage in the inverse direction—that which goes from laws of information to laws of nature—must be also: it is that very passage which for millennia has been operating savage thought (Cuisenier: 549; my trans.).

But really, any dreamed-of final *structure*—the *esprit* itself—should not concern us too much. For if it were ever derived science would be past and Nature attained. Yet positing the *esprit* is crucial, even though we analyzers are restricted to occasional and partial glimpses of it; for it is no less than *the denial of chaos in the absence of determinism*. Nevertheless, a structural analysis can proceed quite adequately without espousing a totalized view of the nature of *l'esprit humain*. A recommendation by Cuisenier helps us make the point:

> . . . *The Savage Mind* ought to be submitted to two different readings. On the one hand it is necessary to seek in the work a theory of the forms of thought, which explains observable conceptual configurations by properties which belong intrinsically to certain logical structures. But on the other hand, it is necessary to follow the argument supporting a thesis on thought, which identifies mental processes with the most general laws of information (Cuisenier: 563; my trans.).

The Savage Mind can be read for the first interest alone, or for both the arguments mentioned above. Finally, with the aid of considerable self-identification, *La Pensée sauvage* can be taken as a means of insight into man's *esprit*, ultimately derived from (at one with) nature, especially insofar as that book preludes *Mythologiques*. Yet the three types of readings are relatively independent. I personally find rather reassuring the final notion that human communication is limited by the same sort of structural principles that appear to govern natural phenomena; my sense of dignity remains unscathed, as I would sooner fall within the limitations of nature than the liberty of free-thinkers. However, the validity of Lévi-Strauss' structural analysis does not rest on this point. One proceeds without ever situating *l'esprit*, perhaps occasionally *sensing* its locus to be nature, but never foreseeing a *proof* of this. All that is certain is that man's *esprit* is *social*, is located outside conscious awareness, is irreducibly manifested in *exchange*, and is most readily reflected in language.

From there perhaps Uitti through an interpretation of Katz interpreting Chomsky suggests, at least provisionally, the best outlook to assume:

> Katz defends the generative grammar of Chomsky, a new 'structuralism' based, we recall, on rationalist theory of conceptualization—innate ideas. He declares that 'the genetic endowment of a human being qua human being is the only

Q

invariant feature of language acquisition contexts which can causally account for non-verbal infants achieving a successful internalization of languages having the universal properties described in the theory of language' (p. 273). Cartesian doctrine 'works.' What about the question of a priori knowledge? Discussing this question, Katz hits on the essence of structuralist freedom: its 'objectivity' and the nature of the 'informed opinion' on which its statements are based: 'That any particular one of the principles in the theory of language is a priori is, then, a consequence of the empirical success of the explanation of language acquisition which employs it *and so accords it the status of an innate principle*' (p. 282, italics mine). Evidence contradicting the innate principle, as stated, merely leads to the formulation of a better 'innate principle.' What is important here, then, is the *activity* Katz associates with 'philosophy' (Uitti 1969: 252–3).[3]

The analogy to be drawn is between this variety of 'innate principle' and Lévi-Strauss' *structures*. Any final structure is never known but always approached; empirical data can be ever more adequately informed.[4] Lévi-Strauss likewise emphasizes the activity of methodological analysis, foregoing any chance for *final* results, as priority falls to the process of translating 'texts' to 'texts' to ...:

Il ne s'agit pas de voguer vers d'autres terres, leur situation fût-elle inconnue et leur existence hypothétique. Le renversement qu'on propose est beaucoup plus radical: seul le voyage est réel, non la terre, et les routes sont remplacées par les règles de navigation (L-S 1964a: 33).

. . . .

It is not a question of sailing towards other lands, were their situation unknown and their existence hypothetical. The in-

---

[3] Compare Panofsky's discussion of his *circulus methodicus* (see p. 130).
[4] For a more thorough and systematic treatment of these basic epistemological issues in Lévi-Strauss' work, see the series of articles by Hugo G. Nutini (1965, 1970, 1971).

version proposed is much more radical: only the voyage is real, not the land; and routes are replaced by rules of navigation (my trans.).

It is precisely such rules of navigation that are at once the conditions for and the object of *Mythologiques*—this comparativist course Lévi-Strauss steers through New World preliterate 'texts'. The *structures* he uncovers are in fact directions for how to *undo* various operations (i.e. correspondences, inversion, transformation) that the ethnographic evidence suggests have been done. (Note that this is not the same as deriving directions which presume to show how to *reproduce* the operations that have been done.) He uses the analytic device of binary opposition to detect possible operations (we might say 'encodings') that are evidenced in compounded fashion throughout some mythic corpus (he also uses the operations detected to delineate a 'corpus'). In sum, the structures are retrospective, large scale representations *of* paths that operations connecting sensory items-as-conceived have followed, and more precisely of paths followed by those operations most involved in cross-cultural borrowing (*exchange* of mythic motifs) across different language groups. Finally, the structures are deterministic in the sense that they embody the 'conditions for the possibility' of conceiving any mythic organization.

Yet only the voyage is real. The social-textual data is never fully grasped, never definitively reached. We do not grasp the myth; we employ the myth to carry us on to another. In the absence of grasping, satisfaction lies in portraying the dawn of significant forms, arising out of freshly tapped orders—orders that do not obviously pertain to the behavioristic needs of the human organism. It is such dawns of complex significative-normative systems that Lévi-Strauss finds recorded in the mythic order of New World preliterates—dawns of musical forms keyed to rite, of cooking and eating customs keyed to moral necessity, of solar constellations keyed to varieties of periodicity. (As we have seen, it is likewise the discernment of such dawns that Lévi-Strauss appreciates in Saussure's concept of linguistics and in Jakobson's poetics.) The dawns occur as discontinuous features are precipitated out of what might (it seems) well have remained insignificant continuity (call it Nothingness). The precipitation of such features has as its prerequisite that other features be already precipitated for the former to be differentiated *according to*. That is why we can never attain knowledge of 'cultural' origins; but at least such dawns smack of principles of originality (albeit 'later on'). Finally, these principles of originality that inform vast amounts of empirical data are analogous to the principles programmed into Symbolists' texts—texts which reveal their authors' personal dawns of multivocal, sensory-based, now normative, corresponding significations.

Only the voyage is real. This conservative view strikes me as the spirit of so-called modern criticism, one text being beyond itself the means towards yet another. This view has licensed my often using secondary and tertiary sources (e.g. Uitti on Katz on Chomsky) in lieu of primary ones, since critics are themselves efforts toward interpretations, and I am in this study at most a tertiary source. No doubt, though, Proust tells us better than anyone what Proust is about; and I would say the same of Lévi-Strauss. But if it were as simple as that, where would that have left us and this? Well, likewise preliterates themselves tell us best what they are about—but, more obviously in their case, not necessarily in the most communicable fashion from the addressee's point of view. Thus, I have drawn on critics trying to make their Symbolist subjects more communicable to more addressees, in order to make Lévi-Strauss (really my interpretations of Lévi-Strauss) more communicable to more addressees—not better. Be that as it may, 'only the work itself, completed and understood, is proof that there was *something* rather than *nothing* to be said' (Merleau-Ponty 1964c: 19). *Understood?* That leaves the matter in your hands. If the 'odds and ends' of the first chapter seem no more ordered now than then, we can both take heart in the belief that 'a sketchy knowledge or a total misunderstanding can be a fruitful aesthetic stimulus' (C. Brown: 77). This book—a dialectic between Symbolist poetics and structural mythologics—attempts to establish harmonious correspondences between the analytically isolated

approaches of literary criticism and anthropology and to surmount certain contradictions between the two. As such, the
book embraces the goal of all myth-like classificatory systems,
which 'however well or badly made, aim always to make sense'
(L-S 1966a: 228). And since an all-encompassing myth, even
a very personal one, should never be terminated, I take this
opportunity to direct us more or less full circle, hopefully at a
higher vantage point than our place of departure, 'epigram-
matically':

> When you notice a cat in profound meditation,
> The reason, I tell you, is always the same:
> His mind is engaged in a rapt contemplation
> Of the thought, of the thought, of the thought of his name:
> His ineffable effable
> Effanineffable
> Deep and inscrutable singular Name
> —from T. S. Eliot (1939)
> *The Naming of Cats.*

Le dossier n'est jamais clos (L-S 1964a: 13).[5]

[5] As if to verify this closing remark, while proofs of this study were
being corrected, there appeared the final volume of *Mythologiques* (L-S
1971 *L'Homme nu*. Paris, Plon). Some passages in volume IV which
corroborate our interpretation include epigrams from Baudelaire, Mallarmé, Wagner, and Proust (pp. 75, 317, 409, 502, etc.); praise of Proust's
musical sensitivity (p. 586) and a revitalization of the music-mythic
analogy; rebuttal of criticisms that he ignores affectivity (p. 596; cf. p. 182
above); reassertion of the Baudelarian position that portions of 'texts' can
be analytically interpreted only insofar as 'they participate in the same
intellectual nature as that activity which strives to understand them'
(p. 596; cf. p. 118 above)—hence a 'myth of mythology'; and finally a
bold summary of the *comparative* basis of mythological analysis: '. . . these
relations of opposition between myths emerge vigorously from a comparative analysis. If the philological study of myths does not constitute an
indispensable preliminary approach, the reason lies in what one might
call myths' diacritical nature. Every transformation of myths results from
a dialectical opposition to another transformation, and their essence resides
in the irreducible fact of translation *by* and *for* opposition. [A myth] is
situated not *in* a language and *in* a culture or sub-culture, but at the
point of articulation of cultures with other languages and other cultures.
Myth is thus never in its language [*de sa langue*], it is a perspective on
another language . . .' (p. 577). There is much more; for even with
L'Homme nu in hand, 'le dossier n'est jamais clos'.

References

ABEL, Lionel. 1970 'Sartre vs. Lévi-Strauss'. *In* (Hayes and Hayes 1970: 235–46).

ARNOLD, Paul. 1968 Charles Baudelaire and the sense of engulfment'. In *Perspectives in literary symbolism*. Joseph Strelka, ed. University Park, The Pennsylvania State University Press.

AUERBACH, Eric. 1957 *Mimesis: the representation of reality in Western literature*. Willard Trask, trans. New York, Doubleday Anchor Books.

BACKÈS-CLÉMENT, Catherine. 1970 *Lévi-Strauss ou la structure et le malheur*. Paris, Éditions Seghers.

BALAKIAN, Anna Elizabeth. 1967 *The symbolist movement: a critical appraisal*. New York, Random House.

BARTHES, Roland. 1967 'Proust et les noms'. In *To honor Roman Jakobson*, vol. I. The Hague, Mouton, pp. 150–8.

BATAILLE, Georges. 1956 'Un livre humain, un grand livre'. *Critique* 10 (105): 99–112.

BAUDELAIRE,Charles. 1925 *L'Art romantique*. Paris, L. Conard.

BAUDELAIRE, Charles. 1951 *Œuvres complètes*. Paris, Gallimard.

BAUDELAIRE, Charles. 1961 *Les Fleurs du mal*. Paris, Garnier Frères.

BAUDELAIRE, Charles. 1964 *The painter of modern life and other essays*. Jonathan Mayne, ed. and trans. London, Phaidon Press.

BECKER, Ernest. 1968 *The structure of evil: an essay on the unification of the sciences of man*. New York, George Braziller.

BECKETT, Samuel. 1931 *Proust*. London, Chatto & Windus.

BERNSTEIN, Leonard. 1959 *The joy of music*. New York, Simon and Schuster.

BLAKE, William. 1953 Selected poetry and prose. Northrop Frye, ed. New York, Random House.

BOHANNAN, Paul. 1960 *'Conscience collective* and culture'. In *Essays on sociology and philosophy by Emile Durkheim* et al. Kurt H. Wolf, ed. New York, Harper Torchbooks, pp. 77–96.

BOON, James A. 1970 'Lévi-Strauss and narrative'. *Man* 5 (4): 702–3.

BOON, James A. 1971 'Lévi-Strauss, Claude'. *The Encyclopaedia Britannica*, 1971 edition.

BRAUN, Sidney D., ed. 1958 *Dictionary of French literature.* Greenwich, Conn., Fawcett Publications.

BROOKS, Cleanth. 1947 *The well wrought urn.* New York, Harcourt, Brace & World.

BROWN, Calvin S. 1967 'The musical analogies in Mallarmé's *Un coup de dés'. Comparative Literature Studies,* 4 (1–2): 67–79.

BROWN, Norman O. 1968 *Love's body.* New York, Vintage Books.

BUCHLER, Ira R. and SELBY, Henry A. 1968 *Kinship and social organization.* New York, Macmillan.

BURKE, Kenneth. 1962 *A grammar of motives and a rhetoric of motives.* New York, Meridian Books.

BURKE, Kenneth. 1964 *Terms for order.* Stanley Edgar Hyman, ed. Bloomington, Indiana University Press.

BURRIDGE, K. L. O. 1967 'Lévi-Strauss and myth'. *In* (Leach 1967a: 91–115).

CASSIRER, Ernst. 1953 *The philosophy of symbolic forms, vol. I: language.* Ralph Manheim, trans. Introduction by Charles W. Hendel. New Haven, Yale University Press.

CAWS, Peter. 1968 'What is structuralism?' *Partisan Review* XXXV (1): 75–91.

CHAMPIGNY, Robert. 1967 'Trois définitions du symbolisme'. *Comparative Literature Studies* 4 (1–2): 127–33.

CHARBONNIER, Georges. 1961 *Entretiens avec Claude Lévi-Strauss.* Paris, Plon-Julliard.

CHARVET, P. E. 1967 *A literary history of France, vol. V, 1870–1940.* New York, Barnes & Noble.

CHENEY, Theodore. 1968 'The power of irrelevant thinking'. *Moderator*, February, 1968.

CHOMSKY, Noam. 1966 *Cartesian linguistics: a chapter in the history of rationalist thought*. New York, Harper & Row.

CLASTRES, Pierre. 1965 'Entre silence et dialogue'. *L'Arc* 26.

COHEN, Percy S. 1969 'Theories of myth'. *Man* 4 (3): 337–53.

COHN, Robert Greer. 1965 *Toward the poems of Mallarmé*. Berkeley, University of California Press.

CUISENIER, Jean. 1963 'Formes de la parenté et formes de la pensée'. *Esprit* 322: 547–63.

DOUGLAS, Mary. 1967 'The meaning of myth'. *In* (Leach 1967a: 49–69.

DUMONT, Louis. 1966 'Descent or intermarriage? a relational view of Australian section systems'. *Southwestern Journal of Anthropology* 22 (3): 231–50.

DUMONT, Louis. 1967 *Homo hierarchicus*. Paris, Gallimard.

DURKHEIM, Émile. 1897 'La prohibition de l'inceste et ses origines'. *L'Année Sociologique I*: 1–70.

DURKHEIM, Émile. 1963. *Incest: the nature and origin of the taboo*. Edward Sagarin, trans. New York, Lyle Stuart, Inc.

DURKHEIM, Émile. 1965 *The elementary forms of the religious life*. New York, The Free Press.

DURKHEIM, Émile and MAUSS, Marcel. 1963 *Primitive classification*. Rodney Needham, trans. Chicago, University of Chicago Press.

ELIADE, Mircea. 1959 *The sacred and the profane*. Willard R. Trask, trans. New York, Harper Torchbooks.

ELIOT, T. S. 1939 *Old Possum's book of practical cats*. London, Faber & Faber.

ESBROECK, Michel van. 1968 *Herméneutique, structuralisme et exégèse*. Paris, Desclée.

Esprit. 1963 322.

EVANS-PRITCHARD, E. E. 1965 *Theories of primitive religion*. Oxford, Clarendon Press.

FISER, Emeric. 1943 *Le symbole littéraire; essai sur la significa-tion du symbole chez Wagner, Baudelaire, Mallarmé, Bergson et Marcel Proust.* Paris, Librairie José Corti.

FOWLIE, Wallace. 1962 *Mallarmé.* Chicago, Phoenix books.

FOWLIE, Wallace. 1968 *The French critic: 1549–1967.* Carbon-dale, Southern Illinois University Press.

FREEDMAN, Ralph. 1967 'Symbol as terminus: some notes on symbolist narrative', *Comparative Literature Studies* 4 (1–2): 135–43.

FURET, François. 1967 'Les intellectuels français et le structural-isme'. *Preuves* 192: 3–12.

GABORIAU, Marc. 1963 'Anthropologie structurale et histoire'. *Esprit* 322: 579–95.

GAUSS, Charles Edward. 1949 *The aesthetic theories of French artists, 1855 to the present.* Baltimore, John Hopkins Press.

GEERTZ, Clifford. 1967 'The cerebral savage: on the work of Claude Lévi-Strauss'. *Encounter* XXVIII (4): 25–32.

GELLNER, Ernest. 1958 'Time and theory in social anthropology'. *Mind* LXVII (266): 182–202.

GENETTE, Gérard. 1965 'Structuralisme et critique littéraire'. *L'Arc* 26.

GIBSON, Robert. 1961 *Modern French poets on poetry.* Cam-bridge University Press.

GODDARD, David. 1965 'Conceptions of structure in Lévi-Strauss and in British anthropology'. *Social Research* 32 (4): 408–27.

GOODENOUGH, Ward H. 1969 'Frontiers of cultural anthropology: social organization'. *Proceedings of the American Philoso-phical Society* 113 (5): 329–35.

GOODENOUGH, Ward H. 1970 *Description and comparison in cultural anthropology.* Chicago, Aldine Publishing Company.

GOODY, Jack, ed. 1968 *Literacy in traditional societies.* Cam-bridge University Press.

GRAMONT, Sanche de. 1968 'There are no superior societies'. *New York Times Magazine*, January 28, 1968.

GUTHRIE, Ramon and DILLER, George E. eds. 1942 *French litera-ture and thought since the revolution.* New York, Harcourt, Brace and World.

R

HARRIS, Marvin. 1968 *The rise of anthropological theory*. New York, Thomas Y. Crowell Company.

HARTLEY, Anthony, ed. and trans. 1965 *Mallarmé*. Baltimore, Penguin Books.

HAYES, E. Nelson and HAYES, Tanya, eds. 1970 *Claude Lévi-Strauss: The anthropologist as hero*. Cambridge: M.I.T. Press.

HEUSCH, Luc de. 1963 'Anthropologie structurale et symbolisme'. *Cahiers Internationaux de symbolisme* 2, pp. 51–66.

HEUSCH, Luc de. 1968 'Les points de vue structuralistes en anthropologie et leurs principaux champs d'application'. In *The Social Sciences, Problems and Orientations*. The Hague, Mouton/UNESCO.

HYMES, Dell. 1964 'Directions in (ethno-) linguistic theory. Transcultural Studies in Cognition'. *American Anthropologist* 66 (3, part 2): 6–56.

HYSLOP, Lois Boe and HYSLOP, Francis E. Jr., intro. and trans. 1964 *Baudelaire as a literary critic*. University Park, Pennsylvania State University Press.

JAKOBSON, Roman. 1960 'Concluding statement: linguistics and poetics'. In *Style and Language*. Thomas A. Sebeok, ed. Cambridge, M.I.T. Press, pp. 350–77.

JACKOBSON, Roman. 1970 Chapter on linguistics in *International study on the main trends of research in the social and human sciences*, vol. I. The Hague, Mouton/UNESCO.

JAKOBSON, Roman and HALLE, Morris. 1956 'Fundamentals of language'. *Janua Linguarum* I, The Hague, Mouton.

JAKOBSON, Roman and LÉVI-STRAUSS, Claude. 1962 ' "Les Chats" de Charles Baudelaire'. *L'Homme* II (1): 5–21.

JOHANSEN, Svend. 1945 *Le symbolisme*. Copenhagen, Einar Munksgaard.

JONAS, Hans. 1966 *The phenomenon of life: toward a philosophical biology*. New York, Delta Books.

KAHN, Jean-François. 1967 'La minutieuse conquête du structuralisme'. *L'Express* 844: 39–41.

KATZ, Jerrold J. 1966 *The philosophy of language*. New York, Harper & Row.

KAY, Paul. 1970 'Some theoretical implications of ethnographic semantics'. *Current Directions in Anthropology, Bulletin of the American Anthropological Association* 3 (3, part 2).

KIDDER, Alfred II. 1968 'Two Peruvian frogs'. *Expedition* 10 (4): 8–9.

KORN, F. 1969 'An analysis of the use of the term "model" in some of Lévi-Strauss' works'. *Bijdragen tot de Taal-, Land-en Volkenkunde* 125 (1): 1–11.

LANE, Michael, ed. 1970 *Structuralism: a reader*. London, Jonathan Cape.

LANGER, Suzanne K. 1951 *Philosophy in a new key*. New York, Mentor Books.

LANGER, Suzanne K. 1953 *Feeling and form*. New York, Scribner's.

LEACH, Edmund. 1965a 'Claude Lévi-Strauss—anthropologist and philosopher'. *New Left Review* 34.

LEACH, Edmund. 1965b 'Lévi-Strauss in the Garden of Eden'. In *Reader in comparative religion*. William A. Lessa and Evon Z. Vogt, eds. New York, Harper & Row, pp. 574–81.

LEACH, Edmund. 1965c Review of *Mythologiques I: Le Cru et le cuit. American Anthropologist* 67 (3): 776–80.

LEACH, Edmund. 1967a *The structural study of myth and totemism*, London, Tavistock Publications.

LEACH, Edmund. 1967b 'Brain-twister'. *New York Review of Books* 9 (6): 6–10.

LEACH, Edmund. 1968 'The comparative method in anthropology'. *International Encyclopaedia of the Social Sciences, vol. I*, pp. 339–45. Macmillan & The Free Press.

LEACH, Edmund. 1969 'The legitimacy of Soloman'. In *Genesis as myth and other essays*. London, Jonathan Cape.

LEACH, Edmund. 1970 *Lévi-Strauss*. London, Fontana Modern Masters Series.

LEFEBVRE, Henri. 1966 'Claude Lévi-Strauss et le nouvel éléatisme'. *L'Homme et la Société* 1 (1–2).

LEHMANN, A. G. 1950 *The symbolist aesthetic in France, 1885–1895*. Oxford, Basil Blackwell. (Second edition, 1968).

Lévi-Strauss, Claude. 1944 'The social and psychological aspect of chieftainship in a primitive tribe'. *Transactions of the New York Academy of Sciences*, series II, 7: 16–32.

Lévi-Strauss, Claude. 1946a 'French sociology'. In *Sociology in the twentieth century*. Georges Gurvitch and Wilbert E. Moore, eds. New York, The Philosophical Library, pp. 503–37.

Lévi-Strauss, Claude. 1946b 'The name of the Nambikware'. *American Anthropologist* 48: 139–40.

Lévi-Strauss, Claude. 1949 *Les structures élémentaires de la parenté*. Paris, Presses Universitaires de France.

Lévi-Strauss, Claude. 1950 'Introduction à l'oeuvre de Marcel Mauss'. In Marcel Mauss, *Sociologie et anthropologie*. Paris, Presses Universitaires de France.

Lévi-Strauss, Claude. 1952 *Race and history*. Paris, UNESCO.

Lévi-Strauss, Claude. 1954a 'What is a primitive?' *Le Courrier* 8–9, Paris, UNESCO.

Lévi-Strauss, Claude. 1954b 'The art of deciphering symbols'. *Diogenes* 5: 102–8.

Lévi-Strauss, Claude. 1955 *Tristes tropiques*. Paris, Plon.

Lévi-Strauss, Claude. 1956 'The family'. In *Man, culture, and society*. Harry L. Shapiro, ed. New York, Oxford University Press.

Lévi-Strauss, Claude. 1958 *Anthropologie structurale*. Paris, Plon.

Lévi-Strauss, Claude. 1960a 'Four Winnebago myths. A structural sketch'. In *Culture and history*. S. Diamond, ed. New York, Columbia University Press.

Lévi-Strauss, Claude. 1960b 'La structure et la forme. Réflexions sur un ouvrage de Vladimir Propp'. *Cahiers de l'Institut de Sciences Economiques Appliquées (Recherches et dialogues philosophiques et économiques)* 7 (99).

Lévi-Strauss, Claude. 1961a (Charbonnier, G.) *Entretiens avec Claude Lévi-Strauss*. Paris, Plon.

Lévi-Strauss, Claude. 1961b *Tristes tropiques*. John Russell, trans. New York, Atheneum.

Lévi-Strauss, Claude. 1962a *La Pensée sauvage*. Paris, Plon.

Lévi-Strauss, Claude. 1962b (with Roman Jakobson). ' "Les Chats" de Charles Baudelaire'. *L'Homme* 2 (1): 5–21.

LÉVI-STRAUSS, Claude. 1962c 'Rousseau, father of anthropology'. UNESCO *Courier*, 1963, 16 (3): 10–15.

LÉVI-STRAUSS, Claude. 1962d 'Les limites de la notion de structure en ethnologie'. In *Sens et usages du terme structure*. R. Bastide, ed. *Janua Linguarum* 16. The Hague, Mouton, pp. 40–5.

LÉVI-STRAUSS, Claude. 1963a *Totemism*. Rodney Needham, trans. Boston, Beacon Press.

LÉVI-STRAUSS, Claude. 1963b *Structural anthropology*. C. Jacobson and B. Grundfest Schoepf, trans. New York, Basic Books.

LÉVI-STRAUSS, Claude. 1963c 'Réponses'. *Esprit* 322, pp. 628–53.

LÉVI-STRAUSS, Claude. 1963d 'The bear and the barber'. *Journal of the Royal Anthropological Institute* 93 (1): 1–11.

LÉVI-STRAUSS, Claude. 1964a *Mythologiques I: le cru et le cuit*. Paris, Plon.

LÉVI-STRAUSS, Claude. 1964b 'Scientific criteria in the social and human disciplines'. *Revue Internationale des Sciences Sociales* 16 (4). Paris, UNESCO.

LÉVI-STRAUSS, Claude. 1964c 'Reciprocity, the essence of social life'. In *The family: its structure and functions*. R. L. Coser, ed. New York, St. Martin's Press, pp. 36–48.

LÉVI-STRAUSS, Claude. 1965a 'Risposte a un questionario sullo structturalismo'. *Paragone* 16 (182): 125–8.

LÉVI-STRAUSS, Claude. 1965b 'Le triangle culinaire'. *L'Arc* 26.

LÉVI-STRAUSS, Claude. 1966a *The savage mind*. Chicago. University of Chicago Press.

LÉVI-STRAUSS, Claude. 1966b *Mythologiques II: du miel aux cendres*. Paris, Plon.

LÉVI-STRAUSS, Claude. 1967a 'À contre-courant'. *Le Nouvel Observateur* 115.

LÉVI-STRAUSS, Claude. 1967b 'The story of Asdiwal'. *In* (Leach 1967a: 1–47).

LÉVI-STRAUSS, Claude. 1967c *The scope of anthropology*. Sherry Ortner Paul and R. A. Paul, trans. London, Jonathan Cape.

LÉVI-STRAUSS, Claude. 1968 *Mythologiques III: l'origine des manières de table*. Paris, Plon.

Lévi-Strauss, Claude. 1969a *The elementary structures of kinship*. James Harle Bell and John Richard von Sturmer, trans. Rodney Needham, ed. Boston, Beacon Press.

Lévi-Strauss, Claude. 1969b *The raw and the cooked. Introduction to a science of mythology, Vol. I*. John and Doreen Weightman, trans. New York, Harper Torchbooks.

Lévi-Strauss, Claude. 1970 'Les champignons dans la culture. À propos d'un livre de M. R. G. Wasson'. *L'Homme* 10 (1): 5–16.

Levin, David Michael. 1968 'On Lévi-Strauss and existentialism'. *The American Scholar* 38 (1).

Lyons, John. 1968 *Introduction to theoretical linguistics*. Cambridge, Cambridge University Press.

Macksey, Richard. 1962 'Architecture of time: dialectics and structure'. In *Proust*. René Girard, ed. Englewood Cliffs, Prentice-Hall, Inc., pp. 104–21.

McLuhan, Marshall. 1962 *The Gutenberg galaxy*. Toronto, University of Toronto Press.

Mallarmé, Stéphane. 1945 *Œuvres complètes*. Paris, Gallimard.

Mallarmé, Stéphane. 1965 *Mallarmé*. Anthony Hartley, ed. Baltimore, Penguin Books.

Mauss, Marcel. 1950 *Sociologie et anthropologie*. Paris, Presses Universitaires de France.

Maybury-Lewis, David. 1969 Review of *Mythologiques II: du miel aux cendres*. *American Anthropologist* 71 (1): 114–22.

Mein, Margaret. 1962 *Proust's challenge to time*. Manchester, The University Press.

Mendelson, E. Michael. 1967 'The "uninvited guest": ancilla to Lévi-Strauss on totemism and primitive thought'. *In* (Leach 1967a: 119–39).

Merleau-Ponty, Maurice. 1964a *Signs*. Richard C. McCleary, trans. Evanston, Northwestern University Press.

Merleau-Ponty, Maurice. 1964b *The Primacy of Perception*. James M. Edie, ed. Evanston, Northwestern University Press.

Merleau-Ponty, Maurice. 1964c *Sense and non-sense*. H. L. Dreyfus and P. A. Dreyfus, trans. Evanston, Northwestern University Press.

MICHAUD, Guy. 1966 *Message poétique du symbolisme*. Paris, Nizet.

MILNER, G. B. 1969 'Siamese twins, birds and the double helix'. *Man* 4 (1): 5–23.

MONDOR, Henri. 1948 *Histoire d'un faune*. Paris, Gallimard.

MOORE, F. C. T. 1969 Review of *The elementary structures of kinship*. *Man* 4 (4): 660–1.

MOSS, Howard. 1962 *The magic lantern of Marcel Proust*. New York, Macmillan Company.

MURPHY, Robert F. 1963 'On Zen Marxism: filiation and alliance'. *Man* LXIII (21–42): 17–19.

MURPHY, Robert F. 1970 'Connaissez-vous Lévi-Strauss?' *In* (Hayes and Hayes 1970: 164–9).

NEEDHAM, Rodney. 1962 *Structure and sentiment*. Chicago, University of Chicago Press.

NUTINI, Hugo G. 1965 'Some considerations on the nature of social structure and model building: a critique of Claude Lévi-Strauss and Edmund Leach'. *American Anthropologist* 67 (3): 707–31.

NUTINI, Hugo G. 1970 'A comparison of Lévi-Strauss' structuralism and Chomsky's transformational generative grammar'. In *Essays in structural anthropology: in honor of Claude Lévi-Strauss*. Hugo G. Nutini and Ira R. Buchler, eds. New York, Appleton-Century-Crofts.

NUTINI, Hugo G. 1971 'Science and ideology'. *Bijdragen tot de Taal-, Land- en Volkenkunde* 127 (1): 1–14.

ORLIAC, Antoine. 1948 *La cathédrale symboliste: Mallarmé tel qu'en lui-même*. Paris, Mercure de France.

ORTIGUES, Edmond. 1963 'Nature et culture dans l'œuvre de Claude Lévi-Strauss'. *Critique* 15 (189): 142–57.

PANOFSKY, Erwin. 1955 *Meaning in the visual arts*. Garden City, Doubleday Anchor Books.

PAZ, Octavio. 1970 *Claude Lévi-Strauss: an introduction*. Ithaca, Cornell University Press.

PICON, Gaëton. 1963 *Lecture de Proust*. Paris, Gallimard.

PINGAUD, Bernard. 1965 'Comment on devient structuraliste'. *L'Arc* 26.

POUILLON, Jean. 1956 'L'Œuvre de Claude Lévi-Strauss'. *Les Temps Modernes* 12.

POUILLON, Jean. 1966 'L'Analyse des mythes'. *L'Homme* 6 (1): 100–5.

PRAZSKY linguistický kroužek. 1929 'Travaux du cercle linguistique de Prague'. *Mélanges linguistiques* I.

PROUST, Marcel. 1956a *Swann's way*. C. K. Scott Moncrieff, trans. New York, Random House, The Modern Library, London, Chatto & Windus.

PROUST, Marcel. 1956b *Within a budding grove*. C. K. Scott Moncrieff, trans. New York, Random House, The Modern Library, London, Chatto & Windus.

PROUST, Marcel. 1956c *The captive*. C. K. Scott Moncrieff, trans. New York, Random House, The Modern Library, London, Chatto & Windus.

PROUST, Marcel. 1956d *The past recaptured*. Frederick A. Blossom, trans. New York, Random House, The Modern Library, London, Chatto & Windus, under the title *Time regained*.

RADCLIFFE-BROWN, A. R. 1965 *Structure and function in primitive society*. New York, The Free Press.

RAYMOND, Marcel. 1947 *De Baudelaire au surréalisme*. Paris, Librairie José Corti.

RICHARD, Philippe. 1967 'Analyse des mythologiques de Claude Lévi-Strauss'. *L'Homme et la Société* 4.

RICOEUR, Paul. 1963 'Structure et herméneutique'. *Esprit* 322.

RICOEUR, Paul. 1964 'Le symbolisme et l'explication structurale'. *Cahiers Internationaux de Symbolisme* 4.

RIFFATERRE, Michael. 1967 'Describing poetic structures: two approaches to Baudelaire's "les Chats".' *Yale French Studies* 36–7.

RIMBAUD, Arthur. 1966 *Complete works, selected letters*. Wallace Fowlie, trans. Chicago, The University of Chicago Press.

ROUSSEAU, Jean-Jacques. 1864 *Œuvres complètes de Jean-Jacques Rousseau, Vol. III, IV*. Paris Librairie de Firmin Didot Frères.

Rousseau, Jean-Jacques. 1960 *Les Rêveries du promeneur solitaire*. Paris, Garnier Frères.

Rousseau, Jean-Jacques. 1965 *Les Confessions, Tome I*. Paris, Gallimard, Livre de Poche.

Rousseau, Jean-Jacques. 1967 *The social contract and Discourse on the origin and foundation of inequality among mankind*. Lester G. Crocker, ed. New York, Washington Square Press, Inc.

Ruwet, Nicolas. 1963 'Linguistique et sciences de l'homme'. *Esprit* 322: 564–78.

Ryle, Gilbert. 1949 *The concept of mind*. London, Hutchinson; New York, Barnes & Noble.

Sahlins, Marshall D. 1966 'On the Delphic writings of Claude Lévi-Strauss'. *Scientific American* 214 (6).

Santayana, George. 1896 *The sense of beauty*. New York, Dover Publications, 1955.

Saussure, Ferdinand de. 1959 *Course in general linguistics*. Wade Baskin, trans. New York, McGraw-Hill.

Scarfe, Francis, ed. and trans. 1964 *Baudelaire*. Baltimore, Penguin Books.

Scheffler, Harold W. 1967 'Structuralism in anthropology'. *Yale French Studies* 36–7.

Schneider, David M. 1965a 'Some muddles in the models: or, how the system really works'. In *The relevance of models for social anthropology*. Michael Banton, ed. New York, Praeger.

Schneider, David M. 1965b 'American kin terms and terms for kinsmen: a critique of Goodenough's Componential analysis of Yankee kinship terminology'. *American Anthropologist* 67 (5, part 2), pp. 288–308.

Schneider, David M. 1969 'Componential analysis: a state-of-the-art review'. Prepared for the Wenner-Gren Foundation symposium on 'Cognitive studies and artificial intelligence research', March 2–8, 1969.

Scholte, Bob. 1970 'Epistemic paradigms: some problems in cross-cultural research on social anthropological history and theory'. *In* (Hayes and Hayes 1970: 108–22).

SHANKMAN, Paul. 1969 'Le rôti et le bouilli: Lévi-Strauss' theory of cannibalism'. *American Anthropologist* 71 (1): 54–69.

SIMONIS, Yvan. 1968 *Claude Lévi-Strauss ou la 'passion de l'inceste'*. Paris, Aubier Montaigne.

SIMPSON, Robert, ed. 1966 *The symphony: vol. I. Haydn to Dvořák*. Baltimore, Penguin Books.

SONTAG, Susan. 1963 'A hero of our time'. *New York Review of Books* 1 (7): 6–8.

STEINER, George. 1967 *Language and silence: essays on language, literature and the inhuman*. New York, Atheneum.

STRAUSS, Walter A. 1962 'Criticism and creation'. In *Proust*. René Girard, ed. Englewood Cliffs, Prentice-Hall, Inc., pp. 53–68.

STURTEVANT, William C. 1964 'Studies in ethnoscience. Transcultural studies in cognition'. *American Anthropologist* 66 (3, part 2): 99–131.

TASSART, Maurice. 1963 Introduction to libretto for Saint-Saen's *Samson and Delila*. Gwynn Morris, trans. Angel Records R 63–1315.

TATE, Allen. 1948 *On the limits of poetry*. New York, The Swallow Press.

TAX, Sol, ed. 1953 *An appraisal of anthropology today*. Chicago, University of Chicago Press.

Times Literary Supplement 1967 'Matrix and myth'. 66 (3407): 521–22.

Times Literary Supplement. 1968 'Anthropology's pope'. 67 (3453): 445–47.

TIRYAKIAN, Edward A. 1965 'Existential phenomenology and the sociological tradition'. *American Sociological Review* 30 (5): 674–88.

TYLER, Stephen A., ed. 1969 *Cognitive anthropology*. New York, Holt, Rinehart and Winston.

UITTI, Karl D. 1961 *The concept of self in the symbolist novel*. The Hague, Mouton.

UITTI, Karl D. 1963 'Le Temps retrouvé: sens, composition et langue'. *Romanische Forschungen* 75.

UITTI, Karl D. 1967 'Le problème de *Sixtine*: rhétorique et structure'. *Modern Language Notes* 82 (3): 347–66.

UITTI, Karl D. 1969 *Linguistics and literary theory*, Princeton, Princeton University Press.

ULLMANN, Stephen. 1967 *Semantics: an introduction to the science of meaning*. Oxford, Basil Blackwell.

VALÉRY, Paul. 1957 *Œuvres*. Paris, Gallimard.

VANOR, Georges. 1889 *L'Art symboliste*. Paris, Vanier.

VERLAINE, Paul. 1942 *Œuvres poétiques complètes*. Paris, Gallimard.

VOLTAIRE. 1964 *Lettres philosophiques*. Paris, Garnier-Flammarion.

WALLACE, Anthony F. C. 1967 'Dreams and the wishes of the soul: a type of psychoanalytic theory'. In *Magic, witchcraft, and curing*. John Middleton, ed. Garden City, The Natural History Press, pp. 171–90.

WELLEK, René. 1970 *Discriminations*. New Haven, Yale.

WHEELWRIGHT, Philip. 1955 'The semantic approach to myth'. In *Myth: a symposium*. Thomas A. Sebeok, ed. Philadelphia, American Folklore Society, pp. 95–110.

WILD, John. 1970 *The radical empiricism of William James*. Garden City, Doubleday Anchor Books.

WILDE, Oscar. 1969 *The artist as critic; critical writings of Oscar Wilde*. Richard Ellmann, ed. New York, Random House.

WOLF, Eric R. 1964 *Anthropology*. Englewood Cliffs, Prentice-Hall.

WYLIE, Laurence. 1964 *Village in the Vaucluse*. New York, Harper and Row.

YALMAN, Nur. 1964 Review of *La Pensée sauvage*. *American Anthropologist* 66 (5): 1179–82.

YALMAN, Nur. 1967 ' "The raw: the cooked :: nature: culture" —observations'. *In* (Leach 1967a: 71–89).

ZIEGLER, Jean. 1965 'Sartre et Lévi-Strauss'. *Le Nouvel Observateur* 25.

ZIMMERMAN, Robert L. 1968 'Lévi-Strauss and the primitive'. *Commentary* 45 (5): 54–61.

Index

Abel, L., 19
Albee, E., 119
Alienation, 86
Americans, 64, 101
Analogy, *passim*
Andersen, H. C., 92
Animism, 113
Apollo 11 moon shot, 101, 182
Arbitrariness (in Saussurian linguistics), 70–1, 191
Aristotle, 34, 102
Arnold, P., 32
Auerbach, E., 147–8
Australian tribes, 56, 88, 131, 218

Bach, J. S., 172, 173, 176, 177
Bachès-Clément, C., 128, 171
Balakian, A. E., 20, 30, 59, 116, 122, 123, 153–4
Barrès, M., 214
Barthes, R., 28, 145
Bataille, G., 30
Baudelaire, C., 2–6, 14, 20–2, 27, 30–3, ch. II, 89, 101, 104–5, 107–110, 115–16, 118–19, 121–3, 125, 134, 136, 139, 148, 154–5, 162, 165–6, 169, 171–2, 175, 178, 183, 194, 199, 202–3, 206, 213–14, 216
Becker, E., 197
Beckett, S., 193
Bees, 85, 87–9, 157
Beethoven, 176
Benveniste, E., 70
Bergson, H., 121, 148–9, 174, 211–212
Bernard, S., 167
Bernstein, L., 173
Binary:
    principle, 44
    opposition, 50, 68, 71–2, 75–6, 126, 183, 229

Blake, W., 175, 189, 212
Boas, F., 192
Bohannan, P., 96
Boon, J. A., 127, 128
Bricoleur, 52–3, 104, 147, 193, 210, 221
Brooks, C., 38, 187
Brown, C. S., 155, 167, 212, 230
Brown, N. O., 62, 212
Buchler, I. and Selby, H., 8
Buddhism, 217
Burke, K., vii, 49
Burridge, K. L. O., 8, 127–8

Cassirer, E., 215
Caste, 128, 131
Cats, ch. II, 89, 97, 101, 105, 106, 111, 115, 123–4, 131, 158, 183, 231
Caws, P., 28, 133–4, 211, 213
Cézanne, P., 204–5, 207
Champigny, R., 214, 215
Charbonnier, G., 139
'Les Chats', ch. II, 69, 98, 99, 104–107, 111, 126, 174, 210, 213
Cheney, T. A., 209–10
Chomsky, N., 227
Chopin, 168–9
Cinderella legend, 100
Circulus methodicus, 130, 228
Code, definition, 3, 73, 78–9, 81, 83, 85, 88, 91, 163, 184
Cohen, P. S., 22
Cohn, R. G., 156, 165–7
Coleridge, S. T., 185
Communication, *passim*
    theory, 11, 140, 201–2
Componential analysis, 90
Conscience collective, 96
Constructionism, 4–5
Contiguity, 46, 72–3, 103–4

Continuous/discontinuous, 80, 212, 229
Cooking, 78–9, 90, 229
'Correspondances', 115, 122, 154, 194, 203
Correspondence, *passim*
Counterpoint, 172–4
Criticism, literary, 14, 17, 19, 26–9, 54, 113, 131, 166, 230, 231
Cross-cousins, 75
Cubism, 84
Cuisenier, J., 134, 226, 227
Culture (versus Nature), 77–81, 131

Déjà vu, 180
Diachrony, 65–9, 124, 154, 157, 195, 212
Distinctive features, 71, 72, 126, 158, 159, 183, 214, 226
'Domain', definition, 14
Donne, J., 99, 187
Douglas, M., 56, 57
Dualism, 201, 222, 223, 228
    death of, 221
Dumont, L., 200, 201
Durkheim, E., 10, 34, 76, 92–6, 103, 203, 204, 212, 219

Eliade, M., 100
Eliot, T. S., 231
Ellman, R., 28
Emic, 14
Empiricism, 8, 13, 95, 99
Equivalence, 50, 72
Esbroeck, M. van, 121
Esprit, 5, 63, 116, 117, 122, 145, 146, 150, 153, 157, 162, 163, 201, 209, 215, 218, 221, 227
    humain, 6, 8, 9, 63, 113, 163, 225–7
Ethnoscience, 89, 91
Etic, 14
Evans-Pritchard, E. E., 93, 94
Exchange, 63, 77, 78, 80, 81, 90, 92, 94, 111, 135, 151, 204, 227, 229
Existentialism, 193
'Extension', 98, 99, 106

Fiser, E., 4, 5, 148–9, 178, 192, 209, 219
Formalism, 121
Foucault, M., 211
Fowlie, W., 29, 62, 112, 155, 168

Frazer, J., 22, 212
Freedman, R., 146
Freud, S., 7, 113, 179, 191, 212
Frogs, 157–9
Frye, N., 28
'Function', 100
Functionalism, 97, 98, 111, 112
Furet, F., 217, 221

Gaboriau, M., 225
Gaultier, J. de, 62
Gauss, C. E., 34
Geertz, C., 31, 36, 43, 50, 118, 125, 149, 210
Generative grammar, 227
Genette, G., 119, 120
Gibson, R., 1
Gide, A., 134
Goddard, D., 75
Goodenough, W. H., 89–91
Goody, J., 86
Gourmont, R. de, 146, 194
Gramont, S. de, 80, 149, 219
Guthrie, R. and Diller, G., 4, 134, 168, 171

Habit (in Proust), 179, 181
Hamlet, 4, 107
Harris, M., 12, 94, 95
Hartley, A., 34, 111–12, 156
Haydn, 173
Hegel, 192, 206, 217
Hermaphrodite, 51, 53, 57, 58
Heusch, L. de, 110
'Historical seepage', 6, 112
Hjelmslev, 91
Hoffman, E. T. A., 92
Homophony, 172–6
Homo religiosus, 100
Honey, 161
Hugo, V., 114
Hymes, D. H., 89
Hyslop, L. B. and F. E., 3, 27, 108

Idealism, definition 34; 109, 111, 114, 115, 136, 166, 186, 213–15, 220, 223
'Imagination', 139, 162
Impressionistes, 29
Incest, 18, 57, 75–9, 171
Indian tribes:
    Eskimo, 64
    Iroquois, 7–8

Indian tribes—*contd.*
Nambikuara, 128
Sioux, 10, 211–12
Indirect statement in poems, 59, 65, 105, 164
'Intension', 98–9, 106

Jakobson, R., 10, ch. II, 65, 70, 72, 91–2, 96, 98, 103, 106, 126, 229
James, W., 223
Johansen, S., 122
Jonas, H., 222–3
Jung, C., 22, 192

Kahn, J-F., 217
Kant, 34, 221, 223
Katz, J. J., 227–8
Kay, P., 90
Keats, J., 49
Kidder, A., 158
Kinship, 8, 47, 64, 75–6, 79, 82, 89–91, 171, 195, 226
Korn, F., 207

Langer, S. K., 174, 178, 209
Language, *passim*
linguistics, ch. III
Langue, 65–7, 72–3, 91, 126, 174–176, 179–180
Leach, E. R., title page, 8, 30, 55, 57, 78, 79, 95, 96, 112, 125, 126, 129, 130, 131, 147, 160–1, 169, 193, 210, 221
Lefebvre, H., 19
Lehmann, A. G., 3, 31, 32, 62, 64, 95, 107, 108, 109, 114, 118, 122, 134, 171–2, 214
Levin, D. M., 218
Lévy-Bruhl, L., 114
Lyons, J., 86–8

Macksey, R., 181, 184–5, 187, 195, 198
McLuhan, M., 35, 86, 176, 213
Magic lantern, 188
Malinowski, B., 127, 192
Mallarmé, S., 4, 16, 18–19, 31–4, 59, 62, 74, 105–6, 108, 110–12, 124–5, 133–4, 137, 141, 143, 148, 155–7, 161, 163–9, 172, 174–5, 199, 210, 212, 214, 218–19
Marxism, 12, 113, 140, 206, 217, 221

Mauclair, C., title page
Mauss, M., 10, 17, 30, 34, 35, 76, 92, 94, 143, 145, 225
Maybury-Lewis, D., 8
Mein, M., 186, 189, 194, 199
Memory (voluntary, involuntary, conscious, and unconscious), 26, 154–155, 179, 180–5, 189, 209, 212
Mendelson, E. M., 128
Mentality (traditional and modern), 200–1
Merleau-Ponty, M., 30, 47, 81, 202, 204–7, 216, 218, 223–5, 230
Message (in information theory), 25, 73, 91, 124, 133, 134, 159, 160, 162, 177, 202, 204–6, 218, 220
Metaphor, *passim*
definition, 74
metaphoric function, 41
Metonymy, 41, 46, 60, 61, 72–7, 81, 83, 85, 88, 103–6, 173–7
Michaud, G., 27, 29, 218–19
Milner, G. B., 121
'Modern poetry model', 96
Mondor, H., 164
Moss, H., 70, 177, 179–81, 185
'Motivation' (in Saussurian linguistics), 68–70, 120
Mozart, 173
Murphy, R. F., 75, 220
Music, 62–4, 84, 150, 167–78, 182, 186, 202, 204, 219, 229
Myth, *passim*
definition, 28, 39
pregnant boy, 22
mythic operator, 90
Mythologiques, 15, 51, 117, 128–30, 135, 137, 157–70, 175, 178, 187–193, 195, 225, 227, 229

Narcissus, 95, 135, 214
Naturalism, 34, 111, 129
Nature (versus Culture), 77–81, 129, 131
Needham, R., 19
'Neologics', 209–12
New Critics, 26
New ethnography, 89
'New humanism', 215, 218
New World Indians, 7, 8, 51, 117, 137, 151, 157–62, 187–91, 217, 229
Nietzsche, F., 213

Nuer, 121
Nutini, H., 228

Oedipus myth, 92, 191
Opera, 26
Operational theory of semantics, 86
Opposition, *passim*
'Order', *passim*
definition, 14–15
Orliac, A., 163, 165
Ortigues, E., 216

Panofsky, E., 130, 131, 228
Parole, 65, 66, 72, 91, 179, 180
Pascal, B., 213
Paz, O., 167
Pensée sauvage, elucidation of title, 36, 37, 58, 81, 83, 102, 121, 122, 127, 145, 163, 186, 201
Phenomenology, 22, 223
Phonetic model, 71, 183
Picon, G., 178, 181, 195
Pingaud, B., 210
Plato, 34, 35, 109, 114, 115, 186
Polyphony, 172–7
Positivism, 94, 220
Pouillon, J., 77, 78, 143–4, 162–3, 202
Pražský linguistický kroužek (Travaux du Cercle Linguistique de Prague), 65–7
Preconscious, 179, 182
'Prelogic', 114
'Primitive', criteria of, 9
Propp, V., 92
Protestant ethic, 101
Protestant literalism, 212, 213
Proust, M., 4, 6, 10, 11, 16, 18, 23–6, 28, 33, 70, 91, 134, 144, 145, 147–9, 154, 155, 167, 168, 171, 172, 177–82, 184–99, 202, 207, 208, 212, 219, 230

Quakers, 150

Racine, 24
Radcliffe-Brown, A. R., 88–9
Rationalism, 75, 79, 106, 116, 151, 227
Raymond, M., 163
Realism, definition, 34; 103–6, 208
Réalité concrète, notion of, 81
Reciprocity, 75, 77, 94, 95

'Referential' theory of semantics, 85
Reflexive verbs, 203, 204
Richard, P., 129
Ricoeur, P., 120
Riffaterre, M., 51–4
Rimbaud, A., 1, 2, 4, 6, 22, 82, 106, 119, 132, 134
Romanticism, 22, 27, 33, 98, 103–6, 112, 113
Rousseau, J. J., 4, 6–8, 16, 140, 149–155, 176, 197–9, 201, 211, 212
Ruwet, N., 91, 120, 175
Ryle, G., 201

Sahlins, M. D., 20
Sainte-Beuve, 192
Saint Pierre, Bernardin de, 13
Samoa, 121
Santayana, G., 15
Sartre, J. P., 19, 217, 218
Saussure, F. de, 10, 11, 65, 68–74, 84, 87, 91, 120, 136, 183, 191, 206, 229
Scarfe, F., 32
Scheffler, H. W., 47
Schneider, D. M., 19, 90
Scholte, B., 20
Schopenhauer, 109, 111, 114
Self, 133–5, 145, 150–3, 185, 194, 199, 201, 213, 223
Semantics, 73, 84–6, and *passim*
Sens, 116, 117, 122
Shakespeare, 4, 107
Shankman, P., 8, 90, 140
Simonis, Y., 140
Simpson, R., 174
Signs, definition 69; 3, 28, 70, 84, 85, 132, 168
'Significant forms', 178
Signification, *passim*
and *value*, 73
Signified, 69–71, 134, 162
Signifiers, 69–71, 134
Sixtine, 146, 147, 194
'The social', 55, 58, 77, 92, 95, 96, 131, 204, 219
'Social contract', 151
'Social discourse', 75, 93, 100–2, 117
'Social fact', 95
Socio-logic, 76, 90
Sociologie, 10, 92, 203, 204
Solipsism, 95, 166, 214, 215, 220

Sontag, S., 141
Sophocles, 191
Sound image (*signifiant*), 69, 85
Steiner, G., 169
Steno-language, 86
Strauss, W. A., 172
Structuralism, definition 17, 22–3;
  passim
  structural analysis, 50, 120, 126–7
  structural method, 2, 114
  structural processes, 117
  structuralist goals, 83–4
Structure, definition 8, 183; and
  passim
Sturtevant, W. C., 89
'Subliminal communal censorship',
  92
Symbol, *passim*
  Symbolic conception of Symbol-
  ism, 98
Symbolism, criteria of 4–5; and
  passim
Synchrony, 65–7, 124, 157, 212
Synecdoche, 46, 74, 82, 103, 104
Synesthesia, 122, 123, 133, 187
Syntagmatic, 72, 104, 173

Taboo, 76
Taine, H., 29
Tassart, M., 98
Tate, A., 98–9, 106
'Tension', 98, 106
'Text', notion of 37, 9–15; and
  passim
Thibaudet, A., 194
Tiryakian, E. A., 94
Totemism, 18, 33, 36, 72, 78, 79,
  88, 100–3, 119, 123–5, 128, 131,
  183, 211
Transformational grammar, 86

Transformations, *passim*
  and synesthesia, 122
Transposition (in Wagner), 171
Trobriands, 127, 161
Tyler, S. A., 89
Tylor, E. B., 22

Uitti, K. D., 34, 111, 132, 146–7,
  180, 194, 213, 227–8
Ullmann, S., 85, 105
Unconscious, *passim*
  collective nature of, 92

Valéry, P., 19, 110, 111
Value (in Saussurian linguistics), 71,
  73, 84, 120
Vanor, G., 29
Verlaine, P., 1, 4, 167–8
Voltaire, 10, 150

Wagner, 148, 170–3
Wallace, A. F. C., 7–8
Warens, Mme de, 151
Wasson, M. R. G., 159
Weberian theory, 113
WE/THEY, 75
Wheelwright, P., 86
Wild, J., 62, 223
Wilde, O., 4, 28
Wolf, E. R., 17
Woolf, V., 147, 148
Writing, 86
Wylie, L., 36
Wyzéwa, T. de, 171–2

Yalman, N., 55, 96–7, 125–7, 129

'Zen Marxism', 220
Zimmerman, R. L., 140
Zoo keepers, 78